Italian Horror Films of the 1960s

Italian Horror Films of the 1960s

A Critical Catalog of 62 Chillers

by LAWRENCE MCCALLUM

McFarland & Company, Inc., Publishers
Jefferson, North Carolina, and London

Dedicated to Forrest J Ackerman,
filmland's most famous monster

The present work is a reprint of the library bound edition of Italian Horror Films of the 1960s: A Critical Catalog of 62 Chillers, *first published in 1998 by McFarland.*

Acknowledgments: I am very grateful for the assistance provided by my long-time associate Camden Carter, *Scary Monsters* editor Dennis Druktenis, and Peter Enfantino (editor of the late, lamented *The Scream Factory*). The information, illustrations, small favors and helpful hints of these gentlemen made the compilation of essays a much easier task.

Frontispiece: A still from *Caltiki, the Immortal Monster* (1960).

LIBRARY OF CONGRESS CATALOGUING-IN-PUBLICATION DATA

McCallum, Lawrence.
    Italian horror films of the 1960s : a critical catalog of 62 chillers / by Lawrence McCallum.
       p.   cm.
    Includes bibliographical references and index.
    ISBN 0-7864-1968-7 (softcover : 50# alkaline paper) ∞

    1. Horror films — Italy — Catalogs.   I. Title.
PN1995.9.H6M3249   2004
016.79143'6164'0945 — dc21   98-22473 CIP

British Library cataloguing data are available

©1998 Lawrence McCallum. All rights reserved

No part of this book may be reproduced or transmitted in any form or by any means, electronic or mechanical, including photocopying or recording, or by any information storage and retrieval system, without permission in writing from the publisher.

On the cover: Poster art for the 1963 film *Atom Age Vampire*, originally titled *Seddok: L'erede di Satana* (Photofest)

Manufactured in the United States of America

McFarland & Company, Inc., Publishers
  Box 611, Jefferson, North Carolina 28640
    www.mcfarlandpub.com

Contents

Acknowledgments iv
Introduction 1

An Angel for Satan 7
Assignment Terror 9
Atlas in the Land of the Cyclops 13
Atom Age Vampire 14
Black Sabbath 22
Black Sunday 31
Blood and Black Lace 39
The Bloody Pit of Horror 43
Caltiki, the Immortal Monster 47
Castle of Blood 55
Castle of the Living Dead 61
The Embalmer 68
The Evil Eye 71
Fangs of the Living Dead 75
The Ghost 80
Ghosts, Italian Style 82
Ghosts of Rome 85
The Giant of Metropolis 88
Goliath Against the Giants 95

Goliath and the Dragon   96
Goliath and the Vampires   98
Hatchet for a Honeymoon   102
Hercules Against the Moon Men   104
Hercules and the Captive Women   109
Hercules in the Haunted World   114
The Horrible Dr. Hichcock   120
Horror Castle   124
Isabel, Duchess of the Devils   131
Kill Baby Kill   133
The Last Man on Earth   137
Libido   145
The Long Hair of Death   147
Mill of the Stone Women   150
The Minotaur, Wild Beast of Crete   154
The Murder Clinic   158
My Friend, Jekyll   161
Nightmare Castle   163
Planet of the Vampires   166
The Planets Against Us   172
The Playgirls and the Vampire   176
The Possessed   179
Satanik   181
Sex Party   184
She Beast   186
Slaughter of the Vampires   190
Snow Devils   192
Spirits of the Dead   194
Terror-Creatures from the Grave   198
Terror in the Crypt   201
The Thief of Baghdad   205

Uncle Was a Vampire   209
The Unnaturals   213
The Vampire and the Ballerina   215
The Vampire of the Opera   217
Venus in Furs   219
War of the Zombies   223
Werewolf in a Girls' Dormitory   229
What!   234
The Wild, Wild Planet   239
The Witch   242
The Witch's Curse   245
The Young, the Evil and the Savage   251

Appendix: Chronological List of Films   255
Bibliography   257
Index   259

Introduction

A young woman walks briskly along a darkened, narrow, deserted street. Only the clicking of her high heels and the mournful howling of the wind break the silence — but somehow the girl senses that she is not alone. Her suspicions are verified when the footsteps of another are heard very faintly, somewhere within a cloud of swirling mist. As the footsteps become louder, the woman's apprehension turns to genuine fright. We see glimpses of hurrying pale legs, eyes grown wide in horror, a mouth now shaped in an "O" of terror. From out of the luminous, blue-grey fog comes a silent figure clad in a black cape and a slouch hat. There is a long moment of silence as prey and predator face one another...

The images evoked by this description should be quite familiar to any fan of a Mario Bava chiller of the 1960s. Bava has toyed with our fear of the unknown, rooted in dark fantasies that come alive on lonely nights, in such films as *The Evil Eye* (1964), *What!* (1964) and *Blood and Black Lace* (1965). Other Italian filmmakers have developed their own brands of horror. Director Antonio Margheriti chilled audiences with tales of vengeance that reached from beyond the grave in *Castle of Blood* (1964) and *The Long Hair of Death* (1964). Riccardo Freda, already known for his handsome costume dramas, combined mystery and horror in such haunted house thrillers as *The Horrible Dr. Hichcock* (1964) and *The Ghost* (1965). Such efforts enjoyed international popularity after a fallow period of several decades in which the genre practically ceased to exist in Italy.

Throughout much of the silent film era, horror was greeted

with revulsion in Italy, where strict censorship controlled the depiction of volatile themes and horrific images. One of the few examples of silent Italian horror is *Frankenstein's Monster* (*Il mostro de Frankenstein*, 1920), an extremely rare film adaptation of Mary Shelley's novel directed by Eugenio Testa. Producer Luciano Albertino played Baron Frankenstein, while his tormented creation was portrayed by Umberto Guarracino. Following that work, a period of some 35 years passed before straight horror melodrama emerged as a distinct genre within the Italian film industry.

On the other hand, fantasy-adventures with mythological roots were quite popular in the Italian silents. Guido Birgnone's *Cabiria* (1914) introduced the character named "Maciste," a quixotic crusader who fought injustice in a series of adventure films produced between 1914 and 1928. The muscle-bound hero, portrayed by wrestler Bartolomeo Pagano, encountered opponents both human and somewhat *less* than human. One of his most horrific adventures was depicted in the visually striking *Maciste in Hell* (*Maciste all'inferno*, 1926).

Around the end of the silent film era, Italian fantasy quickly declined in favor of the neo-realist influence. Colorful heroes and mythological menaces were replaced by dramas emphasizing an austere simplicity, believable characters and natural settings with which the average man could identify. Although fantasy and spectacle still enjoyed some popularity domestically, the international market first began to emerge in the 1950s. The familiar but well-produced *Fabiola* (1951), produced in 1947, thrilled American audiences with its story of Roman decadence and Christian suffering. Kirk Douglas starred in Mario Camerini's *Ulysses* (1955), an epic (with horrific overtones) that became a box office hit in the United States. Horror fans watched with pleasure and excitement as Ulysses and his men confronted Polyphemus, the cannibalistic Cyclops who imprisoned the adventurers in his cave.

Other spectacles laced with elements of horror and suspense became quite popular near the end of the fifties, beginning with Pietro Francisci's *Hercules* (1959) and *Hercules Unchained* (1960), both starring Steve Reeves. Maciste was revived in the early sixties, while other sword-and-sandal epics featured muscle-bound heroes such as Goliath, Samson and Ursus. The prodigious feats of these characters sometimes involved struggles against gorgons, dragons, one-eyed ogres and other hideous creatures.

In the meantime, straight horror melodramas emerged with Riccardo Freda's *The Vampires* (*I vampiri*, 1956). This creepy tale was a variation on the legend of Countess Elizabeth Bathory, who bathed in the blood of young girls in an attempt to maintain her youth and strength. Transposed to modern times the story featured a mad doctor who revitalized his lover with blood drained from young women. Although handled with considerable horrific flair, the film was a commercial failure in the United States. Freda followed with the more successful *Caltiki, the Immortal Monster*, released in the U.S. in 1960. A variation on the "undying monster" scenario, it seemed to have borrowed concepts from Howard Hawks' *The Thing from Another World* (1951), Hammer's *Enemy from Space* (1957) and the infamous *The Blob* (1958).

Horror-suspense...science-horror...the juxtaposition of horror and humor. All of these styles flourished in Italian chillers of the 1960s. Treatments varied from the comic-strip flavor of *The Wild, Wild Planet* (1966) to the surrealistic mixture of supernatural horror and social commentary in Federico Fellini's "Toby Dammit" segment of *Spirits of the Dead* (1969).

The book covers all Italian horror productions of the 1960s, regardless of quality. It provides plot synopses and information on each film's personnel. The films are listed in alphabetical order (an Appendix lists them chronologically). The following abbreviations are used in the lists of credits:

Dir : Director
Prod : Producer
Writ : Writer
Ph : Photographer
Mus : Music
Spfx : Special Effects

Ed : Editor
Cos : Costumes
Chor : Choreography
ORD : Original release date
ORT : Original running time

Distributors are abbreviated as follows:

AA : Allied Artists
AIP : American International Pictures

MGM : Metro-Goldwyn-Mayer
Fox : 20th Century–Fox
UA : United Artists

THE FILMS

An Angel for Satan
(Un angelo per Satana)

Discobolo Cinematografica. 93 minutes. 1966. B&W. Dir: Camillo Mastrocinque. Prod: Liliana Biancini, Giuliano Simonetti. Writ: Mastrocinque, Giuseppe Mangione. Story: Luigi Emmanuele. Ph: Giuseppe Acquari. Spfx: Antonio Ricci. Cast: Barbara Steele, Anthony Steffen (Antonio De Teffé), Claudio Gora, Ursula Davis (Pier Ana Quaglis), Aldo Berti, Maureen Melrose (Marina Berti), Vassili Karamesinis, Betty Delon.

A small cult dotes over this flick, partly because it is the only Barbara Steele horror film never released to theaters in the U.S. *An Angel for Satan* has a few strong points, but it is basically an ordinary mystery with supernatural overtones.

Steele plays an aristocratic young woman named Harriet who begins to experience bizarre and frightening personality changes after an ancient statue is recovered from a pond on the family estate. Harriet alternates between interludes of manic fury and periods in which she exhibits the more typical projection of soft, coquettish charm. A handsome young artist (Anthony Steffen) begins the slow process of restoring the statue, while forming a relationship with the troubled Harriet.

The girl's schizophrenic behavior continues until the truth about the situation finally comes to light. An evil, envious woman named Ilda (Marina Berti) has used hypnosis on the sensitive and vulnerable Harriet, convincing her that she is possessed by an evil spirit ("Belinda") that has emerged from the statue. The weak-willed Count of Montebruno (Claudio Gora) has been manipulated by Ilda into accepting the plot to destroy Harriet. Luckily, the perceptive aesthete Steffen uncovers the plot and ferrets out the villains.

Steele delivers an admirable schizo acting job, much like her portrayal of Asa/Katia in Mario Bava's *Black Sunday* (1961). *An Angel for Satan* borrows a few plot twists from the Bava classic as well as from director Camillo Mastrocinque's *Terror in the Crypt* (1963). The scenario also seems to incorporate the basic premise of *The Frozen Ghost* (1945), and Inner Sanctum thriller in which a hypnotist (Lon Chaney, Jr.) learns that his fearsome "power of life and death" is actually an illusion created by a manipulative colleague.

Screenwriter Giuseppe Mangione was already known for his predictable, heavy-handed treatments. His previous credits included the screenplay for the dull tearjerker *Angels of Darkness* (1956), distinguished mainly by the presence of a strong leading man (Anthony Quinn). Mangione also wrote the hackneyed scripts for a pair of spectacle films — *The Queen of Babylon* (1956) starring Rhonda Fleming and *The Mighty Ursus* (1963). Mangione's *Hypnosis* (1966), released shortly before *An Angel for Satan* reached theaters, was a routine mystery in which a series of murders have a bizarre link to a nightclub act.

Director Mastrocinque fails to handle Mangione's amalgam of clichés with any noticeable flair. Much as in his *Terror in the Crypt*, there are a few striking images and several scenes enhanced by considerable visual appeal and good camerawork. The rest is a flat and uninteresting presentation of a few familiar concepts. Mastrocinque's entire career, for that matter, remained an exceedingly inauspicious one as he wobbled from comedy to romance and eventually concentrated on horror melodrama. Among his previous credits are the mediocre *Toto in Hell* (*Toto all'inferno*, 1954) and a weak tale of romance and tragedy entitled *Duel Without Honor* (1953). The director fared even worse with an insipid romantic comedy originally titled *Eighteen in the Sun* (*Diciottenni al sole*, 1964). The latter flick, dealing with youthful hijinks at a seaside location, was retitled *Beach Party Italian Style* by its American distributors.

However, *An Angel for Satan* contains two competent supporting performances by male stars familiar to fans of Italian adventure and horror-fantasy efforts. Male lead Antonio De Teffé ("Anthony Steffen") previously played an Indian brave named Strongheart in the European Western *The Last Tomahawk*, a.k.a. *The Last Mohican* (*Der letze Mohikaner*, 1965), which was loosely based on James Fenimore Cooper's *The Last of the Mohicans*. The rugged De Teffé later played the gun-toting nemesis of a gang of murderous outlaws in *No Room to Die* (*Una lunga fila di croci*, 1969). He was also cast as a supposedly haunted widower in the routine horror-suspenser *The Night Evelyn Came Out of the Grave* (1971).

Claudio Gora, billed third as the Count of Montebruno, was well-established in the European cinema and adequately filled a number of character roles. His screen credits are quite diverse, ranging from period epics (*Goddess of Love* [1960], *The Swordsman of Siena* [1962]) to the lightweight teenage romance of *Gidget Goes to Rome* (1963). Gora also acted in the campy Mario Bava fantasy *Danger: Diabolik* (1968).

Camillo Mastrocinque's career declined sharply after the release of *An Angel for Satan*, though producer Giuliano Simonetti later scored a triumph with the brutally exciting Italian Western *The Ugly Ones* (*El precio de un hombre/The Price of One Man*), a 1968 release starring Tomás Milian. As for Barbara Steele's return to the horror genre after a brief absence, she fails to recreate the charisma she generated in such classics as *Black Sunday, Pit and the Pendulum* (1961) and *Castle of Blood* (1964). The reluctant horror star had briefly switched to drama and adventure with roles in *Once Upon a Tractor* (1965), *For Love and Gold* (1966) and the award-winning *The Young Torless* (1966), a poignant human interest story with an antifascist message. Steele has since remained highly active in film and television, both as an actress and a producer. Her last solid horror credit of the 1960s was *Curse of the Crimson Altar* (1968), an adaptation of H. P. Lovecraft's "The Dreams in the Witch-House" released in the U.S. by AIP in 1970. The actress was also cast as the sister of Rossano Brazzi in the ABC-TV presentation *Honeymoon with a Stranger* (1969), a mystery with Gothic overtones.

Assignment Terror

Original title: *El Hombre que vino de Ummo* (*The Man Who Came from Ummo*). a.k.a. *Dracula jagt Frankenstein* (*Dracula vs. Frankenstein*). A.k.a. *Los monstruos del terror* (*The Monsters of Terror*). Producciones Jaime Prades/Eichberg Film/International Jaguar, AIP. 86 minutes (ORT: 89 minutes.) 1969. Eastman Color, totalscope. Dir: Tullio Demichelli. Prod: Jaime Prades. Writ: Jacinto Molina. Ph: Godofredo Pacheco. Spfx: Antonio Molina. Cast: Michael Rennie, Karin Dor, Craig Hill, Paul Naschy (Jacinto Molina), Patty Shepard, Angel del Pozo, Ella Gessler, Peter Damon, Manuel de Blas, Gene Reyes.

An Italian-Spanish-West German co-production, this routine, rather inept SF-horror comes off as an updated rehash of Universal's monster mashes of the 1940s. Classic movie menaces appear together, courtesy of an evil scientist who revives and organizes the motley crew in his Transylvanian castle. What follows is pure corn, though the film isn't quite bad enough to laugh at.

The mysterious Dr. Odo Warnoff (Michael Rennie) is secretly an alien agent who arrives from the planet Ummo and establishes a base of operations in a creepy old castle. Warnoff has plans to conquer the world by synthesizing and releasing upon mankind the most fearsome monsters of legend—Count Dracula, the mummy, Frankenstein's Monster and a werewolf. Only the unfortunate lycanthrope, tormented Count Waldemar Daninsky (Jacinto Molina), is not a synthetic creature. Revived from the dead by Warnoff, the tragic Daninsky is reluctantly being groomed as a warrior who will help enforce the expansionist policies of Ummo. Warnoff has also revived several other deceased individuals, including some medical personnel who will help to create monstrous biological mutations. The winsome, dark-haired Maleva (Karin Dor) is one such scientist who must now do the bidding of the alien.

However, the strength of the human spirit and man's instinct for self-preservation prove to be stronger than Warnoff originally anticipated. One of the alien's female lab assistants has fallen in love with Daninsky, who unexpectedly reveals his social conscience. The werewolf and his new love form an alliance with Warnoff's nemesis, the courageous Dr. Kirian (Craig Hill), whose girlfriend (Patty Shepard) has been imprisoned within the castle. While Daninsky fights the crazed mutants who escape from the castle's lower levels, Kirian runs the gauntlet of monsters who block the path to his lover's rescue. Accompanied by Maleva, Warnoff barricades himself in his laboratory and watches, via electronic surveillance, the amazing progress of the doctor. Using strength, courage and clever strategies, Kirian defeats the Frankenstein Monster, marauding mummy and blood-lusting Count Dracula, in addition to several hungry vampire bats. In the meantime, the lycanthropic fury of Daninsky makes short work of Warnoff's mad minions. Daninsky is released from his accursed existence when his mortally wounded lover mercifully fires a clip of silver bullets into him.

Kirian and his lady love are reunited as heavily armed law enforcement officers arrive to conduct a mop-up operation. The castle hovers on the brink of destruction as flames quickly spread. Kirian and his companions flee while Dr. Warnoff accepts defeat and sends a final communication to his home planet. The alien realizes, too late, that the ability of humans to love one another is a strength and not a weakness. Warnoff even asks his superiors to intervene and save his assistant Maleva from the final destruction of the castle as he begins to feel the human sense of compassion. Sadly, the request cannot be fulfilled since the woman is already dead and is little more than a material illusion. Warnoff and Maleva exchange soft smiles — until the woman suddenly fades from view. Moments later, a massive explosion erupts in the laboratory as the air fills with acrid fumes and deadly shards of concrete and steel. The invasion from Ummo comes to an abrupt end when their agent is buried under tons of rubble.

When one considers the many clichéd characters and hokey situations contained in *Assignment Terror*, it becomes obvious that the film has the makings of a parody rather than a straight SF-horror melodrama. The only bright spot in the hackneyed script is a nice homage to George Waggner's *The Wolf Man* (1941) by naming one character "Maleva" (the name of Maria Ouspenskaya's old gypsy woman in the Universal classic). Acting is more embarrassed than convincing by Michael Rennie, who stoically suffers through a prolonged cameo role. This flick is quite a comedown from his best-known thriller, Robert Wise's *The Day the Earth Stood Still* (1951), which cast him as the benevolent alien Klaatu. Rennie also delivered polished performances in the science-fiction melodramas *Cyborg* 2987 (1966) and George Pal's *The Power* (1968). *Assignment Terror* is about as ineptly made as Rennie's *The Young, the Evil and the Savage* (1969), though the latter is the more boring of the two films.

Other cast members who had seen better days include American Craig Hill and German actress Karin Dor. Hill played supporting roles in such American action movies as Sam Fuller's *Fixed Bayonets* (1951) and the Rudolph Maté Western *Siege at Red River* (1954). He also acted in such inoffensive bits of fluff as *Cheaper by the Dozen* (1950), *Tammy and the Bachelor* (1957) and *Follow the*

Boys (1966), a low-budget fantasy with an anti-bomb message. Karin Dor excelled in such West German thrillers as *The Invisible Dr. Mabuse* (1960), *The Terrible People* (1960) and *The White Spider* (1963) before filling roles in Don Sharp's exciting *The Face of Fu Manchu* (1966) and Lewis Gilbert's *You Only Live Twice* (1967), the fifth James Bond film starring Sean Connery.

Assignment Terror is worth noting mainly for the appearance of "Paul Naschy," who also wrote the screenplay under his real name, Jacinto Molina. Then a 29-year-old former weightlifter, Molina here played the role of werewolf Waldemar Daninsky for the second time. His initial portrayal was featured the previous year in *La marca del hombre lobo* (*The Mark of the Werewolf*, 1968). Molina quickly became the Spanish equivalent of Long Chaney, Jr., delineating roles based on classic horror characters with the original scenarios usually being transposed to a Spanish setting. He played a dual role as a Kharis-like reactivated mummy and the descendant of the cloth-wrapped menace in *Vengeance of the Mummy* (1973). He also portrayed a lycanthropic Henry Jekyll in *Dr. Jekyll and the Wolfman* (*Dr. Jekyll y el Hombre Lobo*, 1971), then starred as Bram Stoker's infamous bloodsucker in *Dracula's Great Love* (*El gran amor de Conde Dracula*, 1972). His most famous role, as werewolf Waldemar Daninsky, was inspired by the Larry Talbot character as portrayed by Chaney in five Universal movies produced between 1941 and 1948. Molina played the Daninsky role in a total of 11 features.

Tullio Demichelli, a barely passable action director, is probably best known for the predictable but colorful *The Son of Captain Blood* (1962). This flick introduced Sean Flynn (son of Errol) as the late captain's offspring, who becomes involved with his father's pirate friends. Demichelli also directed an Italian oater entitled *Gunmen of the Rio Grande* (1965) starring Guy Madison as Wyatt Earp. More recently, he handled a B chiller titled *Cauldron of Blood* (1979). Though exceedingly ordinary, all three efforts are superior to *Assignment Terror*, which was never released to theaters in the U.S. American-International released the film directly to television in 1970.

Atlas in the Land of the Cyclops

Original title: *Maciste nella terra dei Ciclopi* (*Maciste in the Land of the Cyclops*). A.k.a. *Atlas Against the Cyclops*. Leone, Medallion. 100 minutes. 1963 (ORD: 1961.) Eastman Color, Totalscope. Dir: Antonio Leonviola. Prod: Ermanno Donati, Luigi Carpentieri. Writ: O. (Oreste) Biancoli, Gino Manghini. Story: Biancoli. Ph: Riccardo Pallottini. Mus: Carlo Innocenzi. Ed: Mario Serandrei. Art Dir: Alberto Boccianti. Cos: Giuliano Papi. Cast: Gordon Mitchell, Chelo Alonso, Vira Silenti, Paul Wynter, Dante Di Paolo, Aldo Bufi-Landi, Germano Longo, Giotti Tempestini, Massimo Righi, Flavio, Aldo Padinotti.

Maciste, the nemesis of evil, has been featured in a number of inept fantasy-adventures, and this is one of his worst. In this outing, U.S. distributors have renamed him Atlas and the role is played by Gordon Mitchell. Our hero comes up against the evil Queen Capys (Chelo Alonso), who wishes to destroy the rightful heir to the throne — the winsome Penelope (Vira Silenti). Atlas takes Penelope under his protection and must also defend her infant son (Flavio) who will one day assume his proper place upon the throne.

After enduring many sword and sandal clichés, the audience is finally treated to the duel between Atlas and the Cyclops (Aldo Padinotti). Penelope and her son have been kidnapped and forced into the monster's cave by the queen's henchmen, but Atlas comes to the rescue. Man and monster stalk one another in the shadowy cave, until Atlas hurls a sword into its eye. The Cyclops, blinded, is still eager for a scrap and matches strength with Atlas, who finally crushes the monster against a huge rock.

Atlas in the Land of the Cyclops features some familiar talents from the thrillers of Mario Bava and Riccardo Freda. The production team of Ermanno Donati and Luigi Carpentieri managed to provide horror fans with some halfway decent chillers, most notably Freda's *The Horrible Dr. Hichcock* (1964). This time out, they came up with a misguided disaster distinguished mainly by the fine camerawork of Riccardo Pallottini. Beyond its photography, the film features a good performance by Chelo Alonso, who portrays the ruthless and ambitious Queen Capys with great relish. The exotic, olive-skinned actress always delivered sensual performances, whether she played the heroine or the villain of such features as *Goliath and the Barbarians* (1960), *The Pirate and the Slave Girl* (1961) and *Samson and the Seven Miracles of the World* (1963). Gordon Mitchell (Atlas) is good at bulging his muscles, bulging his eyes and grimacing in order to display his great dental work. These are feats that he performed more effectively in the 1964 release *The Giant of Metropolis*.

The rest of the performances are uninspired, with the actors mouthing ridiculous platitudes that are badly dubbed into their mouths. As far as the special effects sequences are concerned, the matte work is only fair; basically, this is on the level of an early Bert I. Gordon flick like *The Cyclops* (1957). The sense of perspective is sometimes lost as the monster seems ten feet tall in one scene, then towers near the roof of the cave in the next sequence. One can almost feel the papier-mâché of the "Cyclops" mask worn by actor Aldo Padinotti.

Not surprisingly, U.S. distributors harbored doubts about the box office potential of *Atlas in the Land of the Cyclops*. The film was released directly to television in 1963, although the title also managed to find exposure in a handful of neighborhood theaters.

Atom Age Vampire

Original Title: *Seddok: L'erede di Satana* (*The Heir of Satan*). Lion's Film, Topaz. 87 minutes (ORT: 107 minutes.) 1963 (ORD: 1961). B&W. Dir: Anton Giulio Majano. Prod: Mario Bava. Writ: Majano, Piero Monviso, Gino De Santis, Alberto Befilacqua, John Hart. Ph: Aldo Giordani. Mus: Armando Trovajoli. Spfx: Ugo Amadoro, Euclide Santoli. Cast: Albert (Alberto) Lupo, Susanne Loret, Sergio Fantoni, Roberto Berta, Franca Parisi Strahl, Ivo Garrani, Andrea Scotti, Rina Franchetti.

This formula SF-horror features little in the way of imagination, although there are some creepy sequences plus excellent black-and-white photography. Nevertheless, *Atom Age Vampire* is definitely a minor effort that remains one of Mario Bava's least impressive screen credits.

Window card for *Atom Age Vampire*.

One night, a lovely cabaret dancer named Jeanete (Susanne Loret) has a heated argument with a suitor over the future of their relationship. The enraged Pierre (Sergio Fantoni) declares he is leaving on a long sea voyage. Jeanete, distraught and nearly hysterical after the fight, later takes to the road in her car in an attempt to reach Pierre before his ship departs. She races furiously and recklessly along a country road. Jeanete pays the price for self-destructive behavior as the car veers off the road and careens crazily down a slope. The fiery crash leaves the girl scarred on one side of her face.

Jeanete's career, as well as her love life, ends on that terrible night. She approaches many doctors, all of whom state that plastic surgery could never repair the severe disfigurement. One day, she learns of a doctor whose experimental techniques may be used to repair the most severe scarring. The brilliant Prof. Levyn (Alberto Lupo) examines her face in his office and seems to accept the conclusions of his colleagues — the case is hopeless.

Jeanete bursts into tears and begins to leave, but he abruptly stops her retreat. Levyn continues his explanation, stating that restoration of her face would be impossible by accepted surgical procedures. However, success could be realized through the application of his new techniques. Levyn and his assistant Monique (Franca Parisi Strahl) begin tests and prepare to administering the techniques.

The laboratory–operating room in the lower levels of the house is utilized by the two scientists, who begin working on Jeanete. An injection of the doctor's vaccine into the damaged area produces startling results. The damaged tissue almost magically regenerates itself into a smooth, healthy layer of skin. As the treatment is completed, Levyn pulls the surgical cap from Jeanete and releases the sheet of lustrous blonde hair that enhances her soft features and flawless, pale skin. Levyn is fascinated by the girl's beauty and seems unable to look away from her. Monique is disturbed by Levyn's new interest in Jeanete, which seems more than professional.

Jeanete awakens in a small recovery room and is allowed to see the amazing results of Levyn's treatment. Elated, Jeanete is overcome by a display of emotion. Her sudden embrace and violent kiss leave the doctor quite startled. Monique is no less disturbed and jealousy burns in her eyes. "Jeanete, you must get back into bed!"

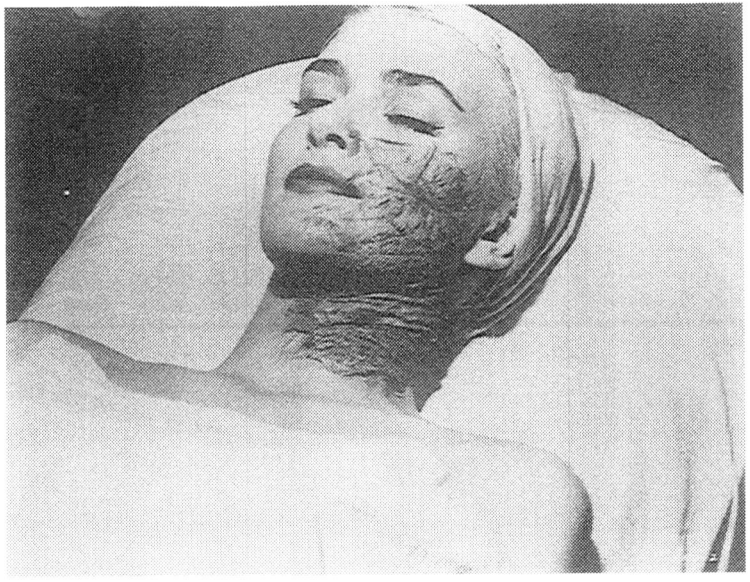

Jeanete (Susanne Loret) is prepared for experimental surgery.

commands Monique. Jeanete complies as Levyn seems to agree that the girl needs rest.

Levyn soon sees his relationship with Jeanete as more than that of a doctor patient. The girl feels gratitude, but assures Levyn as gently as possible that she does not love him. Monique is crushed and heartbroken, having seen Levyn as far more than just a colleague. Alone in her bedroom, she spends the evening crying. Only Sacha (Roberto Berta), the mute gardener, seeks to console her. He quietly enters her room that night and offers a flower from the greenhouse to the distraught woman. But her sense of loss is felt too deeply for the kind gesture of the sad little man to have any healing effect.

One night, as Levyn and Jeanete share cocktails in his parlor, the doctor notices a tiny patch of scar tissue reappearing on the girl's face. Levyn realizes that the initial treatment with his serum has only had temporary results. The production of more serum requires a supply of glandular fluid that Levyn is willing to procure at any cost. He approaches Monique and explains the matter to her, but

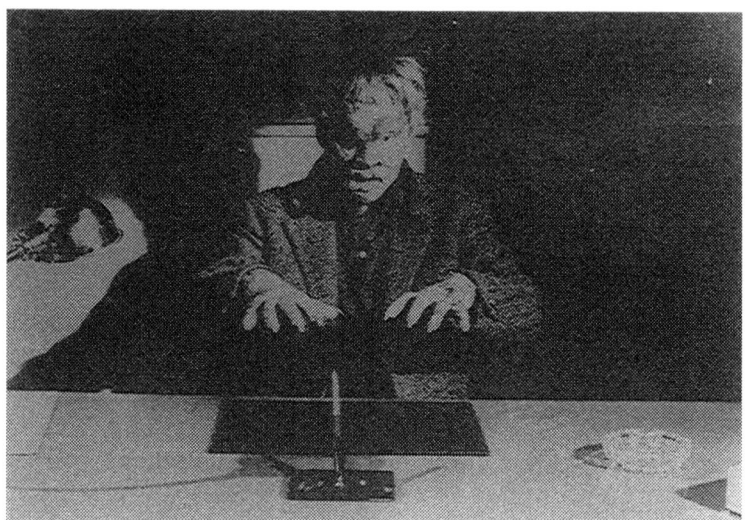

Professor Levyn (Alberto Lupo) transforms himself into a nocturnal menace.

this appeal for help seems more like salt rubbed in fresh wounds. "What do you want me to do?" she cries. "Sacrifice myself for her?" Levyn assures Monique that he would never make such a terrible demand from her, but his actions soon prove otherwise.

Jeanete is administered a second effective treatment and Monique suffers a tragic fate. The police arrive at the Levyn mansion while Jeanete asks Sacha about the strangely absent Monique. Though unable to speak, the gardener makes an obvious reply when he comes near tears at the mention of Monique's name. The lifeless body of Monique has been found in her bedroom. No evidence of foul play can be uncovered and Levyn is not under any suspicion.

Levyn's obsession with Jeanete compels him to continue the search for a permanent cure. He prowls the night, preying on unsuspecting women whose bodily fluids are necessary for production of his serum. He disguises himself by using a variation of his regenerative serum to produce drastic, disfiguring changes in his appearance. Levyn regains his normal appearance by immersing himself in a radioactive fog generated by an atomic-powered device in his laboratory.

After returning from his voyage, Pierre finds that he still harbors

Levyn (Alberto Lupo) prepares to abduct Jeanete (Susanne Loret).

strong feelings about Jeanete and he finds it difficult to accept the girl's reclusive life within the walls of the Levyn estate. His suspicions about Levyn's motives begin to cause problems for the doctor, while police investigators begin to establish a circle of association between Levyn and the grisly murders. Levyn decides to flee the city and demands that Jeanete accompany him.

Ironically, the doctor's treatments have finally cured Jeanete, but Levyn suffers uncontrolled recurrences of his hideous physical distortions. He barks orders at Jeanete, demanding that she get dressed and prepare to leave. As he rages in a nearly incoherent manner, Levyn's speech becomes thick and the malformed features gradually emerge. Jeanete's pleas for mercy are ignored and she runs to a window and desperately cries for help.

Pierre, who has spent much of the evening pacing in front of the Levyn mansion, hears her and climbs over the wall. He forces his way into the house and confronts Levyn, grappling furiously with the madman. Levyn quickly gains the upper hand and deals Pierre a severe beating, while Jeanete ineffectually attempts to intervene. As Pierre lies unconscious, Levyn flees with his female captive.

By now, detectives have arrived with a party of armed men. Levyn finds escape impossible as he enters the greenhouse with his hostage. The startled Sacha cowers in a corner as the structure is surrounded by policemen, one of whom fires a warning burst from a machine-gun. Accepting his fate, Levyn decides that he will not go down alone. He turns toward Jeanete and mutters, "Yes...she has to die."

Sacha is finally moved to violence by this threat. As Levyn advances toward Jeanete, Sacha seizes a gardening tool and thrusts the metal shaft into the madman's back. Levyn staggers backward and collapses as the tormented Sacha kneels at his side. A spark of decency still exists in the monster who gently touches the gardener's shoulder. Levyn weakly nods his head, reassuring the gardener that his intervention was necessary.

As the police enter the greenhouse, the doctor reverts to the striking figure in his middle years who once devoted his life to the betterment of humanity. Torn by anguish, Sacha is led away by the police. Jeanete is reunited with Pierre.

This flick covers just about every genre cliché in the book. We have the mad scientist afflicted with the obligatory mad love for the heroine (a beautiful blonde, of course). We also have the suave, dark-haired hero and a couple of fast-talking detectives (*à la* television's *Dragnet*) who sometimes indulge in a bantering conflict. Toss in the Eternal Triangle and a mute servant and you have an exploiter's delight.

Actually, producer Mario Bava didn't have much to be ashamed of. The film belies its low budget with an impressive "mad lab" and the fine black-and-white photography of Aldo Giordani. The cast is better than the script and includes performers known largely for period adventure films and elaborate spectacles. Alberto Lupo and Susanne Loret excel during the closing scenes. The two performers previously acted in *The Minotaur, Wild Beast of Crete*, with Loret filling a lesser supporting role in that 1963 release. Lupo, a fine character actor, later appeared in the lavish historical drama *The Agony and the Ecstasy* (1965), starring Charlton Heston.

Lupo also appeared together with leading man Sergio Fantoni

in the Steve Reeves adventure *The Giant of Marathon* (1961). Fantoni, a competent actor who resembles Tony Curtis, usually played second male leads or major supporting roles in lavish epics. His other screen credits include *Esther and the King* (1960) and *Hercules Unchained* (1960) plus a pair of World War II epics, Frank Sinatra's *Von Ryan's Express* (1966) and *Hornet's Nest* (1970) with Rock Hudson.

Of the remaining major roles, Franca Parisi Strahl delivers a sympathetic portrayal of the tragic Monique. Strahl remained largely unknown to American audiences, although she acted in other European productions usually given a limited U.S. release. The actress appeared in a maudlin romance entitled *Forever My Love* (1962) and a routine adventure film, *White Slave Ship* (1962).

The best performance, however, is a remarkably sensitive portrayal of the mute Sacha by Roberto Berta. There is an emotional frailty delineated by Berta that rarely emerges in stock horror characterizations. One only wishes that he could have delivered his fine performance in a more worthy effort.

Atom Age Vampire is directed in a suitably grim, visually appealing style by Anton Giulio Majano. A veteran director of radio plays and TV dramas, Majano proved to be quite adept at handling thin programmer material. He is best remembered, however, as a filmmaker with a social conscience who handled such efforts as the 1948 drama *The Wandering Jew*.

Prof. Levyn's grisly procurement of bodily fluids could only be characterized as vampirism in a very broad sense. The inappropriate title of *Atom Age Vampire* was assigned to the film by American distributors for the sake of salability. Vampires, after all, are probably the most popular of movie menaces. The opening credits of the U.S. version are accompanied by an animated sequence in which a bat wings its way across a gray background. The bat freezes in mid-air, its enormous wings forming the "V" for the word vampire as the title appears.

The film also possesses the dark, moody atmosphere of a vampire flick. The compelling nature of its stark black-and-white images often manages to make the very weak story more bearable. However, Alberto Lupo hardly resembles the stereotypical movie vampire, which is usually envisioned as pale and gaunt with darkened eyes and reddened lips. Lupo emotes beneath a swarthy, effectively creepy latex makeup with thick features that make him appear vaguely anthropoid.

Although it is watchable horror fare, the film is somewhat disappointing for a Mario Bava credit. Perhaps if Bava directed as well as produced, we may have seen Bava-esque moments of macabre beauty in addition to a few pleasurably creepy horror interludes. Nevertheless, this flick is more widely known than other Italian chillers dealing with "traditional" vampires such as *The Vampire and the Ballerina* (1962) or *Slaughter of the Vampires* (1962). As a Saturday matinee horror flick, *Atom Age Vampire* was quite adequate.

Black Sabbath

Original title: *I tre volti della paura* (*The Three Faces of Fear*). A.k.a. *Black Christmas*. A.k.a. *Three Faces of Terror*. Galatea/Emmepi/AIP. 99 minutes. 1964. Dir: Mario Bava. Prod: Salvatore Billiteri. Writ: Bava, Marcello Fondato, Alberto Bevilacqua. Based on the short stories "A Drop of Water" by Anton Chekhov, "The Telephone" by Howard Snyder, "The Wurdulak" by Leo Tolstoy. Ph: Ubaldo Terzano. Mus: Les Baxter. Makeup: Otello Fava. Cos: Trini Grani. Cast: Boris Karloff, Mark Damon, Jacqueline Pierreux, Michèle Mercier, Susy Andersen, Lydia Alfonsi, Milli Monti, Glauco Oronato, Rica Dialina, Massimo Righi.

The U.S. box office success of Mario Bava's *Black Sunday* (1961) inspired AIP to enter a co-production deal incorporating the same talents that made that film a triumph of the genre. Bava's stylish direction, superb Ubaldo Terzano camerawork and an intriguing Les Baxter score contribute to the full quality of the tripartite *Black Sabbath*. The film's star, Boris Karloff, had already been "rediscovered" by AIP as a major genre figure shortly after he completed the two-year run of his TV series *Thriller* (NBC, 1960-62). Around this same time, Karloff acted in two of Roger Corman's efforts — *The Raven* (1963) and the no-budget *The Terror* (1963), co-starring Jack Nicholson. *The Comedy of Terrors* (1964) gave Karloff third billing as the father-in-law of murderous funeral director Vincent Price.

AIP decided that it was time for Karloff to star in his own horror vehicle, one beyond a "day labor" flick like *The Terror*. Consequently, Karloff acted as the host of *Black Sabbath* and gave a clever introduction to each story while starring in the final segment, "The Wurdulak."

"A Drop of Water," the first and best segment, begins on a stormy night when nurse Helen Corey (Jacqueline Pierreux) receives a late-night phone call from a woman whose strained voice hints of hysteria. The caller is the housekeeper of a woman who has died suddenly in a grotesque manner. Though annoyed by the demand for her to get to the dead woman's home, Helen reluctantly complies.

Helen arrives at the shadowy mansion of the late, wealthy recluse and is greeted by the nervous housekeeper (Milli Monti). The nurse is shown to the dead woman's bedroom, where the housekeeper will not approach the corpse. Helen quickly understands the woman's fears after her first glimpse of the body—its chalk-white face twisted in pain...teeth bared...eyes wide in death. Helen manages to overcome her revulsion and begins to prepare the corpse for burial. The nurse soon enviously eyes the dead woman's large ruby ring.

After preparation of the corpse is completed, Helen quickly pulls the ring from the woman's finger. She nervously drops it and falls to her knees, groping beneath the bed. Suddenly, the dead woman's hand falls limply against the back of Helen's head. Startled, Helen cries out, but she hastily assures the housekeeper that all is well. Then she carefully hides the ring.

Helen states that the grim task is completed as the housekeeper expresses the desire to leave with her and not spend another moment alone in the house. The nurse passes her hand over the dead woman's face, shutting the mad, staring eyes of the corpse. Helen then turns to inform the housekeeper that it is time to leave. A final look at the corpse fills the nurse with horror as she sees that the dead eyes are wide and staring once again.

There is another strange occurrence that fans her fears to an even higher pitch. A buzzing fly has settled upon the dead woman's finger where the ring once was. Helen attempts to conceal her terror as she joins the housekeeper and quickly leaves the mansion.

However, the words of the housekeeper are firmly planted in the nurse's mind. The dead woman was a medium, killed by the dark forces that she unleashed from the spirit world. A terrible fate was promised by the medium for anyone who stole from her.

Helen returns to her quiet apartment where she feels some sense of security away from the horrid atmosphere of the old mansion. She sits for a time and admires the stolen ring. All seems peaceful until the silence is broken by a steady drip from a faucet. Helen attempts to tighten the handle, but the dripping resumes after a few moments. A second annoyance comes in the form of a housefly that flits noisily about the apartment. The incessant buzzing becomes torture to Helen's ears, as does the steady dripping of water, with each drop resounding like thunder within the small apartment.

Helen is in a near-hysterical state as she cries out, flailing her arms in an attempt to ward off the attacking fly. Both the buzzing and dripping cease abruptly as silence is restored to the darkened apartment. The calm, however, is short-lived as a mournful howling can be heard coming from Helen's bedroom. She slowly approaches the room and opens the door, only to scream in terror at the sight that greets her. The body of the dead medium now rests upon the bed. Although the woman's face is still frozen into a grimace of pain and rage, her body seems imbued with new life. She stiffly begins to rise from the bed.

Helen turns and flees from the horrible sight, but now sees the medium in her parlor — resting in a rocking chair. Glimpses of the undead corpse taunt the nurse as clutching hands reach from darkened corners and the silent, ghostly figure glides toward her with arms outstretched. Escape is impossible as Helen finds herself confronted by the vindictive spirit at every turn. She drops to her knees and begs for mercy while attempting to remove the ring from her finger. A claw-like hand tightens around her throat; joined by a second hand. But they are the hands of Helen and not of the avenging wraith. A death rattle escapes Helen's throat as she drops lifelessly to the floor.

The police are summoned by the landlady, who has no clues to offer in the strange death. Helen is found with eyes wide and staring, her hands locked around her throat. One finger is cut and discolored as though a ring had been torn from it. The landlady takes on a worried look as a detective talks about the missing ring. She is also disturbed by the buzzing of a housefly — that rests upon the dead nurse's damaged finger.

This creepy first episode evokes the same claustrophobic sense of horror present in Roger Corman's *House of Usher* (1960). The scenes in which Jacqueline Pierreux is pursued throughout her darkened apartment manage to equal the best work of Corman, perhaps even of Alfred Hitchcock. The shocks are quite good as clutching hands and unexpected reappearances by the corpse are punctuated by startling blasts from the sound department. Horrors both subtle and overt are present in the story, which begins with a hint of terror and slowly builds into an atmosphere of hysteria. The intriguing final scene leaves open the possibility of new hauntings as the vengeance of the undead will continue to be wreaked upon the living. Did the undead medium reclaim her ring or was it stolen by the landlady? Was Helen Corey actually claimed by a vengeful spirit or did her own guilty conscience create delusions that led to self-destruction? Such questions are never answered, and the ambiguities of the story are part of its fascination.

The second tale has considerably less to recommend it. "The Telephone." Deals with the plight of playgirl Rosie (Michèle Mercier) who finds herself the victim of lurid, threatening phone calls. The mystery caller seems to know her every move and she begins to suspect any stranger (and even neighbors) of involvement in the terrorism by telephone. Rosie's apprehension grows when the caller identifies himself as Frank — her late husband. Frank was convicted of murder and executed after being turned over to the authorities by Rosie. The caller claims that it is time for Rosie to pay the price for her treachery. She will receive a visitor that night and "justice" will be served. Rosie accepts the caller's claim to be the late Frank; his uncanny knowledge of her background and, her every move inside the apartment can only be attributed to supernatural forces. In desperation, she calls a former girlfriend, Mary (Lydia Alfonsi), and asks for help. The two women were once part of a love triangle involving Frank, with Mary losing the man she loved to Rosie. There is still a bitter edge to Mary's words as she rejects the ridiculous notion that "Frank's come back." Nevertheless, Mary finally agrees to stay with Rosie that night.

When Mary arrives, she seems cold and distant at first. She assures Rosie that threatening telephone calls from Frank are quite impossible. Mary insists that Rosie is wracked with guilt over Frank's death and is punishing herself with this delusion. As the two women prepare for bed, Mary slips a mild sedative into a hot drink that she gives to Rosie. The girl quickly drifts off into sleep while Mary begins writing Rosie a letter of explanation stating that the girl's psychological state indicates a need for professional help. When she awakens, Rosie will be in a mental hospital where needed medical help will be administered.

As Mary finishes the letter, the apartment door silently opens. A man quietly creeps up behind her, apparently thinking it is Rosie. He seizes a silk stocking and slips it around Mary's neck. The makeshift noose becomes an effective weapon as the intruder tightens his grip and throttles the innocent woman. As Mary falls lifelessly to the floor, her murderer realizes his mistake but regards the body coldly and emotionlessly.

Rosie is stirred from her light sleep by the sounds of the struggle. She turns to see the intruder now moving toward her and recognizes him as her late husband. "No, Frank...you're dead!" she cries as the stone-faced killer slowly draws near. She slips her hand beneath her pillow and grasps the handle of the butcher knife she hid there earlier in the evening. Frank looms near, preparing to wrap the stocking around her neck. Rosie plunges the knife into Frank's chest. He emits a guttural cry before falling backward and collapsing with the blade still imbedded in his chest.

The bloodied corpse lies still for one terrible moment until Frank's taunting voice can be heard coming from the telephone receiver. "Rosie...Rosie...I'll always be here to call you...on the telephone." A final cry of terror and despair escapes her throat as Rosie realizes that her torment will continue.

The ear-splitting scream practically leaps at the audience and is the only startling moment in this lurid, uninvolving segment. Tales of horror-suspense in which a threatening voice provides the source of terror have been highly effective in such thrillers as *Midnight Lace* (1960), Blake Edwards' *Experiment in Terror* (1962) and, much more recently, the opening scenes of *Scream* (1977). *Experiment in Terror* is especially disturbing as the rasping vocal intonations of Ross Martin are accompanied by background music that sounds like an iron lung set in neutral. However, the soft and melodious voice of the undead Frank seems to indicate the presence of a charmer rather than that of a menace. His lewd, bizarre comments are more funny than frightening, and little else is done to suggest the growing sense of horror within the hapless Rosie.

The story might have been somewhat more effective if shot in black-and-white since color finally dispels any atmosphere of tension that may have existed. Rosie's colorful wardrobe and her tastefully decorated apartment seem more like a set from *Butterfield 8* (1960), another story of a tragic playgirl.

Michèle Mercier (born 1942) is well-cast physically as Rosie and delivers a restrained performance. Mercier is known mainly for her "Angelique" features which typecast her as an amorous adventuress. She also played the female lead in Antonio Margheriti's *Web of the Spider* (1970), a remake of the director's chilling *Castle of Blood* (1964). Though not a good chiller, "The Telephone" may be remembered for the presence of Mercier, if nothing more.

"The Wurdulak" is the final segment, set in Russia during the early 19th century. As the story opens, aristocratic young traveler Vladimir d'Urfe (Mark Damon) is journeying on horseback through a dark forest. He comes upon a corpse clad in black and lying near the side of the dirt road, dismounts and approaches the lifeless form. The man has been decapitated and the head is nowhere in sight.

Shaken by the grisly scene, he continues his travels for a brief time until a peasant farm comes into view. Vladimir describes his encounter with the headless corpse to a strapping young farmer named Giorgio (Glauco Oronato). Giorgio, his wife (Rica Dialina) and child are awaiting the return of the aging but still rugged family patriarch, Gorka. Also present are Giorgio's brother Pyotr (Massimo Righi) and a lovely girl with ash-blonde hair named Sdenka (Susy Andersen).

Vladimir shares quiet conversations with members of the close-knit family and senses the great fear that lingers beneath the placid exterior. The sound of distant footsteps can be faintly heard as someone walks across a rickety wooden bridge and slowly approaches the cottage. The two brothers rush outside, followed by the others, who nervously anticipate the arrival of the grandfather. A slouching figure clad in a black cape draws near, silently passing those who await his return before bracing himself against the door of the cottage. He turns abruptly to face the others and seems surprised that his family does not greet him warmly. It is the patriarch — Gorka (Boris Karloff). The family, now complete, enters the cottage. Any words exchanged with Gorka are few and cautious, as though the slightest offense might provoke a confrontation. Gorka has returned with a horrendous prize that he carries in a burlap bag: the severed head of an infamous bandit, given to one of the brothers for him to place on display on the cottage's gatepost. "Tell them old Gorka killed him!" the old man proudly proclaims.

Gorka's behavior has changed drastically and there is little of the kindly grandfather left. Though hungry, he rejects a plate of boiled rabbit, striking it from his daughter's hands. When the baying of a hound plays upon his nerves, Gorka hands a musket to Giorgio and demands that he shoot the animal — once his favorite dog. The cruel command convinces other family members that Gorka has returned to them as a "Wurdulak" — a vampire who preys upon those he loves.

The bandit slain by Gorka was said to be a Wurdulak and, according to legend, the slayer of a Wurdulak must become such a monster himself. Sdenka explains the fearsome legend to Vladimir and expresses concern for her family's safety. The peasant girl has won the affection of the young man, although he is not convinced of any threat to Sdenka and the others. However, Sdenka's fears are realized when Gorka abducts his grandson in the dead of night. The child's mother senses that something is wrong and finds that the boy is missing from his crib. Giorgio dresses quickly and rushes downstairs, where he finds Pyotr apparently asleep at the table. When Giorgio tries to rouse his brother from sleep, the limp figure falls heavily to the floor. The body of Pyotr bears bloody wounds upon the neck, apparently inflicted by fangs.

The boy is cradled in the arms of Gorka, who madly flees into the night on horseback. Pursuit by Giorgio and Vladimir is futile as the old man soon eludes them. Little time passes before the boy is found, drained of blood. The remaining members of the family seem to accept their inevitable doom, but Vladimir is determined to save Sdenka. Although she first resists the demands by Vladimir to flee the region, Sdenka finally agrees to leave with him.

Giorgio is stirred from his sleep by a faint cry from amid a dark cluster of trees. He fearfully approaches a window and sees his murdered son — now a Wurdulak — walking toward the cottage. "I'm cold, mama…I'm cold," moans the child-vampire.

When the mother awakens, Giorgio insists that it is only the howling of the wind that they hear. The woman, however, is not convinced and must see the truth for herself. Overjoyed that her child has returned, she demands that he be allowed to enter the house. Her reasoning now gone, she stabs her husband and rushes to the door, crying, "Mama's coming!" She undoes the latch and opens the door, finding the cold-eyed Gorka waiting on the doorstep. The woman cries out in terror as Gorka closes in for the kill.

Vladimir and Sdenka are several miles away from the horrendous scene, taking shelter within the ruins of a large house. As Vladimir goes off to search for firewood, Sdenka is left alone for a time. To her horror, she sees Gorka. His words are almost a taunting reminder of the kindly grandfather he once was, as Gorka assures Sdenka that he means her no harm. Giorgio and his wife also appear and the three undead intruders encircle Sdenka, slowly drawing closer.

When Vladimir returns, Sdenka is nowhere in sight. Believing that she has returned home, Vladimir makes his way back to the cottage. Quickly searching the house, he enters Sdenka's bedroom. After pushing back the bed-curtains, he finds the girl cowering within. Sdenka asks Vladimir to forgive her and explains that she could not desert her family.

The girl still expresses her love for Vladimir and pleads with him to stay with her. Looking into the dark, piercing eyes of Sdenka, Vladimir seems to be completely mesmerized. They kiss softly…the girl's lips slowly move toward the young man's throat. Vladimir gasps as he is claimed by Sdenka, who is now a Wurdulak. Gorka and his vampiric brood watch the climax of the grim drama from outside the window. Vladimir's horse, sensing the presence of great evil, breaks away and races along the country road. The animal disappears in the distance as a cloud of dust fills the night air.

Though sometimes marred by heavy-handed dialogue, "The Wurdulak" features the most impressive visual composition of the three stories. Glaring faces, bathed in streaks of blue or red light, emerge from the night shadows and glide toward the camera in a strikingly eerie fashion. The light of the moon reflects coldly upon silent, staring figures who position themselves in doorways or windows. Lonely travelers seem dwarfed by immense black skies and bleak landscapes dotted with gnarled trees. The skeletal branches of these trees seem ready to reach out and grasp unsuspecting interlopers.

Much as in Bava's *Black Sunday*, the original music of Roberto Nicolosi was replaced by a richly symphonic Les Baxter score. His use of strings lends a darkly ethereal quality to the gliding figures of Karloff's vampiric brood as they seemingly "float on air" toward other victims. Sdenka's vampiric seduction of Vladimir is accompanied by a pounding percussion that slowly builds, much like the heartbeat of a man filled with terror. Shrill violins are introduced during Vladimir's final moments as his fate is sealed and the music peaks.

Boris Karloff (1887–1969) earned his second Italian horror credit with *Black Sabbath*. His first Italian "chiller" was the 1953 production *Il mostro dell'isola* (*The Monster of the Island*) with Karloff as a kindly fellow who becomes involved with smugglers. It was never released theatrically in the U.S. and is rarely televised.

Karloff's characterization of old Gorka in *Black Sabbath* is a mixture of crude virility and stubborn pride, with just a hint of the common humanity that once existed. Many years earlier, Karloff brought these same elements to his portrayal of an oppressed Russian peasant in a 1928 play entitled *Windowpanes* which co-starred John Carradine. "[Karloff] looked like Rasputin with a typical peasant shirt and boots," remarked Carradine in a 1972 *Castle of Frankenstein* interview. "It was a superb characterization." *Windowpanes* netted Karloff $75 weekly, which was a paltry amount compared to his salary for *Black Sabbath*—about $25,000.

Mark Damon (born 1935) was a comparative newcomer whose "pretty boy" roles had him briefly competing with actors like Robert Vaughn and John Saxon in portraying rebellious youths unable to express their emotions. Damon first filled bit parts in war movies like *Between Heaven and Hell* (1956) and *The Screaming Eagles* (1956). He played a rich kid in trouble in *Life Begins at 17* (1958) before settling into AIP lo-budgeters with the suspenseful *House of*

Usher (1960). In the latter film, Damon portrayed innocent Philip Winthrop, a young gentleman who encounters the madness and mayhem of the Usher family. His portrayal of Vladimir d'Urfe is also a smooth blend of elegance, courage and common decency. The actor settled into the European action market with AIP's *The Young Racers* (1964), directed by Roger Corman.

Other of Damon's roles have included that of the title gunslinger in the spaghetti western *Johnny Yuma* (1967) and also that of a courageous G.I. in the big-budget *Anzio* (1968), starring Robert Mitchum and Peter Falk. Damon kept his hand in horror, however, starring in *The Devil's Wedding Night* (1973), an Italian chiller directed by Luigi Batzella. Damon more recently turned from acting to become a producer.

The rich color texture, creepy exuberance and often dreamlike quality of *Black Sabbath* are elements injected by Mario Bava into such succeeding efforts as *Planet of the Vampires* (1965) and *Kill Baby Kill* (1966). Sadly, the latter two thrillers suffered from scripting flaws and a lack of originality. It is in *Black Sabbath* that sound plotting managed to gel with various other elements to create a minor genre classic.

Black Sunday

Original title: *La maschera del demonio* (*The Mask of the Demon*). Galatea/Jolly, AIP. 83 minutes. 1961 (ORD: 1960). B&W. Dir: Mario Bava. Prod: Massimo DeRita. Writ: Ennio DeConcini, Mario Serandrei. Based on the short story "The Vij" by Nicolai Gogol. Ph: Bava, Ubaldo Terzano. Mus: Les Baxter. Ed: Serandrei. Art Dir: Giorgio Giovanni. Cast: Barbara Steele, John Richardson, Ivo Garrani, Andrea Cecci, Arturo Dominici, Enrico Olivieri, Antonio Pierfederici, Clara Bindi, Germana Dominici, Mario Passante, Tino Bianchi.

This is Mario Bava's great one, marking the horror debut of Barbara Steele in her first starring vehicle. Though mildly grisly, there is a dark, dream-like quality that pervades the entire film. *Black Sunday* remained Mario Bava's best chiller, despite the many other genre efforts that were to follow.

In 19th-century Moldavia, the fear of Satan is felt strongly by both the common folk and aristocrats. One practitioner of the black arts has been sentenced to death by a group of inquisitors which include members of her own family. The fate of Asa (Barbara Steele) will be execution by impalement: a hideous steel mask lined with spikes will be driven into her face. Asa's faithful manservant Javutich (Arturo Dominici) has already suffered such a fate.

As the mask is set into place, Asa's terror turns into defiance and vindictive fury. She laughs maniacally and curses her descendants for all time. Asa continues to shout threats as the executioner wields a sledgehammer that drives the spikes into her skull.

A full century passes, but Asa's descendants still live in fear of the curse that may one day be fulfilled. The family members live lives of quiet desperation.

A pair of doctors arrive by carriage in the primitive region. Dr. Choma (Andrea Cecci), a striking figure in his middle years, is accompanied by young Dr. Gorobec (John Richardson). The men lack sufficient knowledge of the village history, but will soon learn more than they wanted to know. Choma and Gorobec wander through an old crypt where they find a windowed coffin occupied by the body of a woman, its face covered by a demon-like mask. A large stone cross has been affixed to one end of the coffin. Intrigued by the strange remains, Choma decides to remove the mask. Some effort is required to loosen the deeply embedded spikes, but the mask finally pulls free. The woman's face bears several deep punctures while a few small scorpions emerge from her empty eye-sockets. The corpse is remarkably well preserved.

The men are suddenly distracted by a bat that begins flying in circles around them. Choma begins striking out at the creature with a walking stick, accidentally shattering the stone cross. During the sudden commotion, Choma suffers a minor cut. A few drops of blood fall upon the pale lips of the corpse.

The men depart from the crypt, unaware of the chain of events that they have inadvertently set into motion. The small amount of blood "offered" by Choma has been enough to partially revitalize the corpse of Asa. Whitish orbs fill her eye-sockets, and pupils soon form. The witch regains consciousness and her malevolent influence soon begins to work against her descendants and other innocents.

Dr. Gorobec has a chance encounter with Princess Katia (Steele again), who bears an amazing resemblance to the long-dead Asa. The resemblance is quite understandable since the girl is a direct descendant of the witch. Katia is a strikingly beautiful woman, yet quite mysterious with her somber expression and penchant for black clothing. Her raven hair and coal-black eyes are the same color as the long cape and high boots she wears. Gorobec is immediately drawn to the girl.

Katia's father, the aging Prince Vaida (Ivo Garrani), is troubled by a growing sense of foreboding as he paces the floors of the family castle. His fear intensifies as a servant fetches him wine and he brings the goblet to his lips. Within the dark liquid is the shimmering

Pressbook art for *Black Sunday* (1961).

image of a figure wearing a demonic mask. He casts the goblet away and glances about the room, but no such figure is present. Perhaps the image was a mere delusion produced by his weariness and long-festering fears. Nevertheless, such fears are shared by Katia and her brother Constantin (Enrico Olivieri).

A village priest reveals the source of such fears to the two doctors, explaining the evil practices of Asa and her servant, the horrendous fate of the evil pair and Asa's curse. It is a frightening story that would certainly intimidate simple peasants, but it is somewhat less disturbing to men of science like Gorobec and Choma.

Choma returns to the crypt in search of additional information. Any factors relating to the health of the prince would have value to Choma, including superstitious fears that produce anxieties.

Choma finds Asa in her coffin in a half-rejuvenated state. The heavy door of the crypt suddenly slams shut and Choma is unable to open it. Sudden tremors shake the coffin of Asa as Choma watches in horror. Following the brief disturbance, all is quiet for several moments — until the coffin explodes with a deafening roar. The voice of Asa can be heard calling out to Choma. "Embrace me, human," she commands. "You will die...and I will show you pleasures no mortal could ever know!" Now in a mesmerized state, the doctor walks slowly to Asa's side. The witch bares her teeth in eager anticipation of the life-giving blood he will provide.

After claiming Choma, Asa's power has increased to the point that she is able to call forth Javutich from his unmarked grave. The undead manservant walks the night, beginning a campaign of vengeance against the Vaida family. Javutich materializes within the castle, entering the bedroom of the prince. As the stone-faced figure draws near, the aging nobleman awakens with a start. He seizes a cross and thrusts it forward, then buries his face in the pillow. Javutich flees, unable to withstand the sight of the Christian symbol. Servants and family members respond to the cries for help, though no intruder is in sight. Katia and Constantin are concerned about their father's physical condition, prompting them to summon a physician.

Dr. Choma soon arrives, but he is not the congenial and vibrant figure that he was just a few days earlier. His face expressionless and pale, the doctor coldly performs the physical examination of the prince. Choma insists that the man requires a great rest. Servants and family members must avoid disturbing him for several hours.

The next morning, a servant quietly enters the master's room and discovers the corpse of the prince — his face bloodied and frozen in horror. Dr. Gorobec is joined by the village priest as both men fully comprehend the conflict that they must now face. The two men scour the surrounding area, searching the crypt and nearby ruins. A coffin bearing the corpse of Choma is finally discovered. The priest deals with the vampiric Choma in the prescribed fashion — impalement, followed by a needle through the eye. It is a shattering experience for Gorobec, who is consoled by the priest. The young doctor must remember that this is not the Dr. Choma he once knew, but only a shell occupied by an evil spirit.

The terror grows as the prince is prepared for burial. His body rests peacefully in a coffin as members of the household await the arrival of other mourners. Katia enters the dimly lit chamber and is overcome by grief. Tears begin to flow as the sobbing girl kneels at the side of the coffin. Katia watches in horror as the corpse opens its eyes and stares into her face. She cries out in terror and backs away as the body rises from the coffin. Summoning her courage, she calls out to her father and evokes a chilling response. "You must not call me that now," he rasps. "Your blood is all that I want."

As he moves threateningly toward Katia, the undead prince meets an unexpected adversary. Javutich enters the chamber and seizes the reactivated corpse, hurling it into the flames of an open hearth. The silent, murderous minion of Asa then seizes innocent Katia and spirits her away to the secluded chamber of the witch. It is there that Asa uses her powers to further restore her strength and vigor. Katia becomes pale and gaunt while her evil ancestor takes on a healthy glow.

Javutich continues to wreak vengeance upon the Vaida family as he confronts Constantin in the shadowy corridors of the castle. The youth backs away fearfully from the undead fiend, falling into a pit. Dr. Gorobec soon confronts Javutich in the same corridor and the two opponents engage in a tense struggle that leads to the edge of the pit. Surprisingly, it is Javutich who tumbles into the huge cavity as he is seized from below. Gorobec's rescuer is the mortally wounded Constantin who, during his final moments, informs the doctor of Katia's plight. The girl is held captive in the lower levels, at the mercy of the vengeance-seeking witch.

Gorobec rushes to the rescue, but it is the revitalized witch whom he mistakenly embraces. Asa continues the deception, expressing "relief" at his arrival and fear of the "witch" who lies before them on a slab of stone. Gorobec states his intention to slay the woman he believes to be the witch by driving a needle through one eye. Luckily, he notices a tiny cross around Katia's neck — a symbol that could never be worn by a witch. He removes the cross and approaches the real Asa, who retreats from the symbol of purity. Gorobec reaches out and grasps her cape, which opens to reveal the

Lobby card for *Black Sunday* (1961).

dried flesh and exposed bones beneath. With her identity revealed, Asa attempts to wield her influence upon Gorobec. She promises him the same power and pleasure that she enjoys if he will embrace the dark forces of Satan.

The door suddenly bursts open as the priest arrives with a horde of villagers. Asa is seized and carried out into a clearing where she is bound to a wooden stake. Huge piles of branches encircle the fiendish witch, who watches as torches are touched to the dry wood. Flames envelop Asa, who reverts to her corpse-like state while Katia returns to normal. Gorobec, who kneels praying by her side, is elated at her recovery. The two young people may now hope for a future together as the family curse is lifted by the flames of Asa's funeral pyre.

Black Sunday is the best of Mario Bava's directorial efforts and succeeds on every level of quality. Subtle underplaying by a competent cast, excellent sets and fine camerawork by Bava and Ubaldo Terzano contribute to the overall success of the film. There is an effective use of chiaroscuro that helps establish a grim undercurrent of horror much like that of Dreyer's *Vampyr* (1932). Terzano's camerawork brought the same visual appeal to Bava's *Black Sabbath* (1964) and *Blood and Black Lace* (1965).

Bava avoids violence for its own sake and keeps the visual horror to a minimum. The needle-through-the-eye means of dispatching the vampire, for example, would have warranted a graphic depiction in a Hammer horror flick, but not so with *Black Sunday*. As the priest disposes of the vampirized Choma, Bava's camera switches to a closeup of Gorobec turning away from the grisly sight. Audiences identify strongly with Gorobec as he witnesses the violation of his moral sensibilities. The film also features one of Bava's favorite visual gimmicks — the sudden appearance of a ghastly reflection that provides a warning of horrors yet to come. The demon's mask appearing in a goblet of wine provides one of the film's most startling and pleasurably frightening moments. Bava used a variation of this gimmick in *Hercules in the Haunted World* (a face seen in a pool of blood) and *Planet of the Vampires* (a threatening figure reflected in burnished metal).

Another asset is the richly symphonic score composed by Les Baxter. The original score, composed by Roberto Nicolosi, was deleted by American-International in favor of background music that was deemed more appropriate by the studio. The prolific Baxter (1922-1995) worked on a number of record albums and '50s-'60s horror films, including Reginald LeBorg's *Voodoo Island* (1957), starring Boris Karloff. Baxter's fine talents were utilized by AIP for the Roger Corman Poe series, beginning with *House of Usher* (1960). The score of *Black Sunday* features an effective contrast between the personalities of Asa and Katia with appropriate motifs being assigned to each character. The use of sinister, heavy brass expresses the evil nature of the witch, while soft strings and chimes (with their religious implications) express the purity of the innocent Princess Katia. Baxter went on to compose the scores for such AIP thrillers as *X... The Man with the X-Ray Eyes* (1963), Bava's *Black Sabbath* (1964) and *Cry of the Banshee* (1970).

Black Sunday also marks an auspicious horror debut for Barbara Steele, who delivers an enigmatic performance in the dual role of Asa and Katia. Her large, expressive eyes and dark charisma are highly effective in portraying the somber frailties of Katia and the manic fury of her evil ancestor. Steele (born 1938) is the daughter of a concert pianist and the president of a shipping company. She was educated at the Sorbonne and her flair for the arts was carefully cultivated. Though originally trained as a painter, she exhibited a preference for acting and made her screen debut in a lightweight romance entitled *Bachelor of Hearts* (1958). The actress soon filled minor roles in *Operation Scotland Yard* (1958), *Upstairs and Downstairs* (1959), *The 39 Steps* (1959) and *Sapphire* (1959).

Black Sunday was her sixth film and first starring vehicle. She seemed to be a natural for the field and became a major genre figure in the 1960s, especially in the Italian horror cinema. Her other Italian chillers of the 60s include *Castle of Blood* (1964), *The Horrible Dr. Hichcock* (1964), *The Long Hair of Death* (1964), *The Ghost* (1965), *She Beast* (1966), *Terror-Creatures from the Grave* (1966) and *Nightmare Castle* (1966).

The competent supporting cast includes British actor John Richardson, who was later featured in several Hammer fantasy-adventures. He was the male lead in the Hammer version of *She* (1965), played Tumac in *One Million Years B.C.* (1966; a remake of the 1940 men and dinosaurs adventure *One Million B.C.*) and acted in *The Vengeance of She* (1967). Some will remember him best for a highly publicized role that he *didn't* procure: Richardson was considered for the role of James Bond in *On Her Majesty's Secret Service* (1969). He lost the part to George Lazenby.

Familiar faces in Italian horror and fantasy are those of Ivo Garrani and Arturo Dominici, who deliver nicely tuned performances. Garrani, who portrays the doomed Prince Vaida, also acted in the sci-fi thriller *The Day the Sky Exploded* (1961) and the mediocre *Atom Age Vampire* (1963). The talented Dominici brings the sense of sheer evil to the role of Javutich that he also delineated for the role of a ruthless monarch in the remake of *Thief of Baghdad* (1961).

Mario Bava went on to direct *Black Sabbath*, one of several U.S.-Italian co-productions with AIP: the director's visual skills were soon applied to inferior properties. But one may still look back to *Black Sunday* as an example of Italian horror at its best.

Blood and Black Lace

Original title: *Sei donne per l'assassino* (*Six Women for the Murderer*). A.k.a. *Fashion House of Death*. A.k.a. *Blutige Seide* (*Bloody Silk*). Emmepi/Monarchia, Woolner Bros. 88 minutes (ORT: 90 minutes). 1965 (ORD: 1964). Pathe Color. Dir: Mario Bava. Prod: Alfred Mirabel (Alfredo Mirabili), Massimo Patrizi. Writ: Bava, Marcel Fondat (Marcello Fondato), Joe (Giuseppe) Barilla. Ph: Herman Tarzana (Ubaldo Terzano). Mus: Carlo Rustichelli. Ed: Mark Suran. Art Dir: Harry Brest. Cast: Cameron Mitchell, Eva Bartok, Arianna Gorine, Dante De Paolo, Mary Arden, Lea Krugher, Massimo Righi, Claudia Dantes, Giuliano Raffaeli, Thomas Reiner.

As a director, Mario Bava had suffered one disappointment (*Hercules in the Haunted World*) but earned several triumphs before handling the horror-suspenser *Blood and Black Lace*. The film has echoes of his previous, more successful psychological horror flick *The Evil Eye* (1964). Sadly, the good spots only qualify as echoes and nothing more. In fact, the script is so eclectic that *Blood and Black Lace* comes off as being more thinly plotted than the Paolo Heusch quickie *Werewolf in a Girl's Dormitory* (1963).

Several grisly murders occur in Countess Christina's House of High Fashion. This elegant setting hardly seems like the focus of a serial killer who murders each of his victims in an exceptionally gruesome manner. The models employed by Christina (Eva Bartok) are being picked off by a faceless killer. A mute, fiendishly resourceful figure, the killer is clad in a trenchcoat, slouch hat and a pair of heavy gloves. His head is completely covered by a grayish-white cloth that obscures all facial features.

This basic scenario largely describes the events that occur in all but the last 15 minutes of the film in which we discover that Christina's fashion house is a front for a drug-dealing ring. Christina and her partner Max Morlan (Cameron Mitchell) are alarmed by the fact that one of their models has kept a record of drug-dealing transactions in a diary. The identity of the model and the location of the diary are unknown, so all of them have to go.

Soon after the murders begin, the resourceful Insp. Silvester

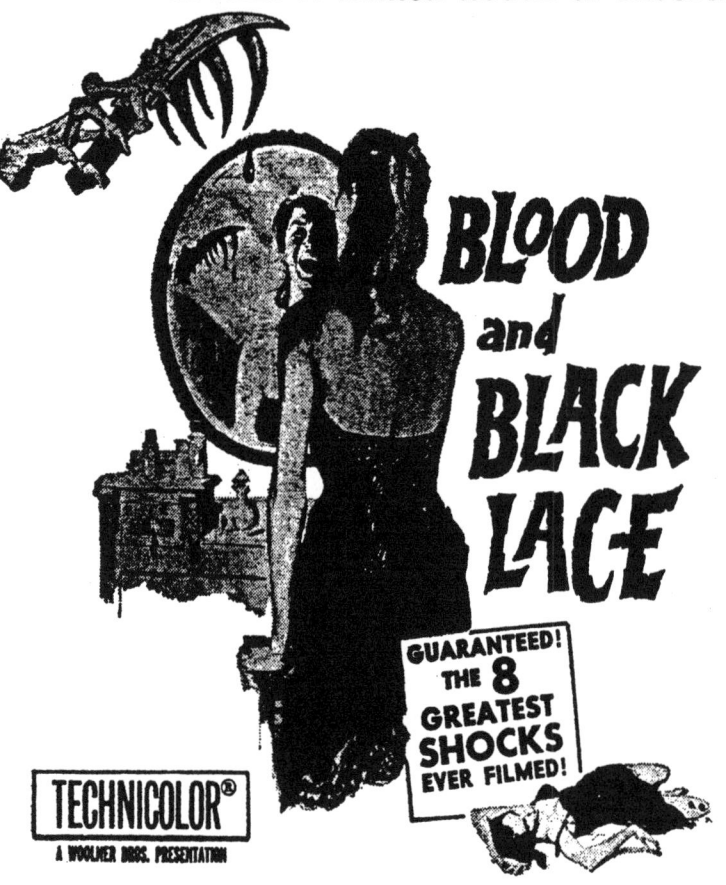

Pressbook art for *Blood and Black Lace* (1965).

(Thomas Reiner) has already uncovered the fact that one of the victims was addicted to cocaine. This development prompts Christina and Max to bring the "purge" of the models to a rapid conclusion. The faceless killer is none other than Christina herself. Her final victim is a voluptuous brunette named Taoli (Claudia Dantes), whom Christina dispatches in a bathtub drowning. Christina then slashes the wrists of the corpse, making the murder appear to be a suicide.

As the foul deed is completed, the murderess prepares to leave Taoli's residence. A sudden, loud rapping on the front door startles Christina, who hears the voice of a man claiming to be a police officer. The shouts continue (as does the pounding on the door) while Christina scampers out the second story window. She attempts to climb down a drainpipe which becomes dislodged, plunging the woman to the ground. Her screams can easily be heard by the "policeman"—who is actually her treacherous partner, Max. The double-dealing Max created the commotion with just this outcome in mind.

Later that night, Max searches through Christina's desk, seeking valuables and documents. A strange noise distracts him, though a search of the premises reveals nothing. Max returns to the desk where he is confronted by a torn and bleeding Christina, who points a revolver at him.

Max does some fast talking and attempts to justify his actions of that night. He speaks softly to Christina as he cautiously approaches the woman and takes her in his arms. She slowly lowers the gun and almost seems to accept his outrageous lies. The moment of weakness quickly passes as Christina's expression suddenly hardens and a gunshot breaks the silence. Max crumbles to the ground and lies still. Only a few moments pass before Christina, fatally wounded, collapses beside him.

Blood and Black Lace features little in the way of character or plot development. The sketchy scenario merely provides another opportunity for Mario Bava to display his technical skills and create a series of disturbing visual experiences.

The routine plot twists and two-dimensional characters could have been incorporated into an adequately plotted half-hour segment of a TV detective series. As a mystery, the film depicts the sort of situation that Peter Gunn or Mike Hammer may have encountered (in a less graphic depiction). This flick is really about the series of exceptionally brutal, sometimes sadistic murders.

The initial killing takes place in a warehouse as petite blonde Nicole is pursued by the murderer through a series of darkened aisles. Horror builds psychologically as the terrified girl attempts to evade her pursuer. The clicking of high heels and painful gasps for air alternate with brief interludes of silence as her eyes scan the darkened showroom. Large crates and piles of boxes create many secluded areas and alcoves that might conceal the fiend.

The cat-and-mouse chase concludes as the maniac seizes her from behind. After locking one arm around her neck, the faceless killer takes brute pleasure in displaying the murder weapon — a glove-like appendage bearing deadly spikes. The weapon is slowly raised, then quickly strikes home as the spikes deeply penetrate the victim's face.

The admirable atmosphere of tension in this sequence, done with a minimum of violence, reminds one of similar moments in Bava's *The Evil Eye*. Unfortunately, the dark tone and psycho-terror soon give way to graphic tortures and mutilations. One especially harrowing scene has a woman being savagely beaten while her hand is seared by a red-hot stove. Eventually, her face is forced against the same glowing metal surface. We see a close-up of the victim with eyes wild as her face is bathed in the red glow of the stove.

Murders by strangulation or suffocation by pillow seem tame in contrast, though the final bathtub drowning is done with the terrible beauty typical of Bava. The voluptuous form of Claudia Dantes relaxes in death with eyes open and sightlessly staring. Her face is expressionless and her pale body, immersed in water, is clad only in flimsy under-clothing. She is nearly presented as an object of necrophilia until her body is enveloped by an expanding pool of blood. Such revolting but strangely compelling sequences need a substantial framing device to provide cohesiveness. An actual story rather than a rough framework would be appropriate.

The murder victims are portrayed by a number of attractive starlets, most of them seen in various states of undress. Their acting styles are wildly divergent, with performances that vary from amateurish to quite fair. Hungarian-born actress Eva Bartok overshadows her glamorous, somewhat younger co-stars with a polished portrayal of the murderous Christina. Then in her late 30s Bartok still retained her considerable physical charms as well as competent acting ability. Sadly, her career was mainly limited to second-rate features, with the exception of the colorful Burt Lancaster adventure *The Crimson Pirate* (1952). Her only previous genre credit was

The Gamma People (1956), a halfway decent SF-horror steeped in Cold War rhetoric.

Cameron Mitchell (1918-1994) delivers the best performance with his smooth portrayal of the devious Max Morlan, Mitchell, a minister's son and World War II bombardier, first became known on the Broadway stage for his portrayal of "Happy" in *Death of a Salesman*. He reprised the role in the first film adaptation of the play in (1951). Many other roles followed, including parts in *Flight to Mars* (1951), the 3-D mystery *Gorilla at Large* (1954) and the offbeat Swedish-made melodrama *Face of Fire* (1959). His European action movie roles included that of Julius Caesar in *Caesar the Conqueror* (1962) and Cesare Borgia in *The Black Duke* (1963). He worked with Bava in a trio of brutally exciting Viking epics, all of them superior to *Blood and Black Lace*.

At this point, Bava had already done his best work in the horror genre with his first directorial effort (*Black Sunday*) remaining his greatest accomplishment. There would still be some variation in quality exhibited in his other chillers, but the director never managed to obtain another decent script for a horror film.

The Bloody Pit of Horror

Original title: *Il boia scarlatto* (*The Scarlet Hangman*). A.k.a. *The Crimson Executioner*. A.k.a. *The Red Hangman*. MBS Cinematografica/International Entertainment, Pacemaker. 87 minutes (some U.S. prints run 74 minutes). 1966 (ORD: 1965). Eastman Color, CinemaScope. Dir: Max Hunter (Massimo Pupillo). Prod: Francesco Merli. Writ: Robert Christmas (Roberto Natale), Romano Migliorini. Ph: John Collins (Luciano Trasatti). Mus: Gino Peguri. Ed: Robert Ardis. Art Dir: Frank Arnold. Cast: Mickey Hargitay, Walter Brandt (Brandi), Louise Barrett (Luisa Baratto), Ralph Zucker (Massimo Pupillo), Alfred Rice (Alfredo Rizzo), Femi Martin (Eufemia Benussi), Rita Klein, Barbara Nelli, Moha Tahi, Nick Angel (Nando Angelini), Albert Gordon.

"Beware the Crimson Executioner!" blared the original newspaper ads for this mixture of gore and sexploitation trash. Mickey

Hargitay was in Italy doing a film with wife Jayne Mansfield entitled *L'amore primitivo* (*Primitive Love*) when he accepted the lead role in this quickie horror job. Supposedly, the film is based on the works of the Marquis DeSade. Which works allegedly provided the basis for the story, however, is anyone's guess. There are the Sadean images of whips, chains and masks intermingled with glimpses of bare female flesh and nothing more.

Hargitay plays a reclusive former actor named Travis Anderson, a narcissistic fellow who takes pleasure mainly in his own exceptional physique. One day, his castle is invaded by a group of the "beautiful people" who want to use the juicy Gothic trappings of Anderson's castle as the background for the book jacket of a horror novel. The lurid cover will cater to sadomasochistic tastes, requiring the use of five well-proportioned models who assume various seductive poses for a sleazy photographer. Also along for the photo session are the publisher, the book's author (Walter Brandi) and the author's fiancée (Luisa Baratto).

About 300 years earlier, the castle was occupied by a mad nobleman who embarked on a killing spree and took great pleasure in torturing to death a number of voluptuous young women. History repeats itself in a grisly fashion when Anderson suddenly feels compelled to re-enact the horrendous murders. Apparently, Anderson experiences uncontrollable rage over any female competition in the body beautiful department. Driven by his strange compulsion, he dresses himself in a black mask, tights and a broad band-belt before subjecting the scantily clad models to a series of grisly tortures. Aided by his psychotic manservant (Massimo Pupillo), Anderson eliminates the girls one by one until the only surviving intruders are the author and his girlfriend. The decent young couple are allowed to flee the castle, apparently because the wholesome Edith (Baratto) presented no threat to Anderson's male ego.

This flimsy framework provides an outlet for all of the voyeurs in the audience who enjoy viewing the well-proportioned anatomies of several starlets as well as that of former Mr. Universe Mickey Hargitay. The girls look fine, though most of them can't act. Nubile bodies in various stages of undress take the place of acting ability with the two-dimensional characters requiring little, if any, exposition. Just what motivates Anderson to become a sadist and a murderer is

In its 1972 reissue, *The Bloody Pit of Horror* (originally released in 1965) was advertised with *Body Snatcher from Hell*.

never explained. Has he been possessed by the Crimson Executioner, whose murderous spirit still lingers in the old castle? Or is his murderous rage the result of impotence? Perhaps he once lost at love — a defeat for a megalomaniac whose mind finally snaps in a blood-spattered welter. Does anyone really care?

Hargitay makes an imposing figure, dressed in the costume of a medieval torturer. As in his other film roles, his body is merely a prop that merges with surroundings. In *The Bloody Pit of Horror*, the black-masked, bare-chested image of the Crimson Executioner blends perfectly with the creepy Gothic setting. Many people have objected to the characterization of Travis Anderson as resembling a negative gay stereotype.

Hargitay's other film roles have made few demands on his limited acting ability. He filled supporting roles in the realistic, hard-edged *Slaughter on 10th Avenue* (1957) and the hilarious satire *Will Success Spoil Rock Hunter?* (1957). The latter effort starred Tony Randall with Jayne Mansfield as the female lead. A ludicrous fantasy entitled *The Loves of Hercules* (1960) featured Hargitay as the fabled demi-god with wife Jayne in a dual role as the heroine and an evil queen. The husband-wife team were again featured in the weak sex farce *Promises, Promises* (1963) with direction by actor King Donovan (who acted in Don Siegel's *Invasion of the Body Snatchers* [1956]). Hargitay chalked up another genre credit with his supporting role in the 1971 Italian horror flick *Lady Frankenstein* (*La figlia de Frankenstein*), starring Joseph Cotten and Sara Bey.

However, the only person who performs with any style in *The Bloody Pit of Horror* is cinematographer Luciano Trasatti. His excellent camerawork was previously featured in such films as *Vitelloni* (1956), *Sign of the Gladiator* (1959) and *Love and Marriage* (1966). Trasatti soon brought a strong color texture to his best job of photography with Franco Zeffirelli's *The Taming of the Shrew* (1967), starring Elizabeth Taylor and Richard Burton.

Massimo Pupillo's unremarkable stint as a director was preceded by a somewhat more successful career as a child actor. Pupillo is adequate as Hargitay's crazy sidekick, acting under the pseudonym of "Ralph Zucker"— a name he also used as the original distributor of the film. He later provided some pleasurably gruesome sequences for a slightly better directorial effort, *Terror-Creatures from the Grave* (1966), starring Barbara Steele. This flick was released by Pacemaker as the bottom half of a double-bill with *The Bloody Pit of Horror*. Unhappily, the Hargitay chiller emerges as a sexist, somewhat homophobic tale that is equally offensive to women and gays.

Caltiki, the Immortal Monster (Caltiki, il mostro immortale)

A.k.a. *Caltiki, the Undying Monster.* AA. 76 minutes. 1960 (ORD: 1958). B&W. Dir: Robert Hampton (Riccardo Freda). Prod: Samuel Schneider. Writ: Phillip Just (Filippano Sanjust). Ph: John Foan (Mario Bava). Cast: John Merivale, Didi Sullivan (Perego), Gerard Herter, Daniela Rocca, Daniel Pitoni, Gay Pearl, Giacomo Rossi-Stuart.

Riccardo Freda is widely known for the elaborate costume dramas that he began directing during the 1940s. However, Freda began turning more to horror melodrama and fantasy laced with horror in the early 1960s. *Caltiki, the Immortal Monster* emerges as Freda's grim, fitfully exciting tribute to the "monster-that-will-not-die" American chillers of the 1950s. Despite an unimaginative script and ordinary performances, Freda provides the audience with an abundance of thrills and several high-powered shock sequences.

Deep within the jungles of Mexico, an archaeological expedition seeks the answer to a centuries-old mystery: What became of the Mayan civilization which vanished without a trace many centuries ago? A previous expedition into the foreboding jungles met with disaster and only one man survived in an incoherent state. A team of well-armed explorers now continues the mission of their predecessors while also attempting to learn the fate of their missing colleagues.

The explorers are a strangely mixed group led by John (John Merivale), an archaeologist whose motives are purely scientific in nature. A German adventurer named Max (Gerard Herter) seeks a treasure of gold. Ruthless and self-centered, the sly Max keeps a lecherous eye on John's wife Ellen (Didi Perego). Max takes advantage of her resentment over the harsh conditions they all must endure. An exotically beautiful Indian girl, Linda (Daniela Rocca), is in love with Max and manages to ignore his callous indifference to her feelings.

An American adventurer named Bob (Daniel Pitoni) is curious about local customs and attempts to investigate aspects of native culture that might help solve the Mayan mystery. He knows that the Indians live in fear of a Goddess of Death that they have named Caltiki. One night, a group of natives watch as an Indian girl performs a ritual dance to the accompaniment of pounding drums. Hiding behind a clump of bushes, Bob watches the strange, compelling performance for several moments. Both the music and the dancing cease abruptly when the girl screams in fear after seeing the white intruder furtively watching the bizarre rites. Bob backs away and manages a nervous smile, but his reckless curiosity will soon prove to have dire consequences.

Bob is certain that there are more treasures and artifacts to be found beyond those already discovered among the ruins of the Mayan town of Tikel. Other clues might be present at the bottom of a small subterranean lake located near the ruins. After donning his diving gear, Bob lowers himself into the lake. Probing the murky depths for a brief time, he sees nothing of any consequence. Suddenly, something comes into view that makes his eyes grow wide with horror. He sounds the alarm signal, which brings a quick response from John and Max. Using the safety line, they pull Bob to the surface. After removing his face mask, the men find near-skeletal remains as though some corrosive substance had eaten away Bob's flesh.

John and Max are distracted from the grisly sight by a sudden turbulence originating from beneath the surface of the lake. A monstrous mass of protoplasm emerges from the water and begins to move inland. The men draw their pistols and open fire, but bullets have no effect on the lumbering monstrosity.

Max turns to flee along with the others until he spies the golden artifacts that lie directly in the path of the monster. He rushes back for the gold, but trips and falls against the writhing mass of organic matter. Max cries out for help as he finds his right arm entangled within a tentacle-like appendage. John seizes an axe and severs the

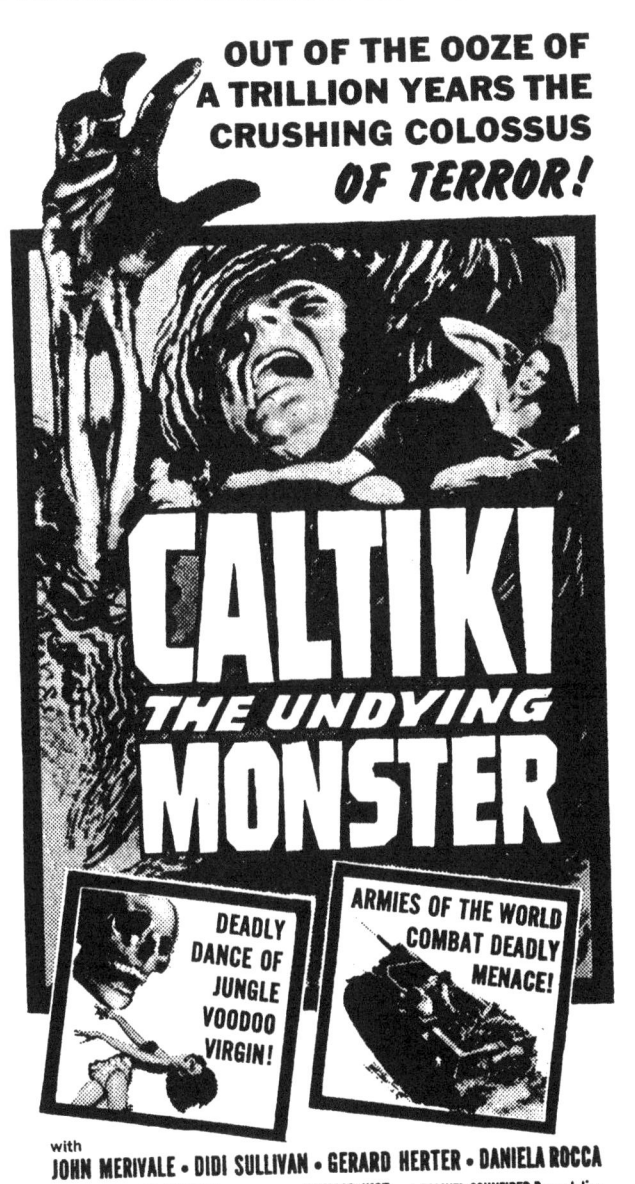

Pressbook art for *Caltiki, the Immortal Monster* (1960).

appendage, freeing Max, who is rushed to safety. The monster continues its slow movement inland.

John rushes to a nearby supply truck, climbs inside and starts the engine. He begins driving at high speed directly toward the monster. With moments to spare, he leaps from the cab and runs from the coming conflagration. A fiery explosion erupts as the truck collides with the horror from the lake. Enveloped by flames, the creature becomes a massive lump of glowing carbon.

Max (Gerard Herter) escapes into the night and embarks on a rampage in *Caltiki, the Immortal Monster* (1960).

Max is rushed to Mexico City, where emergency surgery is performed. There is some scarring on one side of his face, but the horrendous damage is to his right arm, which has been reduced to little more than skeletal remains. The small mass of remaining protoplasm removed from his arm is now apparently inert. Most of the substance is sent to a laboratory where a number of tests are conducted. The growth is subjected to radioactive time-testing and discovered to be quite ancient — older than any living thing on Earth. The organism is the freakish outgrowth of a one-celled structure, much like an amoeba.

Max, recovering from surgery, is visited by John, who tries to be positive about the grim situation. Max bitterly rasps, "You're a lousy liar!" As he departs, John learns from a doctor that a poisonous residue from the organism has entered Max's bloodstream and there is no means to destroy the substance. Max has been secretly listening to their conversation and a frightful plan begins forming in his mind.

As the doctor anticipated, the poison reaches Max's brain and produces psychotic behavior. One night, as a nurse brings medicine

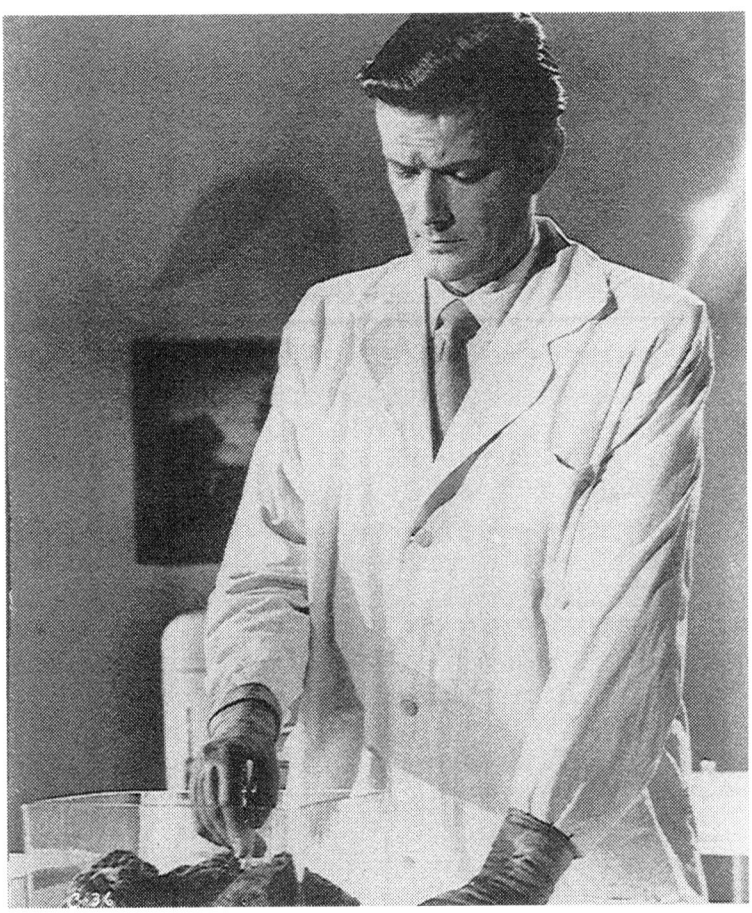

Professor John Fielding (John Merivale) examines a dormant mass of protoplasm in *Caltiki, the Immortal Monster* (1960).

to Max, she is attacked and beaten to death by her patient. Now a homicidal maniac, Max flees the hospital and goes into hiding. Police search the city and surrounding countryside but are unable to locate the murderous fugitive.

In the meantime, a far deadlier situation begins to develop when a radioactive meteorite passes near Earth and revives the remaining pieces of protoplasm. The growth process resumes as the flesh-eaters expand, reproduce and continue growing at an incredible rate. One of the scientists who has been conducting experiments on the substance is killed in a fiery car crash en route to the laboratory. Consequently, the lab is left empty and the now monstrous growth is uncontrolled. Caltiki — the Goddess of Death — lives again and prepares to prey upon mankind as it did centuries earlier. The mystery involving the disappearance of the Mayan people has been solved.

As an unsuspecting Mexico City teeters on the brink of disaster, Max is being hidden by Linda, whose feelings for the now-crazed adventurer have not changed. Max has spent his time in the cellar of John's mansion, where Linda secretly brings him food. Mad Max seizes a revolver and decides to kidnap Ellen.

Max leaves his hiding place and enters the darkened mansion to seek out the woman. He soon confronts Ellen and demands that she run away with him, leaving behind her husband and young daughter. Linda attempts to block the mad scheme as she stands between the gun-wielding Max and the terrified Ellen. Tragically, the Indian girl's courage cannot dissuade him from his evil purpose. Max cold-bloodedly shoots Linda, then proceeds to carry out the mad plan of abducting Ellen.

Unknown to Max, part of the carnivorous organism recovered from Tikel has been kept in an adjoining room. Now of monstrous proportions, the creature overturns lamps and tables while thrashing about. Max thinks John is hiding in the darkness. Pointing his revolver at the sliding doors of the adjoining room, the madman calls out in a threatening fashion. The flesh-eating horror bursts through and hungrily devours Max. Ellen and her child flee the horror that relentlessly pursues them. John arrives in the nick of time and rescues his family; though all of Mexico City is now threatened by the Mayan "god" that devours everything in its path.

John's scientific knowledge comes into play as he provides information to military authorities. Troops and tanks have been mobilized, though John insists that bullets and ordinary projectiles will have little effect upon Caltiki. The creature has no internal organs or central nervous system — it is simply a mass of hungry flesh. Fire was the only effective weapon against the organism when it was first encountered near the ruins of Tikel. The army responds quickly to the scientist's advice as tanks equipped with flame throwers begin their assault on Caltiki. The monster from the dawn of time

Publicity shot of Didi Sullivan as Ellen Fielding in *Caltiki, the Immortal Monster* (1960).

is reduced to a blackened, bubbling mass of dead tissue. John finally shares a tender moment with his family as some semblance of sanity is finally regained.

Caltiki, the Immortal Monster is enriched by the talents of two filmmakers who become very influential in Italian genre efforts of the 60s, Riccardo Freda and Mario Bava. The prolific Freda, born in Egypt in 1914, studied sculpture before entering the film industry in 1937. As a director, he first specialized in adventure films that were usually graced with an elaborate period setting. Some typical credits include *Les Misérables* (1947), the story of Spartacus in *Sins of Rome* (1952), *See Naples and Die* (1952), *Theodora, Slave Empress* (1953) and *Trapped in Tangiers* (1957). Freda began using the name "Robert Hampton" with *Caltiki, the Immortal Monster* and continued using the pseudonym for his other genre efforts *The Horrible Dr. Hichcock* (1964) and *The Ghost* (1965).

Freda creates a number of terrifying images throughout *Caltiki, the Immortal Monster*. Huge, darkened rooms that may conceal unknown menaces, closeups of mad, staring faces and spontaneous outbursts of bestial violence combine to provide considerable tension and shock value for horror addicts. The dark atmosphere and feeling of impending doom are well-maintained, neatly enhanced by Bava's excellent black-and-white photography.

The talented Bava (1914-1980), born in San Remo, Italy, was the son of a sculptor and became a movie cameraman during the 1930s. His first genre credit, Freda's *The Vampires* (1956), not only features Bava's striking camerawork but also provides some early evidence of his skill as a director. After ten days of shooting, Freda walked off the set of *The Vampires* when a conflict erupted with the producers over basic artistic differences. Bava assumed the director's chair and completed the film in just two days, though he only received screen credit as director of photography. A similar situation occurred with Jacques Tourneur's *The Giant of Marathon* (1961), for which Bava directed several action sequences while only being credited for his fine camerawork. Bava's official directorial debut with *Black Sunday* established him as Italy's most skilled purveyor of movie horror during the 60s.

Caltiki, the Immortal Monster delighted both kids and grownups at Saturday matinees. The film earned fairly respectable box office receipts and proved the marketability of the chillers that were emerging from an industry known for elaborate spectacles and austere sociological dramas.

Castle of Blood

Original title: *La danza macabre (Danse macabre)*. A.k.a. *Castle of Terror*. A.k.a. *Coffin of Terror*. A.k.a. *La lunga notte del terrore (The Long Night of Terror)*. A.k.a. *Tombs of Horror*. A.k.a. *Dimensions of Death*. SPA Cinematografica, Woolner Bros. 85 minutes. 1964 (ORD: 1962). B&W. Dir: Anthony Dawson (Antonio Margheriti). Prod: Frank Belty (Marco Vicario), Walter Sarch (Giovanni Addessi). Writ: Jean Grimaud (Gianni Grimaldi), Gordon Wilson, Jr. (Sergio Corbucci). Based on the short story "Danse macabre" by Edgar Allan Poe. Ph: Richard Cramer (Riccardo Pallotini). Mus: Riz Ortolani. Cast: Barbara Steele, Georges Rivière, Margaret Robsahm, Silvia Sorrente, Henry Kruger, Montgomery Glenn (Silvano Tranquilli), Raoul H. Newman (Umberto Raho), Phil Karson, Ben Steffen, Salvo Randone.

Barbara Steele chilled American horror fans in a pair of 1961 AIP releases, Mario Bava's *Black Sunday* and Roger Corman's *Pit and the Pendulum*. Her reputation as the queen of 60s horror helped the salability of *La danza macabre*, which was shot in 1962. The film was completed for two years before being picked up by Bernard Woolner for U.S. release in the fall of 1964. Retitled *Castle of Blood*, it was the bottom half of a double bill with *Hercules in the Haunted World*. Steele fans were not disappointed, either with her performance or with the overall quality of *Castle of Blood*.

The quiet beauty of the English countryside is pleasing to young American tourist Alan Foster (Georges Rivière). Beyond the pleasures offered by verdant landscapes and small villages with their charming simplicity, Foster also enjoys the relaxed contact in a roadside inn. Pleasant conversations and warm pints of beer make the time pass easily enough until Foster meets another American visitor — a diminutive gentleman named Edgar Allan Poe. Poe, a rather impoverished fellow, is the guest of Lord Blackwood, who has accompanied him to the pub. As they indulge in small talk with Foster, the subject of the supernatural is mentioned. Poe is a struggling young author who specializes in the horror field while Blackwood owns a deserted mansion that has the reputation of being haunted.

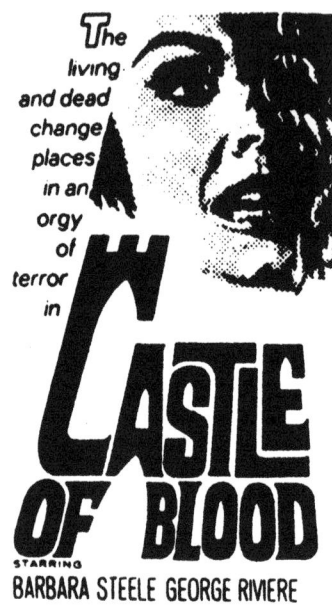

Pressbook art for *Castle of Blood*, 1964.

Foster fails to embrace such superstitions, being the product of a more "enlightened" society. Blackwood promises him a generous cash prize if he spends one night in the eerie mansion. Certain that the offer will provide easy money plus the opportunity to amuse himself with local legends, Foster departs for the eerie abode.

As sunset approaches, Foster and his companions arrive at the house by carriage. Blackwood and Poe quickly depart after informing Foster that they will return for him at dawn. He calmly enters the house and begins to explore the shadowy interior. The dead silence and drab walls fill him with a sense of foreboding.

The door of an adjoining room bursts open and there is a brief glimpse of a young couple dancing to the music of a harpsichord. The door slams shut and the music abruptly ceases. Foster opens the door and rushes into the room, finding it unoccupied. There is a harpsichord, but its surface is covered with a layer of dust. Foster is puzzled by the strange incident, but not deeply disturbed. He mindlessly allows his fingers to play upon the keys of the harpsichord — until a hand touches his shoulder.

The startled Foster turns to face a raven-haired woman dressed in a white nightgown. She introduces herself as Elizabeth Blackwood (Barbara Steele), the only occupant of the mansion. Foster finds her presence to be quite surprising, since Lord Blackwood made no mention of any relatives residing there. The woman takes her unexpected guest on a brief tour of the house.

Elizabeth escorts Foster to her bedroom and the talk becomes more intimate. Sitting on the edge of the bed, she softly smiles and whispers, "Come, Alan...sit by me." Foster complies as the evening seems to be turning into a night of more than pleasant diversions. Unknown to the young man, other figures move furtively throughout the mansion as a plot by supernatural forces begins to unfold.

Lying together now, Foster and Elizabeth share a tender moment. He rests his head upon her breast, but is startled by the fact that he cannot hear the girl's heartbeat. Foster straightens and calls out her name with a hint of a tremor in his voice. Elizabeth softly responds, much to the relief of Foster who states that he feared her heart had stopped beating. Elizabeth informs him that his fear was well-founded. "I'm dead, Alan...dead," she states unemotionally.

The door bursts open as a muscular, bare-chested man storms into the room. Brandishing a knife, he lunges for Elizabeth and thrusts the blade into her heart. Her mad attacker stumbles backward and seems somewhat disoriented as he flees down a dark corridor. Foster withdraws a revolver from his waistcoat and pursues the man, firing a bullet into the broad back of the murderer. The man collapses and mysteriously vanishes as Alan draws near. Foster rushes back to Elizabeth, but finds that she has also disappeared.

The situation becomes even more bizarre and frightening as another man suddenly appears on the scene. A scientist named Dr. Carmus (Henry Kruger) has witnessed the unfolding of the violent drama and provides Alan with some chilling details about the incident. Elizabeth and her attacker, a man named Herbert, are phantoms. Carmus claims that he has been conducting a long investigation of the strange phenomena afflicting the Blackwood mansion. His attempts to penetrate the secrets of life and death are perfectly suited for the spirit-infested structure. Within this large "laboratory," Carmus has studied man's will to survive long after physical death.

Ghostly manifestations continue as Alan witnesses occurrences that preceded the tragic end of a love triangle. An elegant ball was held on the night that Elizabeth married into the Blackwood family. As guests dance gaily or engage in brisk conversation, Elizabeth slips away to meet briefly with her former lover—a manservant named Herbert (Silvano Tranquilli). He pleads with the beautiful woman to run away with him, leaving behind her husband and his estate. Elizabeth tells Herbert that their relationship is over. She tears herself from his embrace and, despite his protests, rejoins the wedding party. Hatred and jealousy burn in Herbert's eyes.

One night, as Elizabeth and her husband are making love, Herbert furtively enters the bedroom and strangles the man with a length of rope. Elizabeth's sister Julia (Margaret Robsahm) sees the murder being committed and does nothing to stop it. As Herbert makes threatening moves toward Elizabeth, Julia approaches from behind. She strikes a fatal blow to Herbert's head with a candelabra before turning to comfort Elizabeth. A demanding and domineering woman, Julia makes clear her intention to control Elizabeth's life once again. The tormented Elizabeth seizes a knife and drives it into Julia's middle. Julia collapses and dies after a brittle scream escapes her throat. Now quite mad, Elizabeth goes into hysterics.

The ectoplasmic manifestations vanish as quickly as they appeared, but the eerie history of the horror-filled mansion soon continues to reveal itself. Dr. Carmus disappears for a brief time, being a phantom himself. However, he soon materializes in a re-enactment of his last night in the house — the night of his death. The figure of Carmus is seen sitting at a desk, making entries in a journal before being distracted by noises in the structure's lower levels. Descending into the shadowy depths of the mansion, Carmus sees a cloud of gray mists emerge from a coffin. Visibly shaken, he fearfully rushes back to his quarters and feverishly scribbles further entries.

Preoccupied with his notes, Carmus fails to notice Herbert emerging from behind heavy curtains. Foster shouts a warning, but these ghostly shadows from the past are doomed to relive this horrid play without interruption. Herbert attacks Carmus savagely, sinking his teeth into the side of the doctor's neck. Carmus pitches forward onto the desk, his neck bearing bloody wounds. Moments later, Foster approaches the desk after both murderer and victim have faded from view. An unfamiliar sound distracts Foster, who instinctively pulls the revolver from his pocket. This puny attempt at self-defense against supernatural predators evokes distant, ghostly laughter. Foster allows the weapon to drop from his fingers, realizing the futility of his response.

Escape seems impossible as one final ghostly vignette is enacted for Foster. Two newlyweds arrive, chattering excitedly. Foster shouts desperate warnings as the phantoms climb a staircase and arrive at their quarters. Their fate is swift and devastating as first the girl and then her horrified spouse are dispatched by the murderous Herbert. The bloodied bodies lie still for a few moments before they vanish. Only a brief time passes before they materialize, hand in hand, slowly walking toward the next victim of the Blackwood curse. "Tonight is your turn...Foster," they grimly chant.

Foster flees the bedchamber, but is pursued throughout the house by Carmus, Herbert and the other phantoms who need his blood. Only Elizabeth intervenes to save him, revealing hidden corridors and passageways that enable Foster to escape the spirits. Foster finally passes through a hidden door into the surrounding grounds. He demands that Elizabeth accompany him, but she insists that escape is impossible for her. Foster seizes the struggling woman and begins moving away from the house, but their flight together is short-lived. Elizabeth falls to the ground and her body disintegrates into a mound of dust.

The horrified Foster is left disoriented by this last terrible experience as he stumbles across the grounds toward the main gate. Strange voices issue threats and the wind howls mournfully as Foster senses the spirits hovering around him. He finally reaches the heavy iron gate which he opens, escaping into the real world. For a few moments, all is quiet as Foster rests against a gate post. In a final irony, the gate swings shut and a protruding spike penetrates the back of Foster's neck. The dead man's impaled body is held erect by the spike.

With the coming of dawn, Poe and Lord Blackwood arrive by carriage. At first, the men are not alarmed as they see Foster "waiting" for them at the gate. As the men draw closer, they realized — to their horror — that Lord Blackwood has won the wager. Foster stares sightlessly as Blackwood reaches for the dead man's pocketbook and withdraws the specified amount of money. The nobleman asks Poe to forgive his lack of respect for the dead as he claims his winnings. Though stunned by Foster's bizarre death, Poe does not object to Blackwood's cold-bloodedness.

The two men depart in the carriage, leaving the disposal of Foster's remains for the authorities to handle. The landscape is shrouded in silence once again as a gentle breeze gives movement to the branches of surrounding trees. A woman's voice softly whispers, "You've come back to me, Alan."

"Yes...Elizabeth," comes a male response.

Despite its horrific nature, *Castle of Blood* ends on a strangely touching note. The joining of two loving spirits is reminiscent of William Wyler's *Wuthering Heights* (1939) with its ghostly reunion between Heathcliff and Cathy. No further comparison seems likely since the Margheriti film displays a generally low level of tragedy and romance.

As a chiller, the film works very well. Director Antonio Margheriti makes effective use of mists and somber, dark rooms enshrouded with cobwebs. The highly atmospheric black-and-white photography of Riccardo Pallotini enhances such Gothic trappings while capturing a sense of foreboding in the blackest nights and the most dismal of mornings. Margheriti and Pallotini were soon teamed again for the visually competent but otherwise less effective *Horror Castle* (1965).

Barbara Steele, having just completed her role in Fellini's *8½* (1963), returns to the horror genre and delivers another polished performance. Her portrayal of the tormented Elizabeth is an intriguing, enigmatic mixture of fragile charm, infinite sadness and outright hysteria. Steele has rarely been more beautiful or more mysterious. Her scenes are neatly complemented by a fine Riz Ortolani score with its haunting, gentle harpsichord and startling use of strings that reach a shrill, hysterical pitch. Several of Ortolani's pieces were soon lifted for another atmospheric Italian chiller, *Castle of the Living Dead* (1964).

Castle of Blood is filled with a number of disturbing images and startling sequences. The quiet wedding night that becomes a scene of carnage is certainly the most horrific. A snake being bisected by a scalpel and refusing to die as it writhes and flicks its forked tongue is repulsive, but more strange than frightening. The most confusing, bone-chilling scene has the terrified Foster fleeing into the night where he is beset by ghostly voices and bodies that suddenly dangle from tall trees. His apparent escape and a few moments of calm are followed by his unexpected, shocking impalement. Images of life and death are just a hair's breadth apart and finally merge in a terrible fashion. It is death that has final dominion over all, no matter how selfishly and frantically the characters cling to their uncertain existence.

Georges Rivière, who neatly portrays the doomed Alan Foster, was soon cast as the hero of Antonio Margheriti's *Horror Castle* (1965). Steele went on to star in another period chiller from Margheriti, *The Long Hair of Death* (1964). Both are comparatively ordinary films with *Castle of Blood* remaining the director's most successful genre effort.

The film failed to draw as much attention as the Corman-AIP Poe adaptations, possibly because of its modest nature. Fans who preferred their horror done in Panavision and Pathe Color, with several major genre figures as cast members, may have been disappointed. It is interesting to note that Margheriti directed a scene-for-scene remake of the film as a widescreen, color feature entitled *Web of the Spider* (1970). A big-name cast included Tony Francoisa, Michèle Mercier, Peter Carsten and Klaus Kinski. Ironically, the film drew even less attention than the Steele version. *Castle of Blood* remains a favorite among cultists who admire its atmosphere, stylish direction and skillful delineation of volatile themes.

Castle of the Living Dead
(Il castello del morti vivi)

A.k.a. *House of Blood*. A.k.a. *House of the Dead*. Serena Films, AIP. 85 minutes. 1964. B&W. Dir/Writ: Herbert Wise (Luciano Ricci). Second Unit Dir: Michael Reeves. Prod: Paul Maslansky. Ph: Aldo Tonti. Cast: Christopher Lee, Donald Sutherland, Gaia Germani, Philippe Leroy, Mirko Valentin, Antonio de Martino, Jacques Stanislawski, Luciano Pigozzi.

Christopher Lee's third Italian horror film was never distributed to theaters in the United States. Instead, *Castle of the Living Dead* was released directly to television by American-International. This was an unfortunate decision by AIP, since this thriller has rarely been seen and would have made a perfect "A" feature for one of the studio's many double bills. Despite its familiar aspects, it is highly atmospheric and contains a few touches of offbeat humor.

Mirko Valentin gleefully subdues a victim in *Castle of the Living Dead* (1964).

It is the beginning of the 19th century — the Napoleonic era in France. Life is difficult in peasant villages, though the austere existence offers a few simple pleasures. Villagers are surprised when a colorful troupe of circus performers arrives in the sparsely populated region. However, the flamboyant entertainers are not without their own troubles and conflicts. Two of the five performers have become embroiled in a terrible argument. One man, who feels slighted by the others, demands his rightful place in the group during a confrontation with their leader, Bruno. When his demands are not met, the disgruntled fellow decides to leave the group.

Fortunately for the others, a former soldier-turned-drifter named Eric (Philippe Leroy) decides to become the fifth member of the group. Eric feels drawn to the comely Laura (Gaia Germani), whose presence may have been the major reason for his attraction to life in a tiny acting troupe.

Their next destination is the eerie castle of Count Drago (Christopher Lee), whom they have been asked to entertain. Along

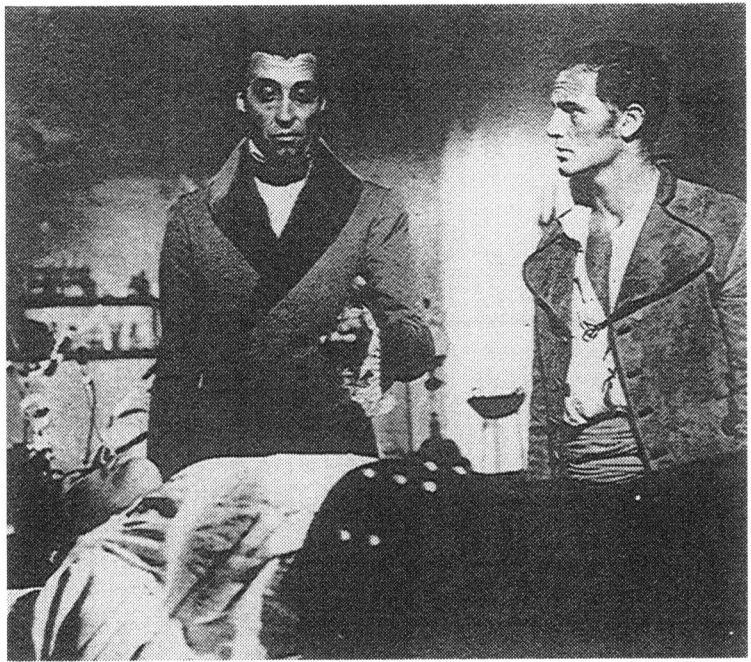

Castle of the Living Dead (1964): Count Drago (Christopher Lee, *left*) explains his bizarre hobby — taxidermy — to Eric (Philippe Leroy).

the way, they encounter a hint of the horrors to come. A raven, long dead and petrified, is perched on the low branch of a tree. This disturbing discovery is followed by the appearance of an old man (Donald Sutherland), clad in black and warning of disaster if they travel to the castle. Nevertheless, the small band continues the journey.

Arriving at their destination, they cautiously enter, but the massive structure seems deserted. The rooms are large but rather drab, distinguished mainly by the embalmed animals that decorate them. Count Drago soon arrives and greets his visitors while his servant Sandro (Mirko Valentin) stands silently in the background. Drago suggests that they rest before the evening performance. The five unsuspecting guests retire to their rooms, unaware of the horrors that await them.

That evening, after a meal, the acrobats begin to perform for the Count and his manservant. Ordinary feats of strength and skill hardly evoke a response, but Drago's interest is aroused by the major act — a mock hanging of Bruno. When the act is over, Drago emits a deep laugh and applauds while Sandro cackles maniacally. However, the act has gone terribly wrong — Bruno is dead. Drago offers his sympathies to the sobbing Laura and her three male companions, expressing regrets over "the terrible tragedy." The acrobats are unaware that Bruno has actually fallen victim to a deadly potion placed in his wine.

Ostensibly, Drago is deeply concerned about the incident and seems to cooperate with the police. A bumbling inspector (Sutherland again) and a pair of equally inept constables arrive to investigate Bruno's strange death. This initial visit fails to dispel the inspector's suspicions of foul play. He intends to visit the Count a second time in a search for the truth. Despite his furtive nature, Drago seems quite sincere in his intentions toward Eric and his friends. The Count's offer to handle Bruno's burial on castle grounds seems to provide adequate proof of his kind nature.

Eric indulges in a friendly chat with Drago after the police depart and learns that the Count pursues an interest in taxidermy. He uses a serum that instantly petrifies any living creature. This strange chemical does more than provide a bizarre pastime for the Count, who is obsessed with "preserving the beauty" of living creatures. The hapless Bruno is only one of the human subjects who have fallen victim to the Count's mad experiments. Other victims of the Count's evil are soon claimed as the acrobat and former member of the troupe finds his way to the castle and is murdered by Sandro. Little time passes before the group's strongman, a powerfully built deaf-mute, wanders into Drago's laboratory and is pierced in one eye by a syringe-like dart filled with Drago's serum. The projectile, fired from a crossbow by Sandro, spells instant death for the unsuspecting intruder.

The lovely Laura nearly consumes a glass of wine containing the potion. Startled by the sudden intrusion of a housecat, she drops the glass and witnesses a blood-curdling sight. The cat begins lapping up the dark liquid and is quickly petrified. Terrified, Laura prepares to flee the castle and searches for her companions. She finds one man, a plucky dwarf (Antonio de Martino), but cannot locate Eric, who has been knocked unconscious by Sandro.

In their flight, Laura and the dwarf blunder into the bedroom of Drago's late wife and find that the woman's corpse has been preserved by the fluid. Sandro arrives — with murder on his mind — and is prepared to kill Laura until Drago intervenes. The crazed manservant pursues the dwarf, seizes his terrified victim and hurls him from the castle battlements. Assuming that the dwarf has been killed, Sandro seeks out Drago for further instructions.

Luckily, the dwarf has fallen into a thick layer of foliage that cushioned the impact. His unconscious form is discovered by the old woman, who drags him away. While Laura and Eric are held prisoner, the dwarf regains consciousness in the woman's hovel. She reveals that many people have fallen victim to Drago's mad experiments, as she did in her youth. She desires revenge and feels that Drago must be stopped, no matter what the cost. Despite the heavy odds, the dwarf leaves for Drago's castle in an attempt to rescue his two surviving companions.

As he reaches the castle, the dwarf encounters Sandro and leads him on a frantic chase across the castle grounds. The dwarf is able to make his way through the narrow spaces between tangles of bushes and clusters of trees that prove to be major obstacles for the evil servant. The dwarf finally manages to seize the fallen pistol of Sandro and slays the murderous fiend with a well-aimed bullet.

Laura and Eric are informed by the pistol-wielding Drago that their fate will be the same as that of other interlopers and innocent drifters who previously arrived at the castle. The two young people are doomed to become frozen, flesh-and-blood statues. However, the dwarf's abrupt intrusion distracts Drago long enough for the captives to flee the laboratory. Drago pursues them to the castle entrance where there is an unexpected encounter with the three policemen. The crazed Count accuses the trio of abusing his hospitality and attempting to steal valuables.

A merry-go-round of madness ensues as Eric squares off against the constables. Though numbered three to one, the ex-soldier is a skilled fighter and his inept opponents are unable to collar him. During the struggle, the old woman suddenly arrives and denounces Drago as a murderous madman whose experiments have taken many innocent lives. The befuddled inspector is visibly stunned by the situation, but the old woman is determined to prove her accusations.

Endowed with strength born of rage, she grapples furiously with Drago, who is punctured by his own serum-soaked needle. His body freezes instantly...eyes wide in horror...teeth bared more in surprise than in pain.

The outlandish story of a chemical that can turn men into stone has been verified in a startling fashion. With the authorities alerted and the old woman vindicated, there are no further scores to settle. A strong new bond now exists between Laura and Eric, who depart in the wagon driven by the courageous dwarf.

Shot in the spring of 1964, this chiller was originally called *House of Blood* and then retitled *House of the Dead* before the more salable *Castle of the Living Dead* was finally chosen. The film is distinguished mainly by its bleak, dismal appearance and believable period setting. It was filmed on the outskirts of Rome in the same 16th century castle where Lee's *Uncle Was a Vampire* was shot in 1959. The striking black-and-white photography of Aldo Tonti makes the most of shadowy rooms and corridors while capturing the sense of foreboding present in mist-enshrouded landscapes. Complementing the bravura cinematics is a haunting musical score that makes effective use of strings and harpsichord. Several pieces were lifted from Anthony Dawson's *Castle of Blood*, shot two years earlier.

The cast is generally adequate, with Donald Sutherland providing most of the fun in his screen debut. He displays a skill for slapstick in his portrayal of the inept policeman, though it is mainly the makeup department that provide an effective characterization of the old woman. Christopher Lee's typical restraint is refreshing as always, despite a rather unsubtle makeup. His status as a madman or a living corpse isn't made clear until the final moments when Drago falls victim to his own lethal formula. Lee certainly looks like a corpse with a chalky complexion, dark, hollow cheeks and black circles beneath the eyes. The actor's fluent Italian comes in handy once again as he is able to dub his own voice in the Italian version while speaking the original role in English.

The film is endowed with an international flavor by a cast that combines the British Lee and the Canadian Sutherland with a Frenchman (Leroy), an Italian (Germani) and a Yugoslavian character actor (Valentin). Lee and Valentin were first paired the previous year in

Anthony Dawson's *Horror Castle*. There Lee portrayed a seemingly sinister butler while Valentin played the psychologically twisted Executioner.

Director-writer Luciano Ricci originally used the pseudonym of Warren Kiefer, though the AIP-TV release credits direction to "Herbert Wise." Ricci's talents lean toward atmospheric horror, light humor and the occasional juxtaposition of these two elements. The most effective sequence is the mock hanging of Bruno in which Drago's true character is revealed. We see the hapless Bruno writhe and emit choking sounds until the death rattle escapes his throat. Drago and his servant are elated by the horrible incident, greeting Bruno's demise with hearty laughter and vigorous applause. People too evil to be real are often quite amusing. This scene evoked laughter from French and Italian movie audiences. Later in the film, we see toy gallows being sold in the village square to people who accept the grisly items with child-like glee (reflecting real-life audience responses).

Such moments of dark humor and sly social commentary are, unfortunately, few and far between. The film as a whole is fairly ordinary with familiar shocks, familiar concepts and the uninspired handling of a few action sequences. Perhaps the most frequently explored premise concerns Drago's preservation of his wife's corpse and his inability to accept her demise. We had previously seen variations of this scenario in such films as *Voodoo Man* (1944), *The Black Sleep* (1956) and *The Horrible Dr. Hichcock* (1962), just to name a few.

Ricci may not have been responsible for all of the film's flaws since the final scenes, which are just sporadically effective, have been credited to assistant director Michael Reeves. A 20-year-old neophyte, Reeves also did some uncredited work on the script. Producer Paul Maslansky saw a great deal of skill and energy in the young man's work. Maslansky soon hired Reeves to direct another production, *She Beast* (1966), starring Barbara Steele.

Not long after its European release, *Castle of the Living Dead* was sold directly to TV by AIP. In fact, the film was reviewed in the "Frankenstein TV Movieguide" of *Castle of Frankenstein #8* (official publication date: April 19, 1966). Fans of Saturday matinee horror flicks were disappointed with the shoddy handling of the film. When the film was in production, it was announced in some of the fanzines while Christopher Lee made a formal statement to his fan club about accepting the role of a baron with "somewhat peculiar habits." AIP certainly had no doubts about the salability of Lee's name, despite a supporting cast that was largely unknown in the United States.

However, the company had been attempting to expand into television and began releasing a number of European and Mexican horror flicks to the small screen, beginning in the 1964-1965 TV season. *Castle of the Living Dead* happened to be one such film, along with *The Invisible Creature* (1960), *Curse of the Doll People* (1960), *The Blancheville Monster* (1964) and many others that never reached American theaters.

Chris Lee and Donald Sutherland were soon teamed again for Freddie Francis' *Dr. Terror's House of Horrors* (1965), the first of many omnibus-style thrillers produced by Amicus. Sutherland also turned up in Hammer's *Die! Die! My Darling!* (1965), portraying a simple-minded handyman, before switching to such major films as *The Dirty Dozen* (1967), *The Split* (1969) and *MASH* (1970). Beyond providing spotty entertainment value for Lee fans, *Castle of the Living Dead* also offers an early look at the talented Donald Sutherland before he achieved stardom.

The Embalmer

Original title: *Il mostro de Venezia* (*The Monster of Venice*). Gondola Film, Europix. 83 minutes (ORT: 85 minutes). 1966 (ORD: 1965). B&W. Dir: Dino Tavella. Prod: Christian Marvel, Walter Manley. Writ: Tavella, G. Muretta. Ph: Mario Contero. Mus: Marcello Gigante. Art Dir: Giuseppe Ranieri. Cast: Maureen Litgard Brown, Gin Mart, Luciano Gasper, Anita Todesco, Alcide Gazzotto, Alba Brotto, Elmo Carusa, Viki del Castro, Carlo Russo, Paolo Vaccari, Antonio Grassi, Jack Judd, Maria Rosa Vizzina, Gaetano Dell'Era, Pietro Walter, Roberto Contero, Francesco Bagarrini.

Of the many Italian horror quickies picked up for double-billing by Europix, *The Embalmer* may be the most trivial. Peopled with a no-name cast and utilizing a predictable, underdeveloped

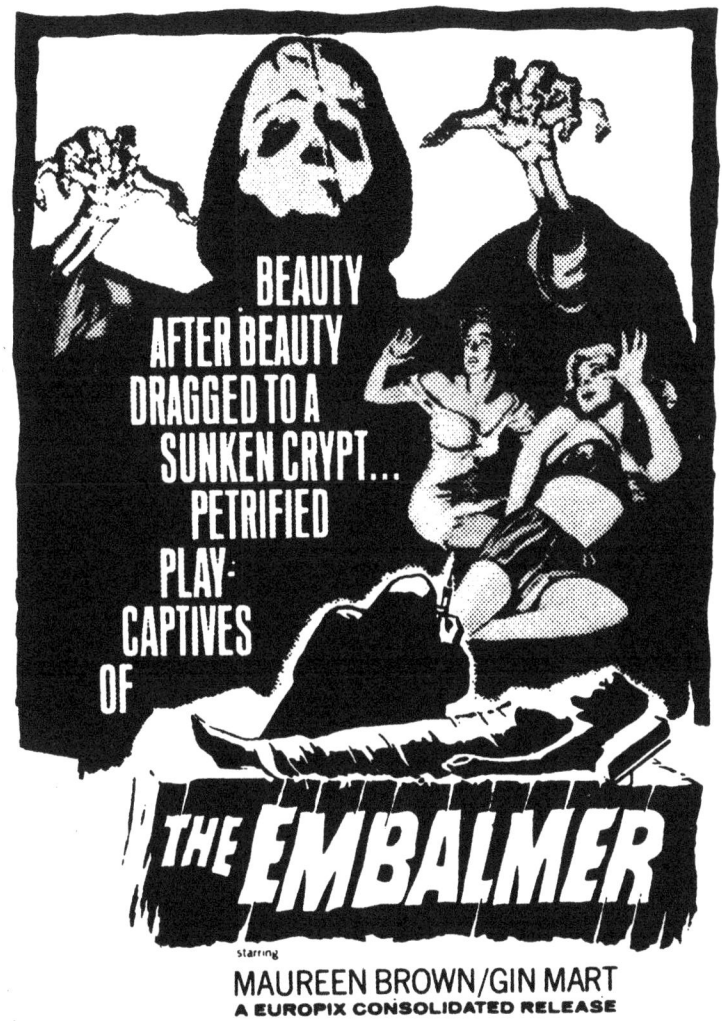

Pressbook art for *The Embalmer* (1966).

script, the film is distinguished mainly by good art direction and occasionally inventive photography.

Probably the only twist to this women-in-peril flick is that the mad stalker is a frogman who emerges from the canals of Venice to seize his victims. Each woman selected by the madman is captured in a freeze-frame for several seconds, allowing a subjective shot from the stalker's point of view. The women are murdered and their bodies stuffed before being placed in the alcoves of the madman's subterranean hideaway. Their murderer periodically removes his aquatic gear, then dresses himself in a cowled robe and a skull-like mask. The motivation for this grisly campaign of terror consists of the same dime store psychology used more effectively in the handsomely produced *House of Wax* (1953) and even in Roger Corman's halfway decent *A Bucket of Blood* (1959). By killing beautiful women who are in their prime, our mentally twisted "crusader" is able to preserve their beauty for all time.

The monster's nemesis turns out to be a shrewd journalist (Gin Mart) whose theory about a serial killer has been rejected by typically bullheaded police officials. A confrontation finally erupts when the journalist falls in love with an attractive young teacher (Maureen Litgard Brown) who has been marked by the madman as his next victim. When one of the teacher's associates (an inquisitive archaeologist) is claimed by the fiend, the woman finds that entry to the sunken crypt can be gained through the basement of the hotel in which she and her friend were staying. She foolishly enters the crypt and is captured by the fiendish killer. Luckily, the journalist has also become aware of the hotel's secret passageway into the crypt. He quickly dons his own diving gear and comes to the rescue in a tense struggle with the monster of Venice.

This thinly plotted effort is filled with countless shots of Venice, its canals, gondolas, buildings, etc. The pointless footage is obviously intended to pad the running time. Male lead Gin Mart probably reached the high point of his career by filling the supporting role of "Marcellus" in 20th Century–Fox's spectacular *Cleopatra* (1963). The unremarkable supporting cast of *The Embalmer* includes Anita Todesco, who previously played minor roles in the costume dramas *Morgan the Pirate* (1961), *The Thief of Baghdad* (1961) and *The Pharaoh's Woman* (1962).

The only real points of interest are provided by the sporadically creepy black-and-white photography of Mario Contero and Giuseppe Ranieri's art direction. Ranieri previously worked as art director on such visually competent films as *Slaughter of the Vampires* (1962), *Atom Age Vampire* (1963) and *The Playgirls and the*

Vampire (1964). As the film's frightened heroine wanders through the series of tunnels and stone chambers, we are treated to a few shadowy gems of suspense. Some good juicy visual horror is provided by closeups of mummified corpses enshrouded by cobwebs. The horrendous, withered faces can be seen with teeth bared in a sardonic grin.

Such brief sequences, largely occurring during the final minutes of the film, compare to the best work of William Castle and Roger Corman. Beyond these few horrific interludes, there is little else to recommend in *The Embalmer*. The film was originally released in the United States as the bottom half of a double-bill with Michael Reeves, *She Beast*, which was just slightly better.

The Evil Eye

Original title: *La ragazza che sapeva troppo* (*The Girl Who Knew Too Much*). Galatea/Coronet, AIP. 92 minutes. 1964 (ORD: 1962). B&W. Dir: Mario Bava. Writ: Bava, Ennio De Concini, Eliana De Sabata, Franco Prosperi, Enzo Corbucci. Ph: Bava. Mus: Les Baxter. Ed: Mario Serandrei. Art Dir: Giorgio Giovaninni. Cast: Leticia Roman, John Saxon, Valentina Cortese, Dante Di Paolo, Robert Buchanan, Gianni di Benedetto, Jim Dolen, Virginia Doro, Chana Coubert, Peggy Nathan, Marta Melecco, John Stacy, Franco Morigi, Milo Quesada, Lucia Modugno.

Mario Bava tried his hand at psychological horror in this flick, avoiding overt horror-fantasy elements and endowing the film with a few supernatural overtones. Bava creates a cold, calculating atmosphere and avoids the use of graphic violence.

A young American woman, Nora Drawlston (Leticia Roman), travels to Italy at the request of her aunt, who is gravely ill. Nora's early stay with the old woman is pleasant, but things go horribly wrong in the middle of a stormy night: The aunt suffers a heart attack and slumps forward in her chair, eyes wide in death. The aunt's face is partially obscured by shadows, but one eye still coldly regards Nora. The effect is quite startling and difficult for the young woman to forget.

A few days later, Nora is subjected to an even more disturbing experience. While taking an evening stroll on a quiet street, she is attacked and knocked to the ground during a robbery. In a semi-conscious state, she sees a woman stabbed to death by an attacker despite the dim light, Nora is able to see the face of a man fleeing the scene.

Nora's recollections of the harrowing events are vague and provide little useful information to the police. Although she clearly remembers the face of the suspect, her dazed condition gives police investigators reason to doubt her reliability. Nora is found to be in reasonably good condition by the sympathetic Dr. Alessi (Robert Buchanan), although his colleague remains concerned about her well being. Dr. Marcello Bassi (John Saxon) takes seriously Nora's fears that she is being stalked by the killer, who wants to silence her. Marcello becomes the girl's frequent companion while police official Landini (Dante Di Paolo) provides whatever security possible.

Despite her fears, Nora tries to lead as normal a life as she can. However, frightening incidents continue to plague Nora during the days that follow. One day, while walking near a seaside location, she is confronted by a burly, cold-eyed fellow whose appearance is quite intimidating. Although she turns to walk in the opposite direction, the stranger grimly follows her. Nora finally overcomes her fear and turns to face him. Surprisingly, the fellow's face breaks into a broad grin as he quips, "Say, beautiful…you want to go out with me tonight?" Relieved that she must only face an ordinary (though obnoxious) masher, Nora delivers a wallop to the side of his head with her handbag. The masher takes the response in stride and goes his way.

Nora's fears are lessened somewhat by her relationship with Marcello. The two young people share afternoon strolls and pleasant dinners as their friendship blossoms into romance. Nora also gets sympathy from shopkeeper Laura Terrani (Valentina Cortese), whose business is near the scene of the murder. Their conversations are pleasant and Laura seems sincere in her desire to be helpful, though she is unable to provide any useful information.

Another frightful incident occurs on a quiet night as Nora lies awake and sees the approach of a dark figure, just outside her curtained window. Despite the drawn curtains, the black-caped figure leans toward the window in an attempt to see into Nora's apartment. The stranger's hands are outstretched threateningly toward the glass. As he approaches the door, Nora's terror grows — until she realizes that the stranger is only a policeman walking his beat.

The "close calls" of recent days have all had rather innocent outcomes, but Nora's fears are not altogether dispelled. One day, she visits Laura's shop and faces a situation that becomes unexpectedly terrifying. The mysterious, middle-aged stranger seen on the night of the murder is cowering in the back of the store. It is Prof. Terrani (Gianni di Benedetto) — Laura's husband. The man nervously eyes Nora before falling from his chair, a knife protruding from his back. Laura confronts Nora, revealing that the furtive stranger of that night was indeed her husband. It was Laura who murdered the woman that night, motivated by intense jealousy. Now, both the man she once loved and innocent Nora must go as well.

Laura withdraws a small pistol from her pocket and, with a mad grin on her face, promises that death will be painless for Nora. The weapon that discharges, however, is not Laura's. As the crazed murderess falls dead, Nora sees a smoking pistol in the hand of the professor. With his dying breath, he took the life of his killer.

The police finally establish the circle of association between the crazed Laura Terrani and the series of unsolved murders in which the victims were young women. Nora's fears are finally laid to rest as she pursues the joys of new love with Marcello.

Mario Bava skillfully provides *The Evil Eye* with a subtle undercurrent of horror, avoiding the lovingly detailed mutilations that filled his succeeding horror-suspense films. Once the basic scenario is established, we see the cat-and-mouse game that exists largely in the mind of the heroine. Nora Drawlston is obviously in danger, but her encounters with malevolent(?) forces are frightening because we experience her paranoia rather than see the presence of any actual threat. A silent, burly stalker is found to be a simple masher who is easily discouraged. A black-cloaked, night-time intruder turns out to be a policeman doing his job.

Even when a suddenly stern-faced Marcello moves silently toward Nora on a deserted beach, we fear that this sundry young man is the mystery killer. "Marcello, what is it?" queries the puzzled Nora. "Don't you know?" comes Marcello's cold response. With that, he drops to Nora's side and embraces the girl who is stunned by his violent kiss. For one moment, we expect the worst from Marcello before realizing that we are only witnessing the open passion that erupts from suppressed desires.

Such moments, in which we mistakenly expect the emergence of the killer, are far more frightening than the actual emergence of the killer herself. An element of irony is neatly introduced by having Nora take elaborate precautions against imagined threats while unconsciously forming a relationship with the killer whose threat is quite real. As always, the fine camerawork of Ubaldo Terzano makes the most of darkened streets and shadowy rooms that may or may not harbor mortal danger. A fine Les Baxter score helps to build the mood of tension in several sequences.

Leticia Roman, who became familiar for her sex kitten roles, is a competent heroine — beautiful but compassionate, vulnerable but tough and resourceful when necessary. Roman previously acted in such efforts as the swashbuckler *The Pirates of Tortuga* (1961) and the Italian Biblical epic *Pontius Pilate* (1962) starring Jean Marais. One of her first major roles was the second female lead in an Elvis Presley musical, *G.I. Blues* (1960). However, Roman's most famous role is probably that of the title character in Russ Meyer's *Fanny Hill* (1965), which told the famous story of the 18th century libertine.

Roman is supported by two fine performers who are more familiar to American audiences. John Saxon brings a great deal of energy and typical charm to the role of Marcello, the young doctor with romance on his mind. Saxon, born in Brooklyn in 1935, was formerly a model whose muscular physique and dark good looks made him a natural for leading man roles. He turned to acting in the mid-1950s, often portraying troubled youths who were rebellious or misunderstood. Such efforts included *The Unguarded Moment* (1956), *The Restless Years* (1958) and *Summer Love* (1958). *The Evil Eye* was Saxon's genre debut and he has since acted in a number of chillers. His other 60s horror credits include *Blood Beast from Outer Space* (1965) and AIP's *Queen of Blood* (1966). Among Saxon's more recent horror credits are such titles as *Blood Beach* (1981) and *A Nightmare on Elm Street* (1984).

Also in fine form is Valentina Cortese (born 1924), who endows the role of Laura Terrani with a matronly charm that conceals the twisted psyche of a serial killer. Her calm demeanor, gentle voice and maddening smile make her murderous acts seem even more monstrous. Cortese began her acting career at age 15, performing in both American and European productions. Her horror and off-trail roles are few but smoothly delineated. She delivered fine performances in Orson Welles' *Black Magic* (1949) and the Fellini fantasy *Juliet of the Spirits* (1965). The actress is best known for her brilliant portrayal of a fading film star in Francois Truffaut's *Day for Night* (1973). This role earned Cortese the New York Film Critics Award for best supporting actress.

Mario Bava's next horror effort, *Black Sabbath* (1964), returned to a period setting for a tale of supernatural terror. However, Bava's *The Evil Eye* provides ample evidence that quiet horrors and monsters of the mind may be just as frightening as the more blatant forms of horror.

Fangs of the Living Dead

Original title: *Malenka, la nipote del vampiro* (*Malenka, the Niece of the Vampire*). A.k.a. *Malenka*. A.k.a. *Malenka, la sobrina del vampiro*. A.k.a. *The Vampire's Niece*. Triton Filmindustria/Victory Films/Cobra Films/Felix, Europix. 80 minutes (ORT: 94 minutes). 1968. Eastman Color, Totalscope. Dir/Writ: Amando de Ossorio. Prod: Audrey Ambert, Rossana Yanni. Ph: Fulvio Testi. Cast: Anita Ekberg, Julian Ugarte, John Hamilton (Gianni Medici), Audrey Ambert (Adrianna Ambessi), Diana Lorys, Maria Luisa de Benedictus, Rossana Yanni, Carlos Casaravilla, Paul Muller, Fernando Bilbao.

Anita Ekberg, stereotypical blond bombshell of the 1950s, acted in a series of low- to medium-budget features before settling into bargain basement quickies like *Fangs of the Living Dead*. The Italo-Spanish co-production is no worse than many of its type, but script and direction offer nothing new to horror addicts.

Ekberg plays a winsome young woman named Silvia whose uncle (Julian Ugarte) welcomes her to the castle she is about to inherit. Silvia expresses optimism over her future in the family castle, which

Pressbook art for *Fangs of the Living Dead* (1968).

will also become the home of her husband-to-be. The handsome structure with its cathedral ceilings, plus the aesthetic value of the surrounding grounds and the posh existence promised by the family fortune, will all make life quite comfortable for the young couple.

Sadly, her dreams are shattered when Ugarte explains the terrible family legacy that is now hers. Many years earlier, a nun named Malenka was accused by local authorities of practicing witchcraft. Seized by angry villagers, she was taken to the village square and burned at the stake. Malenka's demonic spirit has long been expected to return and wreak vengeance upon the village. Now, with the return of her descendant Silvia, the fears of villagers seem to have been realized. Ugarte explains to his niece that she is the image of Malenka—a reincarnation destined to carry out a long-festering vendetta.

During the days that follow, the gloomy revelations of Silvia's uncle seem to be validated by a series of grisly attacks on residents of the surrounding countryside. Silvia is convinced that she is possessed by the spirit of Malenka, who has returned as a vampire seeking the blood of innocent villagers. She breaks off the engagement to her fiancé (Gianni Medici), who refuses to accept the situation. Silvia also fears that her "inherently evil" nature will compel her to slay the man she loves. When the time comes, the woman realizes that she was not born to kill and her illusion of evil is dispelled. The true monster of the castle is her uncle, who has staged elaborate vampiric attacks in order to destroy Silvia and seize her inheritance for himself. In a final confrontation with the heroic Medici, the scheming uncle receives his just desserts.

Fangs of the Living Dead

The predictable series of events and routine plot twists of *Fangs of the Living Dead* come off as a rehash of Edgar G. Ulmer's *Daughter of Dr. Jekyll* (1957). The latter film had evil Arthur Shields convincing Gloria Talbott that she has been tainted with her father's chemically induced ability to transform into a repulsive, homicidal maniac. It is Shields who is finally revealed as the fiend who experiences nightly transformations into a bestial killer and embarks on a reign of terror. He perishes in a tense struggle with Talbott's fiancé (John Agar). Director-writer Amando de Ossorio substitutes a vampiric legend for the Jekyll/Hyde legacy while retaining the remainder of the Ulmer film's scenario.

Fangs of the Living Dead marks an inauspicious genre debut for de Ossorio, who soon became known for the films in his "Blind Dead" series — a quartet of chillers dealing with the gory exploits of long-dead 13th century knights who have been reanimated as vampires. The first entry in the series was the 1971 production *The Night of Blind Terror* (*La noche del terror ciego*), which American-International retitled *Tomb of the Blind Dead* for U.S. release in early 1973. The highly popular effort spawned three sequels: *Return of the Blind Dead*, a.k.a. *The Attack of the Blind Dead* (*El ataque de los muertos sin ojos*, 1973), *Horror of the Zombies*, a.k.a. *Ship of Evil* (*El buque maldito*, 1974) and *Night of the Seagulls* (*La noche de los gaviotas*, 1975). The "Blind Dead" efforts are just as badly written as *Fangs of the Living Dead*, but they are helped by an effective atmosphere of tension plus some high-powered shock sequences.

Horror buffs might find some interest in the presence of four faces familiar from their appearances in Italian and Spanish horror films. Character actor Julian Ugarte, whose best film was probably Stanley Kramer's *The Pride and the Passion* (1957), played a vampire in *Frankenstein's Bloody Terror*. The latter film is the American title for the 1968 chiller *The Mark of the Wolfman* (*La marca del hombre lobo*) starring Paul Naschy as the tormented werewolf Waldemar Daninsky. Ugarte later turned up in such action flicks as *A Man Called Noon* (1973) and *Blood Money* (1974). Paul Muller is more than familiar to fans of European horror films, having portrayed the mad doctor in Riccardo Freda's *The Vampires* (1956). Muller's acting enriched other thrillers such as *Nightmare Castle* (1966) and *Venus in Furs* (1969).

Co-producers/cast members Adrianna Ambessi and Rossana Yanni are also known for their additional acting credits in European horror flicks. Ambessi played the female lead in Camillo Mastrocinque's *Terror in the Crypt* (1963), based on Joseph Sheridan Le Fanu's classic vampire tale "Carmilla." Yanni played supporting roles in a trio of Paul Naschy thrillers *Frankenstein's Bloody Terror*, *The Hunchback of the Morgue* (*El jorobado de la morgue*, 1972) and *Dracula's Great Love* (*El gran amor de Conde Dracula*, 1972).

However, *Fangs of the Living Dead* might be seen mainly as a sad footnote in the declining career of a screen goddess — Anita Ekberg. Born September 19, 1931, in Malmo, Sweden, the actress first came to the United States to compete in the Miss Universe pageant as Miss Sweden in 1951. She soon accepted modeling jobs and did nightclub appearances before obtaining a minor role in the SF comedy *Abbott and Costello Go to Mars* (1953). Despite a misleading title, this outer space yarn has Bud and Lou heading for Venus, where they encounter a race of Amazons — including a statuesque guard played by Ekberg. The actress also filled roles in such efforts as *The Golden Blade* (1953), *Artists and Models* (1956) and King Vidor's *War and Peace* (1957). She played a fairly complex role in *Screaming Mimi* (1958), which cast her as a nightclub dancer left seriously disturbed as the result of a sexual assault. This near-manic thriller received mixed reviews and failed to advance Ekberg's career as a serious dramatic actress. For the most part, American producers continued to offer her sexist "dumb blond" roles, among them *Paris Holiday* (1958), *4 for Texas* (1963) and *Call Me Bwana* (1963).

However, Ekberg was permitted to portray characters endowed with some level of dignity in such Italian productions as *Sign of the Gladiator*, a.k.a. *The Sign of Rome* (*Nel segno di Roma*, 1960) and *The Mongols* (*I mongoli*, 1961). Her screen image of the buxom blond beauty was used to great effect in Fellini's brilliant *La dolce vita* (1960), which had a glamorous movie queen (Ekberg) becoming the obsession of world-weary Marcello Mastroianni. The role also allowed the actress to portray a woman lost beneath her own image — much like the real-life Ekberg. Sadly, the Fellini triumph was one of the last opportunities for Ekberg to delineate a character with some substance. It was back to cheesecake roles as she played a seductive Soviet cosmonaut in Jerry Lewis' *Way...Way Out* (1966)

ANITA EKBERG, as the Vampire's niece, tortures her lover, who has come to save her from the clutches of the Undead, in Europix-International Ltd's ORGY OF THE LIVING DEAD; the triple terror bill now playing at the .... theatre.
MAT 201 A

Pressbook art and copy for *Fangs of the Living Dead* (1968).

a weak mixture of science fiction and sex farce. Even such superficial roles were becoming few and far between for the still lovely actress when producers decide unjustly that, at age 35, Ekberg wasn't quite the sex goddess that she was at 25.

Ekberg competently filled the female leads in a pair of U.S. Italian co-productions released by American-International. *The Cobra* (1967), a James Bond–style thriller, cast her as the doomed companion of secret agent Peter Martell while the colorful *The Glass Sphinx* (1967) had Ekberg playing Robert Taylor's leading lady in a mystical tale of intrigue involving ancient artifacts and the search for an elixir of eternal life. Though no better than second-rate, both films were somewhat better than *Fangs of the Living Dead*. The film wasn't widely released in the United States until 1972, when it was distributed under its original European title (*Malenka, the Niece of the Vampire*). The film remains a mediocrity under any title.

The Ghost
(Lo spettro)

A.k.a. *Lo spettro de Dr. Hichcock* (*The Ghost of Dr. Hichcock*). A.k.a. *The Spectre*. Panda Films, Magna. 93 minutes (ORT: 96 minutes). 1965 (ORD: 1963). Technicolor, Techniscope. Dir: Robert Hampton (Riccardo Freda). Prod: Louis Mann (Luigi Carpentieri), Ermanno Donati. Writ: Hampton, Robert Davidson. Original story: Davidson. Ph: Donald Green (Raffaele Masciocchi). Mus: Frank Wallace (Franco Mannino). Ed: Donna Christie (Ornella Micheli). Art Dir: Samuel Fields (Mario Chiari). Cast: Barbara Steele, Peter Baldwin, Leonard Elliott (Elio Jotta), Harriet White, Raoul H. Newman (Umberto Raho), Reginald Price Anderson, Charles (Carlo) Kechler, Carol Bennet.

Largely a routine tale of horror-suspense endowed with supernatural overtones, *The Ghost* purports to be a sequel to Riccardo Freda's *The Horrible Dr. Hichcock* (1964). Actually, the story has little to do with the original feature beyond the presence of Barbara Steele, whose character is married to an individual named Dr. Hichcock. In addition to these points of reference, the supposed follow-up is directed in the same shadowy style by Freda, who provides the pleasurably creepy atmosphere that horror fans will appreciate rather than the lackluster script.

Margaret Hichcock (Barbara Steele) is a recent widow who resides in the mansion of her late husband, Dr. Hichcock. The woman harbors a terrible secret, however: She murdered her husband with the help of his associate (and her lover), Dr. Charles Livingstone (Peter Baldwin). Their crime seems to have baffled the authorities, but forces beyond the comprehension of man now seem to be intervening. Margaret begins to experience bizarre, terrifying visitations by her murdered spouse. The vindictive spirit of Dr. Hichcock (Leonard Elliott) demands that she find the cache of precious jewels hidden somewhere in the vast, gloomy mansion. Despite the positive contact offered by Livingstone and Catherine the maid (Harriet White), the haunting continues and Margaret slowly descends into madness.

The "late" Dr. Hichcock is very much alive and has engaged in a conspiracy with the double-dealing Catherine to drive Margaret insane before finally eliminating her. With no other surviving relatives to receive the inheritance, money and property would be left to Catherine. Afterwards, she and Hichcock plan to run away together and lead a life of ease. The plot seems to work perfectly until one final turn of the screw spells disaster for both victim and conspirator. Margaret prepares to take her own life before there is another hair-raising appearance by her husband, whom she still sees as a vengeful wraith. Hichcock injects her with a drug that affects the nervous system, inducing paralysis. As he gloats over his final victory, Hichcock partakes in some liquid refreshment — which Margaret had laced with poison. In his death throes, the doctor's last vision is of his wife's face, which is twisted into a sardonic grin.

The Ghost is an obvious rehash of Henri-Georges Clouzot's *Diabolique* (1955), the suspense classic starring Simone Signoret. We had already seen variations on Clouzot's scenario, most notably Seth Holt's creepy *Scream of Fear* (1961) and the sporadically effective *Nightmare* (1964) from director Freddie Francis. Both efforts, produced by England's Hammer Films, achieve a higher level of quality than Freda's horror opus. The trick ending is fairly satisfying, though it is the sort of ironic twist that had already been done a number of times on segments of television's *Alfred Hitchcock Presents* during the 1950s and 60s. A good performance by the inimitable Ms. Steele and the rich atmosphere created by director Freda help to provide passable entertainment.

The fine photography of Raffaele Masciocchi is one of the film's strongest assets; his camera helps to create the proper atmosphere. As in *The Horrible Dr. Hichcock*, there is an effective use of chiaroscuro plus strategic use of color that combine to create a bewildering sense of unreality. Shadows play upon people's faces in an extraordinary fashion while dimly lit rooms conceal unknown horrors that may strike at any moment. Once again, the visual texture of Freda's film helps to compensate for the lack of a good script.

Beyond the presence of Barbara Steele, who vacillates between treachery and hysteria, there are several good supporting performances. Competent portrayals are achieved by Elio Jotta ("Leonard Elliott") as the ruthless Dr. Hichcock, Harriet White as his equally cruel and greedy accomplice and Carlo Kechler as a shrewd police official. The editing is a cut above the ordinary and, as horror buffs and film journalists have often pointed out, Steele's voice is heard in the dubbed version rather than that of some third-rate New York actress. Certainly, this is quite enough to warrant a look from dedicated Steele fans.

Ghosts, Italian Style

Original title: *Questi fantasmi* (*These Ghosts*). A.k.a. *Three Ghosts*. Ponti, MGM. 92 minutes. 1969 (ORD: 1967). Mixture of B&W and Technicolor footage. Dir: Renato Castellani. Prod: Carlo Ponti. Writ: Castellani, Adriano Baracco, Leo Benvenuti, Piero De Bernardi, Ernest Pintoff. Based on the play *Questi fantasmi* by Eduardo De Filippo. Ph: Tonino Delli Colli. Mus: Luís Enrique Bacalov. Ed: Jolende Benvenuti. Art Dir: Piero Poletto. Cos: Piero Tosi, Enrico Sabbatini. Cast: Sophia Loren, Vittorio Gassman, Mario Adorf, Margaret Lee, Aldo Giuffrè, Franceso Tensi, Marcello Mastoianni, Francis DeWolff, Augusta Merola, Piera Degli Esposti, Giovanni Tarollo, Nietta Zocchi, Valentino Macchi. MPAA rating: G.

Here we have the sort of spook comedy that was popular during the 1940s in the United States. Lacking the funny one-liners and occasional visual gags that helped such efforts as *The Ghost Breakers* (1940) to succeed, *Ghosts, Italian Style* must rely on a big-name cast to carry the story through. The results are a bit disappointing when one considers the talent involved.

A beautiful but embittered young woman named Maria (Sophia Loren) and her ineffectual husband Pasquale (Vittorio Gassman) decide that life has dealt them a bad hand. The glamorous life led by some residents of Naples means little to them as they face major financial woes, serious marital problems and a hopeless future. Even an attempt at a double-suicide fails, and they lack the energy to make a second attempt.

Maria encounters a man she has known for much of her life, the burly Alfredo (Mario Adorf). Once the superintendent of the orphanage where she grew up, Alfredo now owns an elaborate mansion which has been turned into a hotel. He seems to take pity on the woman and offers the position of caretaker to Maria, who will work along with Pasquale at the mansion. Alfredo, however, fails to mention that they will be working in a haunted house.

Other details are kept from Maria as well. It is the influence of the wealthy Alfredo that has kept Pasquale in a nearly permanent state of unemployment. Alfredo has secretly desired Maria since she was in her mid-teens and now he sees the opportunity to have the girl as his own. He occupies the room directly above that of the married couple, allowing him to keep a lecherous eye on Maria.

The presence of Maria and her husband imbues the mansion with a new vitality and helps to dispel the rumors of ectoplasmic manifestations. Pasquale feels a sense of purpose as he goes about his daily functions, unaware of Alfredo's intentions toward Maria. Although he means well, Pasquale makes the mistake of renting a room to a voluptuous but scatterbrained prostitute named Sayonara (Margaret Lee). The situation becomes more complicated and bizarre when Pasquale, who is unaware of the ghostly disturbances, sees Alfredo wandering through the shadowy corridors one night and thinks that his employer is a ghost. Alfredo has unknowingly dropped a pouch containing a great deal of money and Pasquale sees the newly obtained wealth as a gift from a benevolent spirit.

Maria learns of Pasquale's nest egg and the fact that he has rented a room to a prostitute. She comes to a disturbing conclusion Pasquale has become a procurer of women and is reaping the profits of his immoral new profession. Maria is enraged and abruptly leaves her husband. Alfredo comes to believe that Pasquale has murdered his wife and notifies the authorities. However, since there is no body and no evidence that Maria has been murdered, Pasquale is eventually released.

Several months pass before Pasquale meets Maria again at their home and the strangely matched couple realize that they still love each other. When they encounter Alfredo, their conniving former employer is convinced that Maria is a vindictive spirit come back to haunt him. Much like Ebenezer Scrooge, Alfredo is suddenly humbled and wants to make amends for his greedy and lustful ways of the past. Maria takes advantage of Alfredo's fears and elicits a promise from him to donate much of his ill-gotten wealth to charity (with the donation being made in her memory). He must also promise to marry Sayonara, giving some respectability to an unfortunate girl of the streets. Pasquale, the "tragic widower," is given a generous amount of money by Alfredo before they part company.

Maria and Pasquale decide to leave Italy and begin a new life in Scotland. An eccentric nobleman asks them to act as caretakers of his drafty old castle, where they will at least have peace of mind as well as a sense of security. The quiet life that they anticipated, however, doesn't quite come about as they discover that this decrepit structure really does have a resident spirit (Marcello Mastroianni).

Shot in 1967, *Ghosts, Italian Style* was completed two years before it was released in the United States. Despite some bawdy subplots, the film was awarded a G rating and yet still failed to draw large crowds. The story was originally written as a stage play in 1946 by Eduardo De Filippo and probably fared much better when endowed with the ambiance of the theater. Sadly, the transition from stage to screen resulted in the loss of some much-needed energy. The elements of TV sitcom humor involving suspicions of infidelity, the misadventures of a stereotypical male boob and the demands of an angry, dissatisfied wife fail to be orchestrated effectively by director Renato Castellani. What we have instead is a horror-comedy presented on the level of television's *I Love Lucy*, without the screwball charm of Lucille Ball and Desi Arnaz.

This isn't to say that there is nothing of value to be found in *Ghosts, Italian Style*. The cast is generally competent, though critics thought this flick was quite a comedown for Loren, who won an Oscar for her electrifying performance in the widely acclaimed *Two Women* (1961). Vittorio Gassman does well as the male lead while Mario Adorf is suitably pompous as the lascivious, over-stuffed Alfredo. Even Marcello Mastroianni does a clever cameo as a congenial spirit. His in-joke appearance is an obvious reference to the 1961 *Ghosts of Rome*, which co-starred Mastroianni with Vittorio Gassman. There is also some fine photography provided by Tonino

Delli Colli, whose skills enriched Arthur Lubin's *The Thief of Baghdad* (1961) and the "William Wilson" segment of AIP's *Spirits of the Dead* (1969).

Pedestrian direction and a lack of pace mar *Ghosts, Italian Style* considerably. The film emerges as a near-miss that could have earned a mild recommendation had it been handled in the loud, boisterous fashion of an AIP horror-comedy. One leaves the theater longing for the naive charm of an entertaining Roger Corman spook like *The Raven* (1963).

Ghosts of Rome (Fantasmi a Roma)

A.k.a. *Phantom Lovers*. Lux Films/Vides/Galatea, MGM. 100 minutes. 1961. Color. Dir: Antonio Pietrangeli. Prod: Franco Cristaldi. Writ: Pietrangeli, Ennio Flaiano, Sergio Amidei, Ettore Scola, Ruggero Maccuri. Ph: Giuseppe Rotunno. Cast: Marcello Mastroianni, Vittorio Gassman, Belinda Lee, Sandra Milo (Alexandra Marini), Eduardo De Filippo, Tino Buazzelli, Claudio Gora, Franca Marzi, Ida Galli, Lilla Brignone.

Despite the talents involved, this occasionally spooky mixture of comedy and the supernatural is just a minor spoof that owes a great deal to a pair of similar efforts based on a similar theme. *Ghosts of Rome* has a down-on-his-luck nobleman (Marcello Mastroianni) meeting an unexpected demise when his defective hot water heater explodes. The family mansion manages to survive the disaster and Mastroianni's spirit joins the small band of specters already haunting the aging structure. It isn't easy becoming accustomed to "life" in the spirit world, but a fetching ghost like Belinda Lee makes the transition less painful than it may have been otherwise. When real estate developers decide that the building should be demolished and the lot used for other purposes, the ghosts become crusaders with a purpose. Mastroianni and his ectoplasmic allies, using supernatural trickery, finally discourage demolition and continue with their harmless, cheerful haunting of the premises.

Mastroianni's predicament seems vaguely inspired by that of

Renato Rascel in *Uncle Was a Vampire*, shot two years earlier. The latter flick had a penniless nobleman (Rascel) losing his family castle to a hotelier before supernatural forces engineer a drastic change in his lifestyle. However, *Ghosts of Rome* borrows considerably from two other horror-comedies. The West German-made *The Spooks of Castle Speisert* (*Das Spukschluss im Speirsert*, 1960) had crusading ghosts fighting against the obnoxious new owners of a castle and intervening on the behalf of the rightful owners. Even more is owed to *Revolt of the Ghosts* (*La rebelión de las fantasmas*, 1943), a clever Mexican horror-comedy in which the ghosts who haunt an old mansion must struggle against the planned demolition of their home. Much as in *Ghosts of Rome*, the wraiths are an oddly mixed group of intellectuals, artists and eccentrics. In this flick, celebrities such as Chopin and Caruso are among the spooks. However, the eerie protagonists in *Revolt of the Ghosts* must accept social change and become accustomed to dwelling in a modern structure. The title characters in *Ghosts of Rome* emerge victorious as the film conveys a message of positive resistance to social progress.

Ghosts of Rome is worth noting, of course, for the fine talents who lend their presence to such trivial but reasonably amusing fantasy fare. Director Antonio Pietrangeli (1919-1968) was previously known for his work within the neo-realist school; he is in fact officially credited for having coined together the word neo-realism. Fans of colorful Italian epics may remember him more as the author of the screenplay for *Fabiola*, a tale of ancient Rome that was shot in 1947. This effort marked the international revival of the Italian spectacle which had received little attention since the end of the silent film era. *Ghosts of Rome*, co-written by Pietrangeli, is one of his lesser accomplishments both as a screenwriter and director. Sadly, the talented Pietrangeli drowned while directing the film *Com, Quando e Con Chi?* (*How, When and With Who?*, 1968).

No less prolific is Eduardo De Filippo (1900-1984), the celebrated author, theater director and actor who plays a supporting role as one of the spirits. De Filippo began acting at the age of 13 with his family troupe before he turned more to writing stage plays. He completed over 25 plays by 1945 when he formed his repertory company, Il Teatro Umoristico. His greatest triumph in the area of fantasy remains the famous *Questi fantasmi* which was written in

1946 and produced a number of times, even at Oxford under the title of "Too Many Ghosts" in the late 1950s. *Questi fantasmi* became the basis of a film adaptation in the late 1960s with Sophia Loren and Vittorio Gassman in the lead roles.

Handsome and haunted — this is so compelling in Fellini's depiction of the true horror of contemporary society *La dolce vita* (*The Sweet Life*, 1960). Mastroianni (born in Fantona Liri, Italy) was always cast very well as a personable but vulnerable hero who feels empty despite having achieved goals that society may see as worthy. His greatest performance can be seen in Fellini's *8½* (1963), which casts Mastroianni as the tormented film director who seeks greatness within a stagnant industry. *Ghosts of Rome* also casts the actor as a quixotic crusader who finds both love and purpose after an empty life comes to an end.

Second male lead Vittorio Gassman (born 1922 in Genoa, Italy) does well in his genre debut, eight years before he would play the hero of another spook spoof (*Ghosts, Italian Style*, 1969). Gassman began studying law in his youth before he switched to life as an actor, first on stage and then in film. The former husband of actress Shelley Winters played rugged leading man parts in such films as *Sombrero* (1953), *Rhapsody* (1956), *The Tiger and the Pussycat* (1967) and *Woman Times Seven* (1967).

The two female leads are also competently filled, with Belinda Lee making an especially winsome ghost in one of her last film roles. Lee (1935-1961) concentrated on portraying seductive characters in such films as *Dangerous Exile* (1957), *The Nights of Lucretia Borgia* (*Le notti di Lucrezia*, 1961) and *Constantine and the Cross*, a.k.a. *Constantine the Great* (*Constantino il grande*) (1962). The closest thing to a horror film in her previous credits is a supporting role in the eerie Victorian era suspenser *Footsteps in the Fog* (1955). Sadly, the actress met an untimely end at age 25 in a fatal traffic accident.

Sandra Milo (born 1935 in Milan as Alexandra Marini) is a more skilled actress who began her career while she was still a college student. She had already worked with director Pietrangeli in *Lo scapolo* (1956), starring Alberto Sordi. Milo later distinguished herself by portraying the mistress of the neurotic director in *8½*, and later played a triple role in the Fellini fantasy *Juliet of the Spirits* (*Giulietta degli spiriti*, 1965).

The color photography of Giuseppe Rotunno is one of the major assets of *Ghosts of Rome*; Rotunno's fine camerawork gives the film the visual flair one might expect in a Corman-Poe flick. Rotunno (born 1923 in Rome) makes effective use of atmosphere and lighting, while he highlights the translucent spirits with an eerie blue aura. While in his early 20s, Rotunno worked as a still photographer for Cinecittà Studios before becoming a newsreel cameraman and finally director of photography in 1955. He also photographed Luchino Visconti's superb *White Nights* (*Le notti bianche*, 1957), then worked on such efforts as *The Witches* (*Le streghe*, 1967) and *The Secret of Santa Vittoria* (1969).

Producer Franco Cristaldi (born 1924 in Turin, Italy), whose previous credits included *White Nights* and *Big Deal on Madonna Street* (a.k.a. *Il soliti ignoti*, 1958), later provided audiences with such critically acclaimed efforts as *Divorce Italian Style* (*Divorzio all'italiana*, 1962) and *Bebo's Girl* (*La ragazza di Bube*, 1964). His *Ghosts of Rome* may be the least of his screen accomplishments, though it qualifies as mildly diverting entertainment done with skill and polish.

Though the film is well played, one can't help but think that the talents involved may have treated the subject matter a bit too respectfully. Like *Ghosts, Italian Style*, *Ghosts of Rome* might have been more interesting had it been endowed with the delightfully blatant humor of AIP spoofs like *The Comedy of Terrors* (1964).

The Giant of Metropolis
(Il gigante di Metropolis)

A.k.a. *Metropolis*. Centro, Seven Arts. 812 minutes. 1964 (ORD: 1961). Color. Dir: Umberto Scarpelli. Prod: Emimmo Salvi. Writ: Salvi, Sabatino Ciuffino, Oreste Palella, Ambrogio Molteni, Gino Stafford. Ph: Mario Sensi. Mus: Armando Trovajoli. Ed: Leo Scuccuglia, Adriana Ballanti. Art Dir: Giorgio Giovannini. Cast: Gordon Mitchell, Roldano Lupi, Bella Cortez, Liana Orfei, Furio Meniconi, Marietto, Omero Gargano, Kronos.

Here is a thriller that is one of Italy's most ambitious experi-

The Giant of Metropolis (1964) was double-billed with *The Invincible Gladiator*.

ments in the juxtaposition of several genres. Horror, science-fiction, adventure and costume drama are merged with sporadically effective results. Despite its failings, the film generates a crude virility while attaining a certain degree of visual flair.

In A.D. 12,000 the many centuries of war, economic ruin and ecological decay have taken their toll upon civilization. Most communities function under crude conditions, but the city of Metropolis has elevated science to the level of magic. Sadly, the leader of Metropolis and his ambitious clique of followers have decided to use their achievements for selfish ends. The ruthlessness of the monarch Yotar (Roldano Lupi) will soon have tragic consequences.

Simple men from nearby villages have not lost their compassion for others and have also maintained a feeling of unity with nature. The courageous, powerful Obro (Gordon Mitchell) and several companions have embarked on a journey to Metropolis to plead for a return to the sense of decency that will placate nature. Obro's aged father dies shortly before the city comes into view. During his final moments, the old man is reassured by Obro that the pilgrimage will be completed.

The tiny band soon encounters one of the booby-traps surrounding Metropolis. A vortex of pure energy is generated as the men pass within the defense perimeter of the city. Enveloped by the whirling blue force-field, Obro and his companions lose consciousness. When he finally awakens, Obro finds that only he has survived the encounter with the devilish force of science. The others have been reduced to skeletal remains.

Obro tries to carry on alone, but he is soon captured by men clad in strange suits of armor. The soldiers of Metropolis bring him to the palace of Yotar, who is amazed that this powerful stranger has survived the force-field trap. "It is you who killed my brothers!" Obro shouts as he is led away. Yotar is determined to learn the secret of Obro's strength — even if the knowledge is obtained at the cost of Obro's life.

Yotar continues to be intrigued by the physical and spiritual strength of Obro, who survives assaults by force-beams and heat rays. The leader of Metropolis becomes obsessed with breaking Obro, forcing him to fight a group of savage, dwarf-like warriors. Obro's defeat by his barbaric opponents seems to appease Yotar's unreasoning vendetta against the quixotic crusader. Yotar orders that Obro be spared, but the future of the still defiant captive remains uncertain.

Yotar's demanding nature and thirst for power have led to the neglect of his second, younger wife, Queen Texon (Liana Orfei), and their child, Elmos (Marietto). The relationship with his wife has become quite superficial as he seeks sensual gratification rather than a valid human relationship. One night, as he wields his mesmeric control over Texon, Yotar eyes her slender form lustfully before proclaiming his love for her. The woman feels no passion in her heart, claiming that it is only her body that he wants to possess. Yotar embraces Texon, who shudders with revulsion.

Yotar soon devises more tests for Obro, including a fight with a club-wielding madman (Kronos) who stands about seven feet tall. The men square off in a shadowy arena as Yotar watches silently, seated upon a glistening throne. Obro deftly avoids the savage blows of the towering fiend, who grunts and groans with each swing of the club. Obro whittles down the brute's strength with intermittent kicks and well-placed punches. Seized from behind, Obro exerts a monumental effort to break free of his opponent's iron grip, then grasps the fallen club and deals several strong blows to the man's middle and one to the back of his skull. The massive body falls face down and lies still. Yotar watches the climax of this mortal combat without displaying the slightest emotion.

Yotar devises a master plan involving his son Elmos, who will one day rule Metropolis. The Immortality Experimentation Machine, constructed by Yotar's most brilliant scientists, may endow Elmos with eternal life. A series of tests must be performed upon a human subject — namely Obro.

Obro survives several ray-bath treatments, though the experiments drain his energy. As he rests, the prisoner seems both helpless and friendless. The hope for deliverance suddenly emerges as Obro finds an ally in Queen Texon, who secretly arranges his rescue from the laboratory. There are a handful of accomplices, including a few slaves and one official, who reject the oppressive nature of the monarchy. Obro's new allies establish a shelter for him in a cave beneath the city while helping to plot a terrorist campaign against the government.

Texon suffers the vengeful wrath of Yotar when he learns that she has betrayed him. Though Yotar threatens to have her killed, Texon cheats him of this victory by cutting her wrist with a poisoned blade. The woman places her dying curse upon him before expiring.

One of Yotar's ministers pronounces Texon dead, drawing a horrified gasp from a nearby corridor. The men turn toward the source of the disturbance and find that it was the startled cry of Princess Mesede (Bella Cortez). She is the winsome, raven-haired daughter of Yotar's first wife. Shocked by her father's ruthlessness, she flees the palace and evades Yotar's men. Obro shelters her in his subterranean hideaway.

Obro uses hit-and-run tactics against the palace guards and elite military units. His few allies perish in the struggle, but he continues to fight alone. Mesede, living under his protection, accepts Obro's claim that his struggle is against the monarchy of Metropolis, not its people. A strong bond forms between Obro and Mesede as Metropolis nears destruction.

Pressures build within the earth as the air turns cold and mists begin to enter the palace. Yotar wanders alone through the throne room and cries out fearfully. The spear-wielding Obro enters the room and bitterly states, "You're mad, Yotar…and I'm going to kill you!" Yotar seizes a trident and attempts to engage in a duel, but is quickly defeated. Before he can finish Yotar with a fatal thrust, palace guards arrive. Obro is soon overpowered and captured by Yotar's men.

Mesede, now considered a traitor to Metropolis, is also apprehended and joins Obro in imprisonment. Although they may face death, Obro avoids bitterness and still hopes that Yotar may one day see the folly of his ways. Mesede embraces the man she loves, refusing to allow such tender moments to escape her as time grows short.

Yotar is moved by the relationship between Obro and his daughter. In the midst of such misery, how could people find love and still be willing to forgive their persecutors? Yotar is informed by a messenger that the frail Elmos seems to be growing weaker. Rushing to the boy's side, Yotar embraces his son, who calls out to his father before fainting.

Realizing the end of Metropolis is near, Yotar orders the release of his daughter and Obro. The spiritual strength of these two young people is more powerful than the super-science of the fabled city. Yotar places the semi-conscious Elmos in Obro's arms, urging him to flee Metropolis with the boy. Elmos cries out to his father as he is carried away by the giant of Metropolis.

The earth quivers as multitudes of angry citizens gather in the streets. Yotar faces the enraged but terrified masses and says that science cannot save Metropolis. He extends his arms in a plaintive gesture toward the heavens and cries, "Nature has defeated me!" Unable to contain their rage, Yotar's subjects storm the pedestal upon which he speaks. The monarch disappears beneath the angry fists and feet of the people.

The earth crumbles, buildings collapse and fires erupt throughout the city. Dams and floodgates burst, releasing waters that drown thousands and shatter many remaining structures. Obro makes his way through the terrible conflagration, determined to survive along with Mesede and Elmos. They move to higher ground with others who are also fleeing the wrath of nature.

Hours pass before the tremors subside and the waters finally lie still. Metropolis has ceased to exist and nature is once more placated. A quiet beach is littered with bodies, some of them lifeless but others still imbued with a vital spark. Obro and Mesede, weakened by the ordeal, rise from the wet sand to embrace one another. Together, they look at the rising sun which marks the start of a new day as well as a new life for those who remain.

There's a lot of frantic action in this flick, much of it enhanced by a rousing Armando Trovajoli score. Mario Sensi's fine camerawork makes effective use of lighting plus odd, occasionally interesting streaks of color that break the foreboding sense of mystery in darkened rooms. Some additional visual appeal is provided by the flowing robes, dramatic capes and elegant gowns reminiscent of those seen in the final sequences in William Cameron Menzies' *Things to Come* (1936).

On the negative side, long shots of the ultra-modern city of Metropolis consist of cheap, unconvincing miniatures. The story shares some of the incongruities usually present in the science-fantasy pulp novels, most notably in the depiction of the culture's military capabilities. Although Metropolis possesses destructive heat-rays and is able to generate powerful force-fields, its soldiers are armed with swords and spears. The considerable excitement value of the action sequences often gives way to stagy, overly theatrical scenes full of heavy-handed dialogue with moral significance. *The Giant of Metropolis* is one of those films in which one can find something negative for every positive aspect.

The cast members handle their roles fairly well, with Roldano Lupi coming off best in the role of Yotar. Lupi's cold-bloodedness is expressed in a steely-eyed projection that is more effective than any amount of sneering or eyeball-rolling could be. The actor was already familiar to audiences from his major supporting roles in such costume dramas as *Duel Without Honor* (1953), the Errol Flynn swashbuckler *Crossed Swords* (1954) and the silly but elaborate *Queen of Babylon* (1956), starring Rhonda Fleming and Riccardo Montalban.

Gordon Mitchell, a comparative newcomer, really isn't much of an actor. His displays of emotion are limited mainly to a grimace that allows us to admire his fabulous dental work. Nevertheless, Mitchell is well-cast physically in the role of Obro and brings a lot of energy to the role. He has since enjoyed a long career in such efforts as *The Fury of Achilles* (1962), *The Secret Seven* (1965), *Reflections in a Golden Eye* (1967) and *Count Frankenstein's Castle of Freaks* (1978), starring Rossano Brazzi and Edmond Purdom. One of Mitchell's more recent appearances was the starring role in the SF-horror *The Alien Within* (1987). The latter flick co-starred Richard Harrison, John Carradine and Forrest J Ackerman.

Liana Orfei brings an appropriate mixture of strength and vulnerability to the role of Queen Texon. Orfei is a strikingly beautiful woman whose fair complexion, soft features and beautifully packaged figure made her a perfect choice for portrayals of ladies of quality. Her other screen credits include such sword-and-sandal flicks as *The Avenger* (1962) and *Damon and Pythias* (1962), starring Guy (Zorro) Williams. She also acted in a pair of costume dramas starring Vincent Price, *Queen of the Nile* (1963) and *Rage of the Buccaneers* (1964). A refreshing departure from period adventure films had Orfei becoming one of Marcello Mastroianni's conquests in the farcical *Casanova '70* (1965).

No less attractive and just as talented is Bella Cortez, a raven-haired, olive-skinned actress usually cast in exotic roles. She brings a slinky sensuality to her portrayal of Mesede while also endowing the character with an undercurrent of sensitivity. Cortez acted with co-star Liana Orfei in *The Tartars* (1962), starring Orson Welles, before showing her villainous side as an evil barbarian queen in *Taur the Mighty* (1963).

Although *The Giant of Metropolis* is an acceptable piece of entertainment, what little attention given to the film was probably earned by lingering interest in Fritz Lang's classic *Metropolis* (1925).

Fanzines occasionally made erroneous claims about the Gordon Mitchell film being a remake of the Lang effort. However, one of the first mentions of the Italian production was in *Spacemen* #4 (July 1962) which expressly stated that the story was vastly different from that of the silent classic. Confusion was understandable since the new production's tentative American release title was *Metropolis*. Meanwhile, producer/director Bert I. Gordon was announcing plans for a remake of the Lang film.

The Gordon project fizzled while Seven Arts finally decided to retain the original title of *The Giant of Metropolis* as part of its double-bill with *Revenge of the Gladiators*. Released in the late winter-early spring of 1964, *The Giant of Metropolis* had already been completed for about three years. A photo-story treatment of the film appeared as an article entitled "Monsters of Metropolis" in *Famous Monsters of Filmland* #31 (December 1964). The piece was fairly amusing and made a few subtle allusions to Fritz Lang's *Metropolis*, editor Forrest J Ackerman's favorite film. There was no sneaky promotion by Seven Arts in attempts to capitalize on the Lang classic. Horror fandom had inadvertently provided such promotion before the effort was even released to American theaters.

Goliath Against the Giants
(Goliath contro i giganti)

A.k.a. *Goliath contra las gigantes*. A.k.a. *Goliath and the Giants*. Cineproduzioni Associati/Procusa, Medallion. 95 minutes. 1963 Eastman Color, Super Totalscope. Dir: Guido Malatesta. Prod: Cesare Seccia, Manuel Perez. Writ: Seccia, Gianfranco Parolini, Giovanni Simonelli, Arpod De Piso, Sergio Sollima. Original Story: Seccia. Ph: Alejandro Ulloa. Mus: Carlo Innocenzi. Ed: Mario Sansoni, Edmondo Lozzi. Art Dir: Ramiro Gomez, Carlo Santonocito. Cast: Brad Harris, Gloria Milland, Fernando Rey, Barbara Carroll, José Rubio, Lina Rosales, Carmen de Lirio, Angel Aranda, Mimmo Palmara, Fernando Sancho, Ray Martino, Ignazio Dolce, Luigi Marturano, Nello Pazzafini, Manuel Arbo, Rufino Ingles, Gianfranco Gasparri, Francisco Bernar, Luis Marco, Angel Ortiz.

Here is another sword-and-sandal epic with elements of horror that fails to frighten or thrill its audience. Goliath (Brad Harris) has been away fighting a war while his kingdom of Beirath has been seized by a murderous usurper named Bokan (Fernando Rey). The new ruler displays his cruelty while watching mortal combat between two gladiators. The surviving combatant is eyed passively by Bokan, who tells one of his men-at-arms that "the poor fellow is suffering...put an end to his misery." The victor receives an arrow through the throat as a reward for his skillful fighting.

Goliath makes his way back to Beirath, saving the life of Bokan's prize female agent, a beauty named Elea (Gloria Milland). The girl falls in love with Goliath and is eventually charged with treason. She is sent to a bleak, mountainous area beset by occasional volcanic disturbances and populated by a race of overgrown Neanderthal types. Clad in animal skins and armed with spears, they make formidable enemies for Goliath, who has come to Elea's rescue. His strength, courage and superior fighting abilities are more than enough to defeat the frightful giants. Bokan, in the meantime, has seen his palace invaded by Goliath's insurgents, who defeat the monarch's brutal guards. The oppressor falls, more quickly studded with arrows than Toshiro Mifune at the end of *Throne of Blood* (1957).

Brad Harris had already acted in such second-rate epics as *The Fury of Hercules* (1960) and *Samson* (1961). It's anyone's guess why Fernando Rey accepted a role in this one. Rey previously acted in a number of exceptional dramas, most notably Luis Bunuel's electrifying *Viridiana* (1961). The prolific Rey later became known for his restrained portrayal of the "cultured" drug lord in *The French Connection* (1971). He just looks embarrassed during a number of badly directed sequences in *Goliath Against the Giants*. Trivia buffs will also note the presence of Angel Aranda, who later played the second male lead in Mario Bava's *Planet of the Vampires* (1965).

Goliath and the Dragon

Original Title: *La vendetta de Ercole* (*The Vengeance of Hercules*). Italo-French, AIP. 90 minutes. 1961 (ORD: 1960). Colorscope. Dir:

Vittorio Cottafavi. Prod: Achille Piazzi, Gianni Fuchs. Writ: Marco Piccolo, Archibald Zounds, Jr. Ph: Mario Montauri. Mus: Les Baxter. Ed: Maurizio Lucidi. Cos: Peruzzi. Cast: Mark Forest, Broderick Crawford, Eleonora Ruffo, Philippe Hersent, Sandro Maretti, Federica Ranchi, Gaby André.

This awful mixture of fantasy-adventure and supernatural horror is occasionally included in "all-time worst" lists compiled by journalists and film critics. The muscular Goliath (Mark Forest) must defeat a number of mythological menaces to rescue his beloved Dejanara (Eleonora Ruffo) from the clutches of evil King Eurystheus (Broderick Crawford). Cerberus, the savage three-headed dog, and a hideous dragon are among the monstrous creatures that are about as convincing as handpuppets. Crawford gets his just desserts in a pleasurably creepy-crawly scene involving a snake pit, the film's only good spot. The rest consists of poor dubbing, cheap color and inadequate English dialogue that make the film frequently ludicrous when not merely unpleasant to look at. One especially laughable scene has a large diamond floating toward the head of a statue, with the connecting "invisible" string clearly visible to the audience.

The original Italian-language version of the film, *The Vengeance of Hercules*, depicted the adventures of the Greek demi-god whose intrusion into the underworld with its various supernatural threats closely resembled the scenario of Mario Bava's *Hercules in the Haunted World*, shot the same year. AIP retitled the Cottafavi film in order to present it as a sequel of sorts to their previous release *Goliath and the Barbarians* (1960), starring Steve Reeves and Bruce Cabot. A new musical score composed by Les Baxter was inserted into the latter flick. The rousing theme that accompanied the opening credits was also utilized for *Goliath and the Dragon*, in order to establish further points of reference. Certainly, the film could not be a source of pride for Baxter, whose exciting score is one of the film's few positive aspects.

Broderick Crawford (1910-1986) sleepwalks through the two-dimensional role of King Eurystheus, acting as though he is just visiting the set. One can hardly blame him since this is quite a comedown after delivering an Oscar-winning portrayal of Huey Long-type senator Willie Stark in Robert Rossen's *All the King's Men* (1949). Many fans, however, prefer to remember Crawford for his forceful characterization of the no-nonsense Chief Dan Matthews on television's *Highway Patrol*.

Another victim of this mess is the talented director Vittorio Cottafavi, who previously worked with Vittorio De Sica during the 1940s. Cottafavi turned to sword-and-sandal efforts for a time, directing such elaborate action flicks as the exciting *Legions of the Nile* (1960) and the occasionally horrific *Hercules and the Captive Women* (1963). His *Goliath and the Dragon*, despite a potentially absorbing premise, is merely a bore.

Goliath and the Vampires

Original title: *Maciste contro il vampiro* (*Maciste Against the Vampire*). A.k.a. *The Vampires*. A.k.a. *Goliath and the Island of Vampires*. A.k.a. *Machiste Against the Vampires*. A.k.a. *Maciste vs. The Vampire*. Ambrosiana Cinematografica, AIP. 92 minutes. 1964 (ORD: 1961). Technicolor, Totalscope. Dir: Giacomo Gentilomo, Sergio Corbucci. Prod: Paolo Moffa. Writ: Corbucci, Duccio Tessari. Ph: Alvaro Mancori. Mus: Angelo Francesco Lavagnino. Ed: Eraldo Da Roma. Art Dir: Gianni Poladori. Cast: Gordon Scott, Gianna Maria Canale, Leonora Ruffo, Jacques Sernas, Guido Celano.

The vampire has probably been the most popular movie menace ever to work in the horror genre. *Goliath and the Vampires* presents a bloodsucker who is not surrounded by typical points of reference (coffins, blood-dripping fangs, hovering bats, etc.). A less familiar approach to the vampire myth, in addition to some adroitly staged horrific sequences, help to compensate for a predictable, heavy-handed treatment of a potentially interesting premise.

Despite his great strength and the admiration of the common folk, the stalwart Goliath (Gordon Scott) has remained a man of the people. He never sets himself above the joys of labor and, one typical day, spends the morning plowing a field like any other peasant farmer. However, this will not be a day like any other: The village is raided by armor-clad mercenaries who take female captives; Goliath's beloved Julia (Leonora Ruffo) is among the women kidnapped by the followers of Kobrak (Guido Celano), the vampiric ruler of a small island.

Kobrak has been involved with slave trade as well as black magic, with some of the kidnap victims providing nourishment for the monster's unholy thirst. The winsome Julia has been spared from such a fate by the burly mercenary leader who, while in a drunken stupor, makes his lecherous interest in the woman quite obvious. Surprisingly, it is the chief female accomplice of Kobrak who rescues Julia from the clutches of her captor. Astra (Gianna Maria Canale) intrudes suddenly and hurls a dagger with great accuracy at the professional soldier. The blade deeply penetrates his chest as he staggers forward in his death throes. Stumbling past Astra, he falls lifelessly over a balcony. Astra takes Julia to a place of safety, knowing that the woman would be a great prize to Kobrak.

Determined to rescue Julia and destroy the monstrous Kobrak, Goliath travels to the island of the despotic vampire. Goliath finds that the monster is an elusive entity, wraith-like and difficult to fight. Kobrak is aided not only by mercenaries, but also by an army of faceless, zombie-like warriors who are seemingly invulnerable in combat. However, Kobrak is resisted by some of the island natives, most notably the mysterious but courageous Blue Men who live in subterranean caves.

Goliath forges an alliance with the Blue Men after contacting Kurtik (Jacques Sernas), the leader of the tribe. Many freedom fighters are killed in clashes with Kobrak's forces. A nighttime confrontation with the zombie-warriors is confusing and terrifying as a regiment of Blue Men is decimated in a mist-covered swamp.

Goliath and Kurtik continue their struggle against heavy odds until Julia is rescued, though a last confrontation with Kobrak is necessary. Astra, once a loyal follower of Kobrak, feels her conscience stirred by the humanity of Goliath and Julia. A spark of decency compels her to side with Goliath and his allies. The sly Kobrak, in a final attempt to crush the insurgents, uses sorcery to transform himself into the exact image of Goliath. He enters the subterranean colony of the Blue Men and attempts to subvert the group until Astra courageously intervenes. She cries out for Kurtik and his men to beware the image of Goliath, which is a magical disguise devised by Kobrak. The ruthless sorcerer seizes a spear from one of the Blue Men, hurls the deadly shaft at Astra and impales her.

The arrival of the real Goliath marks the beginning of a monumental fight to the death between the muscle-bound crusader and the evil, spell-casting despot. Muscles bulge as the men groan, grimace and pit brute force against brute force in a terrible ballet of violence. Kobrak's power wanes, leaving him unable to maintain the Goliath illusion. His own facial features emerge with bluish-green skin, mummified features and a twisted mouth that reveals a row of animal-like teeth.

With his true appearance exposed and his magic uncontrolled, the dark powers become self-destructive. Kobrak's body emits trails of smoke, as though his flesh is beginning to burn from within. He runs madly throughout the stone chamber, gesticulating wildly until he disappears within an adjoining tunnel. An ear-splitting roar can be heard as Kobrak literally explodes in a cloud of fire.

Kobrak and his predatory minions have finally been vanquished and the Blue Men are liberated. The inhabitants of surrounding islands and coastal regions no longer need to fear raids by Kobrak's slave traders. Goliath and Julia depart for their village, bidding farewell to Kurtik and his people.

As in most of the Maciste thrillers, our hero is given a name more familiar to American audiences — this time it's Goliath. Gordon Scott (born in 1927 as Gordon M. Werschkul) is well-cast in the lead role, having played Maciste in one previous feature, *Samson and the Seven Miracles of the World* (1963). His strong physical presence, soft charm and casual style make him the most satisfying Maciste in the 1960s series based on the adventures of the silent film hero. Scott, a former lifeguard from Portland, Oregon, remains best known for his Tarzan characterization which he first delineated in *Tarzan's Hidden Jungle* (1955). He reprised the role of "the white ape" in *Tarzan and the Lost Safari* (1957), *Tarzan's Fight for Life* (1958), *Tarzan's Greatest Adventure* (1959) and *Tarzan the Magnificent* (1960).

Scott's entry into the European action market cast him in a number of other costume dramas, most notably *Duel of the Titans* (1962), which told the story of Romulus (Steve Reeves) and Remus (Scott). After sword-and-sandal epics declined in popularity, Scott tried his hand at Italian westerns with the lead role in a post-Civil War oater, *The Tramplers* (1966). Sadly, the transition was not an effective one and Scott's career faded.

Equally effective is the performance of Gianna Maria Canale (born 1927), a competent actress who was often cast in the films of her director-husband Riccardo Freda. After doing such costume dramas as *Theodora, Slave Empress* (1953) and *The Sword and the Cross* (1956), she starred in Freda's 1956 chiller *I vampiri* (*The Vampires*). The raven-haired actress was featured in other colorful efforts, including *The Warrior and the Empress* (1958), *Hercules* (1959) and *Nights of Rasputin* (1960). Her performance as the ambitious Astra in *Goliath and the Vampires* is typical of her smooth villainy. She projects a mixture of arrogance, avarice and suppressed hostilities tempered with a hint of vulnerability.

Goliath and the Vampires emerges as an interesting scenario padded with routine action sequences. Occasionally, we are treated to effective episodes of supernatural horror. One early segment is a creepy sequence in which one of Kobrak's men offers his master a jewel-encrusted goblet filled with blood. A sinewy arm covered with hair suddenly reaches from behind a wispy, translucent curtain. Kobrak's fearsome hand, displaying deadly talons, grasps the goblet and slowly withdraws the horrid nourishment into his secluded chamber.

Another highly effective scene takes place in a shadowy hovel where an escaped slave girl uncovers a document revealing the origins and identity of Kobrak, the vampire king. As she reads aloud from the parchment, the monstrous monarch appears in the darkened room and silently glides toward her. The girl screams in terror as the taloned hand tears her throat. Blood pours from the fatal wound.

The occasional splashes of gore are usually presented in an unearthly, dream-like manner by director Giacomo Gentilomo. His liking for **gore** and graphic violence was most liberally displayed in the very **rough** and bloody *Last of the Vikings* (1962). Tortures and grisly killings only occur sporadically in *Goliath and the Vampires*, thus avoiding the numbing effect of gratuitous blood-letting. The more blatant forms of horror are more effective when used strategically at the proper moments.

A few scenes were directed by Sergio Corbucci, who co-wrote the script with Duccio Tessari. The prolific Corbucci also directed Gordon Scott in *Duel of the Titans* before elevating the nineteenth century American gunfighter to mythical proportions with *Minnesota Clay* (1865), an Italian western starring Cameron Mitchell. Duccio Tessari co-wrote the script for *Hercules in the Haunted World* (1964), another ambitious but disappointing mixture of horror and fantasy-adventure.

Goliath and the Vampires was released in the United States by American-International in the spring of 1964. The film didn't receive the typically bombastic promotional campaign and newspaper ads usually given to AIP's period horror pieces. Bookings were largely confined to neighborhood theaters and drive-ins where box office receipts were disappointing. *Goliath and the Vampires* lacked the excitement value of many sword-and-sandal adventures, while effective horror interludes occurred too infrequently for the film to attract interest of AIP horror fans. The company fared much better that year with a U.S.-Italian co-production, Mario Bava's *Black Sabbath*.

Hatchet for a Honeymoon (*Una hacha para la luna de miel*)

A.k.a. *Il rosso segno della follia* (*The Red Sign of Madness*). A.k.a. *Un' accetta per la luna di miele* (*An Axe for a Honeymoon*). A.k.a. *Blood Brides*. A.k.a. *A Hatchet for the Honeymoon*. Pan Latina Films/Mercury, G.G.P. 90 minutes. 1969. Color, Techniscope. Dir: Mario Bava. Prod: Manuel Cano Sanciriaco. Writ: Bava, Santiago Moncada, Mario Musy. Ph: Bava, Antonio Rinaldi. Mus: Sante Romitelli. Ed: Soledad Lopez. Cast: Stephen Forsyth, Dagmar Lassander, Laura Betti, Jesús Puente, Femi (Eufemia) Benussi, Antonia Mas, Alan Collins (Luciano Pigozzi), Gérard Tichy, Fortunato Pasquale, Veronica Llimera. MPAA rating: PG/M

Horror films done with deep psychological meanings and shock endings were quite popular in the early to mid–1960s. Alfred Hitchcock's brilliant *Psycho* (1960) spawned a long series of imitations ranging from William Castle's *Homicidal* (1961) to Bert I. Gordon's *Picture Mommy Dead* (1966). Mario Bava's derivative *Hatchet for a Honeymoon* borrows considerably from the Hitchcock classic, but a trowel-like handling of an eclectic script never involves the viewer in the thoroughly nasty story.

A sound, fairly interesting framework deals with the bloody killings carried out by a handsome, seemingly charming fashion designer (Stephen Forsyth). Though his good looks, wealth and prestigious career make him attractive to many women, Forsyth is saddled with a shrewish wife (Laura Betti) who bears a remarkable resemblance to his late mother. It is the love-hate attachment to his domineering mother — whose "spirit" is embodied in an equally demanding wife — that provokes the killer's rampage.

Forsyth maintains a room filled with female mannequins clad in wedding gowns that proved a constant reminder of the pure, virginal image with which he is obsessed. His murder victims, all beautiful women, are clad in such gowns as he hacks them to death with an axe. The startling pinball emotions...love and then hate...love and then hate...repeat themselves with destructive fury as each killing recalls associational aspects of a traumatic boyhood experience. Terrible memories come in brief snippets and finally emerge in a crystal-clear recollection as Forsyth attempts to kill his mistress (Dagmar Lassander). He murdered his own mother — a horrible revelation dredged from his subconscious mind that causes him to break with reality completely. Now quite insane, he is taken away by the police as the mother personality openly haunts him.

Although psychologically sound, the film is dramatically unconvincing. Forsyth is well-cast physically as the male lead, but he lacks emotional strength and seems fairly weightless in the role. The actor was better suited for frothy entertainment as proven by his adequate supporting performances in such films as the romantic comedy *Love and Marriage* (1964) and the lightweight *Seated at His Right* (1968). Laura Betti, as the domineering wife, fares somewhat better. Betti previously excelled in supporting roles for such films as *La dolce vita* (1961), *Red Lips* (1964) and *The Witches* (1969). She later appeared in Bava's gruesome *Twitch of the Death Nerve* (1971). Of remaining cast members, there are only two good performances. Luciano Pigozzi, a dependable genre regular, comes off well, as does Gérard Tichy, whose participation in such "B" movie fare was a rare thing. A more than competent performer, Tichy acted in the major films *El Cid* (1961), *King of Kings* (1961) and *Dr. Zhivago* (1965).

An Italo-Spanish co-production, *Hatchet for a Honeymoon* never rings true as events move with mechanical precision while unconvincing snatches of dialogue and familiar plot twists hardly add to its effectiveness. There is lots of *déjà vu* here as we see a psychotic killer created by the influence of a domineering mother (à la *Psycho*). Forsyth even takes to wearing a wedding dress in one scene to maintain the virgin bride illusion and imbue that illusion with new life (a variation of *Psycho*'s transvestism theme). Although he carries out a series of gruesome murders in which beautiful women are the victims, Forsyth has a fairly normal relationship with an attractive girl. The latter situation was depicted in Jack Hill's Bavaesque chiller *Blood Bath* (1966) as well as in a number of adult features produced in the early to mid-1960s.

Mario Bava directed a pair of lightweight science-fiction efforts before doing *Hatchet for a Honeymoon*. *Dr. Goldfoot and the Girl Bombs* (1966), starring Vincent Price, came off as an embarrassing mixture of sex farce and silly slapstick. Bava fared better with his *Danger: Diabolik* (1967), a spotty comic strip adventure done with the campy approach of television's *Batman* series. The director then decided to return to horror-suspense in the same vein as his wickedly perverse *Blood and Black Lace* (1965). Fluid camerawork, sensuous use of color and high-powered shock sequences are present in *Hatchet for a Honeymoon*, though these bravura cinematics sometimes work against the story. The threadbare plot of *Blood and Black Lace* was enhanced by Bava's fine visuals, but his celebration of film (and an annoying over-use of a zoom lens) often prove distracting for a more complicated chiller like *Hatchet for a Honeymoon*.

Hercules Against the Moon Men

Original title: *Maciste contro gli uomini pietri (Maciste Against the Stone Men)*. A.k.a. *Maciste e la regina di Samar (Maciste and the Queen of Samar)*. A.k.a. *Maciste contro gli uomini della luna (Maciste Against the Men from the Moon)*. A.k.a. *Maciste contre les hommes de pierre (Maciste Against the Men of Stone)*. Nike Cinematografica/ Comptoir Français, Governor. 88 minutes. 1965 (ORD: 1963). East-

Ad for *Hercules Against the Moon Men* (1965), double-billed with *The Black Torment*.

man Color, Cromoscope. Dir: Giacomo Gentilomo. Prod: Luigi Mondello. Writ: Arpod De Piso, Nino Scolaro, Angelo Sangarmano. Ph: Oberdan Trojani. Mus: Carlo Franci. Spfx: Ugo Amadoro. Art Dir: Amedeo Mellone. Cast: Alan Steel (Sergio Ciani), Jany Clair, Anna Maria Polani, Nando Tamberlani, Delia D'Alberti, Jean-Pierre Honoré, Goffredo Unger.

Maciste, the Son of Stone, was nearing the end of his popularity as a movie hero by the mid-1960s. He was the muscle-bound protagonist of many Italian fantasy-spectacles produced between 1960 and 1964, though the character was largely unknown in the United States. As was often the case with epics featuring Maciste, our hero was given the name of a more familiar character in the dubbed American version. The SF-horror slant of *Hercules Against the Moon Men* was new to the genre, but the film is otherwise very ordinary.

A conflict of horrific proportions begins with a bizarre and frightening cosmic disturbance. The inhabitants of the city of Samar witness a ball of fire descend from the heavens and collide with the Earth in a mountainous region. This strange display of nature's fury marks the start of a reign of terror as the ruthless Queen Agar (Jany Clair) forces oppression upon the land, taking hostages and eliminating political opponents. The queen has forged an alliance with an army of stone creatures which arrived in the flaming ball, which was actually a spaceship. These stone monsters have promised fantastic powers to the earthly queen if she assists them in the revival of their Queen Selene.

The misery of the oppressed masses is so great that Gladius (Nando Tamberlani), the prime minister of Samar, summons the demi-god Hercules (Alan Steel). The arrival of the muscle-bound crusader is soon followed by an ambush as a band of brutal mercenaries attempts to block the intervention of Hercules. Their puny efforts prove futile as the motley group is driven away and our hero devotes himself to the task of liberation. Hercules is not alone in his struggle as freedom fighters led by a charismatic insurgent (Jean-Pierre Honoré) join in the fight. The courageous leader of the group is in love with Princess Bilis (Delia D'Alberti), whose life is threatened by the queen and her lunar allies. Hercules, however, feels drawn to the lovely Arga (Anna Maria Polani), daughter of Gladius.

When his investigation leads him to the palace of Queen Agar, Hercules finds that the ambitious woman desires him as well as the powers that the moon men have promised to grant her. The queen boasts of her power to have him grovel at her feet, but makes a point of her decision not to enact such power. She pretends to show hospitality by offering a goblet of wine to Hercules. The wine has been laced with a magical potion able to destroy Hercules' will and make him her psychic slave. However, the son of Zeus is clever and perceptive as well as strong. He recognizes the treachery that lies behind her kind words and winsome smile. When the queen's back is turned, Hercules empties the goblet with a quick jerk of the wrist that flings the tainted wine behind a marble table. When Agar fixes her lovely but evil gaze upon him once again, Hercules pretends to have been drinking. He then feigns sudden weakness and dizziness before pretending to lose consciousness completely.

After a brief time, Hercules "awakens" as a seemingly docile, completely obedient minion of the queen. His simple questions are actually quite devious as he plays the role of slave for as long as necessary. He cleverly manipulates the queen into revealing a frightful plan for conquest. She will share worldwide power with the stone men, who have come from the surface of the moon. They require a human sacrifice to revive their Queen Selene, who exists in a suspended state. The earthly queen will provide the needed sacrifice of royal birth — the lovely Princess Bilis. Having obtained the information that he desires, Hercules admits he never drank her potion. Stunned by her sudden defeat, the queen escapes through a secret panel in her throne room. Open rebellion by her political foes makes her situation even more desperate.

The queen flees to the mountain hideaway of the stone men and appeals to them for help. The lunar high priest states that she has failed them and outlived her usefulness, and she is encircled by a complement of rock creatures. The monsters tighten the circle and crush to death their former ally.

The hapless Bilis, now a captive of the moon men, will become their sacrificial victim when the stars are aligned in a mystical pattern and a proper conjunction has emerged. Cosmic forces will then come into play, thus reviving Queen Selene, who will hold dominion over all mankind. Despite his great strength and resourcefulness, Hercules has also been captured by the monsters and bound with chains as the crucial moment for ritual sacrifice approaches.

Renewed strength born of desperation allows Hercules to break his chains and launch a courageous attack on the stone monsters. Seizing their high priest and lifting him above his head, Hercules hurls the powerfully built monstrosity as though he weighed little more than a pebble. Precious moments pass as the time for sacrifice draws near and Hercules continues his struggle against heavy odds. The crucial moment passes unfulfilled as the stone men are cheated of their victim with Queen Selene doomed to continue existing in her suspended state.

Earth is saved as the lunar invaders are vanquished. Bilis is returned to the kingdom of Samar, which is now free of oppression. Hercules may now turn his attention to Arga as a new romance begins to blossom.

The U. S. distributors recognized the lack of salability in *Hercules Against the Moon Men*, which was released at a time when sword-and-sandal flicks were definitely on the wane. Secret agent thrillers and period horror films were more profitable in the mid-1960s. Consequently, the horrific aspects of the film were emphasized in a promotional campaign that also greatly exaggerated the scale of production as "mighty" and "monumental." This is a film shot in "Cosmicolor" and "Lunarscope," claimed the ads. Hercules "body builders" were sometimes distributed at theaters where the film was booked. *Hercules Against the Moon Men* was widely distributed as the major feature of a double-bill with a handsomely made British chiller, *The Black Torment*, starring Heather Sears and John Turner.

Beyond having its mythological hero do battle against moon monsters instead of earthbound monarchs and menaces, *Hercules Against the Moon Men* has nothing new to offer. Even for its type, the film exhibits a surprisingly low-grade production veneer. Several scenes are poorly shot with the color being a total wash-out. One battle sequence utilizes especially blurred footage that looks as though it was shot through a pea-soup fog. The action sequences are short on extras as well as in technical slickness, defeating any attempt to do horror-fantasy on an epic scale.

Sergio Ciani, starring under his professional name of Alan Steel, is cast in another film that allows him to display his impressive physique. Sadly, Ciani's acting ability fails to match the size of his biceps. He handles the action sequences fairly well, giving audiences ample opportunities to admire his bulging muscles and tanned, hairless chest. Once he opens his mouth, it's downhill as he stiffly recites his dialogue while strutting and posturing like a male model. Although he lacked the casual style of Gordon Scott and the limited charm of Steve Reeves, Ciani did his share of sword-and-sandal fantasies. His credits, previous to *Hercules Against the Moon Men*, include *Hercules Against Rome* (1960), *Hercules and the Masked Rider* (1960), *Hercules and the Black Pirates* (1960), *Hercules and the Treasure of the Incas* (1960), *Samson and the Slave Queen* (1964) and *The Three Avengers* (1964).

Neither the supporting cast nor the mediocre special effects of Ugo Amadoro are much help. Director Giacomo Gentilomo generates a fair amount of tension during the final scenes, but the film lacks both the mysticism of Gentilomo's *Goliath and the Vampires* (1964) and the queasily exciting violence of his *Last of the Vikings* (1962). However, there is one creepy, well-photographed scene in which Hercules and Bilis are captured by the stone men on a foggy night. The massive creatures lumber across a bleak landscape, emerging from the mists that one would expect to see in a Mario Bava chiller. Bilis attempts to escape, but is surrounded on all sides by the monsters, who also overwhelm Hercules. It is a passably good sequence, somewhat out of place in this generally poor film.

Hercules and the Captive Women

Original title: *Ercole alla conquista di Atlantide (Hercules and the Conquest of Atlantis)*. SPA Cinematografica/Comptoir Français du Film, Woolner Bros. 87 minutes (ORT: 93 minutes). 1963 (ORD: 1961). Super Technirama, Technicolor. Dir: Vittorio Cottafavi. Prod: Achille Piazzi. Writ: Cottafavi, Alessandro Continenza, Duccio Tessari. Story: Archibald Zounds, Jr. Ph: Carlo Carlini. Mus: Gino Marinuzzi, Armando Trovajoli. (Additional pieces for U.S. release were composed by Gordon Zahler.) Ed: Maurizio Licudi. (Partial reconstruction for U.S. release was by editor Hugo Grimaldi.) Art Dir: Franco Lolli. Cos: Vittorio Rossi. Cast: Reg Park, Fay Spain, Ettore Manni, Luciano Marin, Laura Alton, Mario Petri, Salvatore Furnari, Gian Maria Volonté, Ivo Garrani, Mario Valdemarin, Enrico Maria Salerno, Mimmo Palmara, Nicola Sperli.

Though critically pasted, this mixture of spectacle and horror-fantasy contains some good ingredients. Photography and color are excellent, several action sequences are fairly well choreographed and there's even an anti-fascist philosophical framework. That's quite a bit for a sword-and-sandal flick from Italy. But the film's intriguing concepts only provide the basis for a series of events that are exceedingly ordinary. Nevertheless, the movie deserves some examination for its ambitious nature.

Pressbook art for *Hercules and the Captive Women* (1963).

When Greece is threatened by the military adventurism of the ruling circles in Atlantis, it is Hercules who must intervene and neutralize the dark forces at work on the lost continent. The demi-god arrives by ship on the shores of the mysterious kingdom. He is aided by the stalwart Androcles (Ettore Manni) and a plucky dwarf (Luciano Marin). Soon they face many dangers, both human and supernatural. Hercules must battle a reptilian creature to save the life of an innocent peasant girl (Laura Alton). He finds the human "monsters" of Atlantis to be even more dangerous.

The intervention of Hercules seems quite appropriate and may coincide with "the game of the gods" that has helped to create the current situation in Atlantis. Sorcery and black magic are employed by Queen Antinea (Fay Spain) in the formation of a powerful army whose warriors seem unmatched in combat skills, physical strength and ruthlessness. These superhuman engines of destruction have been created by the dark forces of the god Uranus, whom the civilization of Atlantis now serves. Uranus, once defeated in battle by Zeus, still remains an evil entity who threatens mankind. The son of Zeus would be a powerful ally as Antinea attempts to win Hercules to her side rather than destroy him.

A confrontation in the throne room reveals the true nature of the warriors who serve Antinea. As Hercules confidently displays his great strength by hurling a massive marble slab across the room, he watches one of the queen's soldiers match the same feat. Several of the men, clad in black armor, form a line and remove their helmets at Antinea's command. Beyond powerful physiques shared by all of them, each reveals similar coloring and facial features. Blond, bearded and with cold blue eyes, the strange men remain as unemotional and expressionless as pieces of sculptured marble.

Hercules makes clear his refusal to cooperate with the plans for world conquest that Atlantis has decided to embark upon. Those in Atlantis who share Hercules' view have been imprisoned in a deep quarry where they are subjected to an austere existence and frequent brutalities by guards. The queens' army of supermen derived their power from exposure to a magical rock that is located within a deep cavern. This vital information is revealed to Hercules by a guilt-ridden priest (Gian Maria Volonté) who now longs for the merciful release of death.

Hercules is not swayed by the beauty of Antinea or the promise of power and great wealth. Her final attempt to "seduce" him with drugged wine proves unsuccessful as Hercules feigns unconsciousness and later flees the palace to enact his plans against the conspiracy of evil. Fomenting rebellion against the monarchy is just a part of Hercules' plan. Frantic encounters by rebels with Antinea's forces precede a final blow against Atlantis. Hercules engineers a situation in which a ray of sunshine penetrates the cavern where the mystical stone rests. This focal point of the dark forces of Uranus cannot survive exposure to the glow of the sun. Complete destruction of the kingdom will then occur.

Androcles and the faithful dwarf aid Hercules in whatever way possible, using trickery, strength and simple courage to fight the occult army of Atlantis. The courageous pair join Hercules and other freedom fighters who prepare to flee the coming destruction of the kingdom. As the day wears on, the sun's rays slowly move toward the magical stone. Contact finally occurs, resulting in a massive explosion. Volcanic eruptions on an apocalyptic scale ravage the land, claiming Antinea and her evil army. Hercules and his friends escape the final conflagration and return to Greece.

Vittorio Cottafavi fares somewhat better with *Hercules and the Captive Women* than he did with his inept *Goliath and the Dragon* (1961). The rubberized monsters, gushing blood and weak villain of the latter flick are gone; *Captive Women* features good camerawork, an imaginative use of color and a horde of superhuman menaces who project an inherent sense of evil. There is one regrettable lizard-monster with which Reg Park must do battle, but there is much more in the way of fast action enhanced by good technical qualities. The final destruction of Atlantis in a volcanic upheaval does not rely on special visual effects — a reliance that was one of the weakest aspects of *Goliath and the Dragon*. Instead, Cottafavi employs Haroun Tazieff's fine documentary footage of an actual volcanic eruption. These documentary sequences are skillfully merged with scenes of the fleeing masses, disintegrating structures and monumental confusion. Shot in 70mm Super Technirama by Carlo Carlini, these sequences project bold images that have a staggering effect on the viewer.

Much like his muscular predecessor Steve Reeves, the new Mr. Universe — Reg Park — proves to be a fair actor. His ability to express a wide range of emotions is limited, though he brings a great deal of energy to the role of Hercules. More interesting than Park's performance is the script's characterization of Hercules. The son of Zeus is no strutting, flawless paragon of virtue. This Hercules enjoys the aesthetic value of a pretty girl, the taste of good wine and a preference for afternoon naps rather than a search for oppressed peoples to liberate. A roguish but idealistic fellow with a lazy streak, he sometimes comes off as a rebel without a cause. When oppression rears its ugly head, however, our hero leaps into action.

The script, written mainly by director Cottafavi, contains many points of reference toward Hitler's Germany in a denunciation of greed and political oppression. The forces of Atlantis seem to be predecessors of the Aryan supermen of the Third Reich. Blond, blue-eyed and powerfully built, they are determined to create an empire that will encompass the entire world. Those who fail to conform are sent to a "concentration camp" where they suffer the miseries of forced labor and corporal punishment. The final conflagration depicting the fiery destruction of Atlantis is not unlike the firebombing of Dresden.

Such high-flown intentions prove to be a bit much for the subject matter, which is given the inauspicious treatment of many early 60s Italian epics. The weak comic touches, predictable attempts at seduction by well-endowed wenches and bombastic displays of physical strength are not handled in any fresh, imaginative ways. It is Cottafavi's inventive characterization of Hercules that remains the most innovative aspect of the story. The talented Cottafavi gave proper treatments to socially significant material after switching from film to Italian TV in the late 60s. His small-screen adaptations of plays and novels included dramas based on the works of Sophocles, Dostoyevsky, Moliere and Pirandello.

Other talents worth mentioning include Fay Spain, who plays the ambitious Antinea with a typically hard edge, though there is also a touch of elegance usually missing from her previous film roles. The actress is known mainly for her portrayals of characters who are hard, flip and cheaply attractive. She filled such roles in contemporary gangster melodramas that include the part of a girl gang leader in Roger Corman's *Teenage Doll* (1958). Spain also played the "moll" of Rod Steiger, who filled the title role in the Allied Artists release *Al Capone* (1959). Although her career began to decline in the mid-1960s, she continued to deliver competent performances in low-budget melodramas. She played the female leads in *Thunder Island* (1963) and *Flight to Fury* (1966), a pair of Monte Hellman thrillers scripted by Jack Nicholson. The actress later reverted to hard-bitten roles by playing the dissipated girlfriend of gangster Mickey Rooney in a creepy segment of Rod Serling's TV series *Night Gallery*.

Among supporting players, horror buffs will recognize the name of Ivo Garrani, who is best remembered as the doomed father of Barbara Steele in *Black Sunday* (1961). Gian Maria Volonté, in the days before his Italian westerns, adequately fills the minor role of a tormented priest. The dark-eyed, brooding Volonté became best known as the psychotic outlaw named Indio in Sergio Leone's *For a Few Dollars More* (1967). Volonté was later featured in an "adult" chiller, *The Witch* (1967), a gangster flick entitled *The Violent Four* (1969) and the powerful *Sacco and Vanzetti* (1971).

However, the best performance is by the robust second male lead, Ettore Manni (1927-1979). His energetic, often romantic roles included the part of Marc Antony in *Two Nights With Cleopatra* (1954). The actor was featured in *Ulysses* (1955), starring Kirk Douglas, and later played the hero of *The Warrior and the Slave Girl* (1958). Manni also confronted the living dead in AIP's *War of the Zombies* (1965).

Despite its good points, *Hercules and the Captive Women* ultimately fails due mainly to mixed intentions. Vittorio Cottafavi's attempt at making a coherent philosophical statement earns some admiration, though he finally spends too much time pandering to thrill seekers. The routine heroics, two-dimensional villains and the simplistic struggle of good vs. evil are often on the same low level of a Kirk Morris or Alan Steel thriller. Only the interesting, multifaceted portrayal of Hercules as a less-than-perfect hero offsets the tedious nature of such material. Reg Park would reprise the role of Hercules in an even more horrific scenario with Mario Bava's *Hercules in the Haunted World* (1964).

Hercules in the Haunted World

Original Title: *Ercole centro della terra* (*Hercules at the Center of the Earth*). A.k.a. *Hercules vs. The Vampires*. A.k.a. *Vampires vs. Hercules*. A.k.a. *With Hercules to the Center of the Earth*. SPA Cinematografica, Woolner Bros. 83 minutes (ORT: 91 minutes). 1964 (ORD: 1961). Technicolor, Totalscope. Dir: Mario Bava. Prod: Achille Piazzi. Writ: Bava, Alessandro Continenza, Duccio Tessari, Franco Prospero. Ph: Bava. Mus: Armando Trovajoli. Ed: Mario Serandrei. Cos: Mario Giorsi. Cast: Reg Park, Christopher Lee, Leonora Ruffo, Giorgio Ardisson, Franco Giacobini, Ida Galli, Marisa Galli, Ely Draco, Mino Doro, Monica Neri.

Mario Bava handled the photography for many colorful epics

Pressbook art for *Hercules in the Haunted World* (1964).

and fantasy-adventures, including such efforts as *Hercules* (1959), *Hercules Unchained* (1960) and *The Colossus of Rhodes* (1962). He brought his visual skills, as well as the sense of horror previously displayed in *Black Sunday* (1961), to this mixture of fantasy, adventure and supernatural horror. The film is Reg Park's second outing as the heroic son of Zeus, following his success in Vittorio Cottafavi's *Hercules and the Captive Women* (1963). Woolner Bros. released the Bava effort as the top half of a double-bill with Antonio Margheritti's *Castle of Blood*.

In times long past, Hercules was often called upon to fight against political oppression and supernatural evils. The struggle against the dark forces of King Lico begins on a pleasant day as Hercules (Park) rests near a sandy beach with two friends. One of his companions, a harmless dolt named Telemachus (Franco Giacobini), has inadvertently angered a burly ruffian. The ax-wielding bully seizes Telemachus and binds his limbs between two teams of horses, preparing to send the beasts galloping in opposite directions.

A muscular blond warrior named Theseus (Giorgio Ardisson) turns his attention from a raven-haired girl, draws his sword and comes to the dolt's rescue. As Theseus fights a duel with the brutish attacker, Hercules seizes the leather straps linking the two horse teams. The beasts are powerful, but they cannot match the strength of the demi-god. Drained of energy, the horses cease straining against the might of Hercules. Their unruly master, in the meantime, is knocked unconscious by Theseus.

Hercules and his friends next confront a band of mercenaries bent on destruction. The defeat of Hercules, however, seems impossible for men of ordinary strength and fighting skills. A confrontation finds Hercules victorious once again as the professional soldiers are driven away.

The leader of the ruthless band reports to his master, King Lico of Ecalia (Christopher Lee). The soldier-of-fortune is told to take his fill of precious gems from a coffer, only to trigger a deadly booby-trap. After being impaled by several gleaming spear-points, the armor-clad corpse seems to become a source of mild amusement of the evil Lico.

The desire to eliminate Hercules is logical, as the courageous, resourceful son of Zeus is needed to perform a critically needed task. Queen Deianira (Leonora Ruffo) has been suffering from a strange malady producing madness, making her unable to perform her royal duties. She can only be cured with the healing properties of the Golden Apple (found on the isle of Hesperides) and a magical stone that must be obtained in Hades. With Hercules eliminated, Lico would have direct control of the kingdom while Deianira would become the victim of a sacrifice to dark gods.

Hercules and his two companions depart for the isle of Hesperides where they obtain the Golden Apple. There is also an encounter with a rock-like monster that is vaguely humanoid in shape. Theseus attempts to fight the creature, but his sword shatters against its rocky exterior. The monster binds both Theseus and Telemachus to stone slabs, stating in a rasping voice the tortures he is about to inflict upon them. Telemachus cries out in terror as Hercules arrives in the nick of time. Seizing the rock monster and lifting him over his head, Hercules hurls the creature against a stone wall. Rubble buries the monster's remains as collapsing stones reveal a portal to the underworld.

The Golden Apple is entrusted to Telemachus as Hercules and Theseus enter Hades. Their dark journey presents other perils that, including a demon who appears in the form of a seductive woman. The weakness of Theseus for the fairer sex is effectively controlled by Hercules, though another obstacle seems to spell the end for the demi-god's companion. The men extend a rope across a chasm at the bottom of which lies a mass of bubbling volcanic mater. The men travel hand-over-hand across the chasm. As his strength gives out, Theseus plunges into the molten material before Hercules is able to rescue him.

Amazingly, Theseus has been transported to an astral plane inhabited by a beautiful goddess who is enamored of him. Although the woman is indeed a temptation to Theseus, his loyalty to Hercules wins out in the end. Reluctantly, she transports him back to the stone portal where Hercules is preparing to tell Telemachus of their friend's apparent demise. The sudden arrival of Theseus amazes his friends, but it is a joyful reunion. Hercules has obtained the magic stone which glows with unearthly energy that has curative powers. With their quest completed, they begin the journey back to the palace of Deianira.

Lico, the sly usurper, is not to be thwarted from his evil goals by Hercules' success. The brutal monarch kills the maidservant of Deianira and abducts the terrified queen for ritual sacrifice to Pluto, god of the underworld. As the night of sacrifice arrives, Deianira rests in a mesmerized state on a stone slab. Lico raises a dagger, made of human bones, above his head as he prepares to thrust the blade into the woman's heart.

Hercules arrives and grapples with the madman. The son of Zeus hurls the villain a good distance away, pinning him beneath a stone pillar. Other disciples of Pluto come to Lico's aid as supernatural forces revive half-decayed corpses from their coffins. The mummified horrors approach the stone altar, which is surrounded by a circle of stone spires. Hercules defends himself by using the spires as projectiles that he hurls at the undead creatures. The attackers are kept at bay long enough for the time of sacrifice to pass unfulfilled. Lico, still entrapped by the stone pillar, rages ineffectively. The powers of black magic turn against Lico, who suddenly bursts into flame and is reduced to a pile of ashes.

With the evil madman gone, the minions of Pluto are also vanquished. Deianira is freed from Lico's mesmeric control and may assume her rightful place as a just ruler of the land. Hercules has not only ended turmoil in Ecalia, but also saved the life of the woman he loves.

Mario Bava endows *Hercules in the Haunted World* with streaks and flashes of color that inspire both a sense of awe and a feeling of revulsion. The scowling face of Christopher Lee reflected in a pool of blood is probably the film's most chilling moment. In contrast, brief scenes of the all-knowing Oracle utilized colored beads and garments that create an atmosphere of mystery and visual beauty. Bava's ability to splatter the audience with cinematic eyewash helps to distract viewers from the limitations of small, inexpensive sets.

Despite a potentially interesting scenario, the film is marred by its largely routine heroics and the interspersion of poorly done comic sequences. Humor is hardly Bava's forte as proven by the silly slapstick involving the character Telemachus (humorously overplayed by Franco Giacobini). The mugging and pratfalls of Giacobini are more tiresome than amusing. Bava later fared even worse with the Vincent Price science-fiction spoof *Dr. Goldfoot and the Girl Bombs* (1966). The latter flick featured the incredibly inept comedy team of Franco and Ciccio.

Despite its often grim scenario, the film has a few touches of fairy tale charm. The story unfolds as the recollections of the Oracle a lithe, winsome figure sitting cross-legged in an ornate temple, her face covered by an exotic mask. Her words are punctuated by sweeping hand or arm gestures that compensate for the lack of facial expressions. Such lightweight moments, done with considerable visual appeal, manage to offset the horrific sequences more effectively than the poor comic interludes.

In the early scenes, Reg Park's Hercules is still a roguish fellow who enjoys harmless mischief but has high ideals and is always ready to help a friend in need. Park soon emerges as just another musclebound hero, ultimately lacking the charm of his character in *Hercules and the Captive Women*. However, the episodes of supernatural horror are quite effective as Hercules confronts a squadron of living corpses during the film's final minutes. The cobwebs, coffins and loathsome reanimated bodies characteristic of Bava's straight horror melodramas are a welcome sight for horror fans. During such pleasurably creepy scenes, Park is required to be little more than an appropriately beefy prop.

The less robust but equally energetic Giorgio Ardisson displays competent acting ability in his portrayal of the rugged, quick-tempered Theseus. Ardisson played the younger brother of Cameron Mitchell in the rough and bloody *The Last of the Vikings* (1963) plus supporting roles in other period action flicks As *George* Ardisson, he later played male leads in contemporary adventure films like *Agent 383: Passport to Hell* (1964) and *Operation Counterspy* (1965). Ardisson also played the male lead in the Barbara Steele chiller *The Long Hair of Death* (1964).

The scenes with Christopher Lee are quite good, allowing us to savor the smooth villainy and cold-eyed ruthlessness that the actor displayed in his Hammer horror films. Lee expressed disappointment over the quality of the film before it was released in the United States. When the Bava effort was announced in some of the fanzines as *Vampire vs. Hercules* in 1963, Lee wrote a letter to *Famous Monsters of Filmland* in regard to a glaring mistake. The letter became part of a feature article entitled "Are Movie Monsters Human?" in FM #29 (July 1964). Lee pointed out an error concerning a still, supposedly featuring the actor as a cobweb-enshrouded corpse rising from an elaborately carved coffin. He used the occasion to rail against exploitive advertising, and he hinted at the film's inherent deficiencies.

Lee pointed out that in FM #23 (June 1963), a still purporting to be that of the actor in a grisly makeup was not him. Nor was the new film in question entitled *Vampires vs. Hercules*. The actor further explained that he was never in a coffin at any time during the film and that his character could just vaguely be described as one of the undead. The Bava effort was originally titled *Hercules at the Center of the Earth*.

The actor continued to discuss the situation as an example of inaccurate advertising designed to exploit Lee's screen image as a vampiric menace. It was a sad situation to Lee, who felt that the film would have been quite competent if the story adhered to the classic portrayal of Hercules' journey to Hades.

The adventures of Hercules in the netherworld could indeed have provided the substance for a creepy, fitfully exciting epic. However, it is the type of story that would require the large-scale treatment associated with such talents as George Pal or Ray Harryhausen.

The Horrible Dr. Hichcock

Original title: *L'orribile segreto del Dr. Hichcock (The Horrible Secret of Dr. Hichcock)*. A.k.a. *The Terrible Secret of Dr. Hichcock.* A.k.a. *The Secret of Dr. Hichcock.* A.k.a. *The Terror of Dr. Hichcock.* A.k.a. *Raptus.* Panda Film, Sigma III. 76 minutes (ORT: 88 minutes). 1964 (ORD: 1962). Technicolor, Panoramic. Dir: Robert Hampton (Riccardo Freda). Prod: Louis Mann (Luigi Carpentieri, Ermanno Donati). Writ: Julyan Berry (Ernesto Gastaldi). Ph: Donald Green (Raffaele Masciocchi). Art Dir: Frank Smokecocks (Franco Fumagalli). Cos: Inoa Starly. Cast: Barbara Steele, Robert Flemyng, Teresa Fitzgerald, (Maria Teresa Vianello), Montgomery Glenn (Silvano Tranquilli), Harriet White, Spencer Williams, Neil Robinson, Al Christianson, Nat Harley.

Here is a chiller based on a disturbing premise that is more sexually convoluted than the themes that most of its type are based upon. Sexual tastes that border on necrophilia are dealt with in this Gothic chiller that is helped by several good performances while being hampered by the unimaginative screenplay of Julyan Berry (Ernesto Gastaldi). Nevertheless, director Riccardo Freda provides several frightening sequences in addition to moments of dark visual beauty.

The setting is the eerie English mansion of Dr. Bernard Hichcock (Robert Flemyng) in the year 1897. About 12 years earlier, Hichcock's wife Margaret (Teresa Fitzgerald) died suddenly under strange circumstances. Since that sad time, the personal life of the doctor has been shrouded in mystery until he meets the lovely Cynthia (Barbara Steele). A whirlwind romance develops into a strong relationship and Cynthia becomes the new Mrs. Hichcock.

Soon, strange events begin to occur in the old mansion as unexpected noises and mysterious voices emanate from rooms that are apparently empty. The mansion proves to be a forbidding structure as Cynthia begins spending most of her days there alone. Darkened

In Great Britain, *The Horrible Dr. Hichcock* (1964) was released under the title *The Terror of Dr. Hichcock*, as shown in this pressbook art.

alcoves and shadowy chambers instill Cynthia with a fear of the unknown. A portrait of the late Margaret, an exquisitely beautiful woman, seems to hold dominion over all.

Hichcock downplays Cynthia's fears and remains devoted mainly to performing his duties at the hospital. His youthful colleague, Dr. Kurt Lowe (Montgomery Glenn), seems more sympathetic to Cynthia's plight and the two young people share a strong friendship. The bizarre, frightening events in the mansion continue to occur, with Cynthia finally discovering a skull in her bed. Obviously, she and her husband are not the only occupants of the house.

The truth about Dr. Hichcock and his "late" wife finally comes to the surface as Kurt and Cynthia piece together bits of information concerning Hichcock's shadowy past. Margaret is still alive and secretly living in the mansion. Her alleged death was announced prematurely after bizarre sexual games placed her in a suspended state. Hichcock administered an anesthetic to Margaret before they engaged in sexual relations. This simulation of death managed to pique their peculiar sexual interests with unexpectedly horrendous results. Margaret returns from the grave, not as the beauty she once was, but as a mummified madwoman who still desires her husband and craves revenge against the woman who "stole" him.

A plan comes together in the brain of Hichcock, who wishes to restore Margaret's beauty. The madman feels that a total blood transfusion is in order, with Cynthia's vital fluids completely rejuvenating Margaret. Luckily, Kurt is aware of Hichcock's views concerning the virility of blood, its powers of revitalization and experiments involving blood samples. He arrives at the mansion in time to save Cynthia and has a startling encounter with Hichcock, who emerges from a darkened room. The cackling voice of Margaret can be heard emanating from the shadows as Hichcock emits a belligerent cry and lunges for Kurt with a knife. During the struggle, a fire is inadvertently ignited with the flames quickly spreading throughout the house. Kurt and Cynthia flee the burning structure which becomes the funeral pyre for the mad Hichcock and the hideous Margaret.

The Horrible Dr. Hichcock has been hailed as a masterpiece by some who see it as a handsomely produced, atmospheric tribute to the thrillers of Alfred Hitchcock. Certainly, the film is visually excellent with the widescreen photography and use of color enhancing the atmosphere rather than detracting from it. The vast, drab mansion seems empty as a tomb, with its occupant's faces being illuminated by dim rays of light and occasional streaks of color. Barbara Steele, a vibrant and desirable woman, provides a strong contrast with the funereal surroundings.

Beyond the strong images, there are a number of disturbing elements that cannot really constitute a homage to Hitchcock as much as a blatant pilferage of his works. The subject of necrophilia was more disturbingly dealt with in *Psycho* (1960), while other ingredients and shock devices are taken from such Hitchcock thrillers as *Jamaica Inn* (1939), *Rebecca* (1940), and *Suspicion* (1941). Ernesto Gastaldi's script rehashes elements not only from Hitchcock's suspense classics but from at least one literary classic. Gastaldi's remise deals with events surrounding a mad wife, supposedly dead for years but actually being hidden in the family mansion by her morose husband. Sound familiar? Anyone who has read *Jane Eyre* by Charlotte Brontë will recognize its basic premise as part of the story in *The Horrible Dr. Hichcock*.

However, the sheer visual pleasure of the film should prove to be diverting enough for horror addicts. Excellent photography and a believable period setting become a feast for the eyes, while Riccardo Freda fills the screen with images familiar from his other chillers. A vulnerable but plucky heroine faces vague, unknown fears obscured by shadows that creep along walls or suddenly come alive with threatening voices. Withered faces become twisted masks of evil that evoke an enigmatic fascination because one is able to recognize traces of the normal human being who once existed. The shrunken, skull-like countenance of Margaret, partially obscured by a veil, becomes even more horrible when her face breaks into a mad grin. She reveals teeth as white and perfect as those of the skull hidden in Cynthia's bed. Freda created equally disturbing images in otherwise less effective thrillers including *Caltiki, the Immortal Monster* (1960) and *The Ghost* (1965).

As always, Steele is mysterious and seductive without flaunting her sexuality. In other words — she does it without doing it! Silvano Tranquilli ("Montgomery Glenn") delivers a nicely tuned performance as the heroic Kurt Lowe. Previously, Tranquilli portrayed Steele's lover in Antonio Margheriti's *Castle of Blood* (1964). We see little of actress Maria Teresa Vianello as the crazed Margaret. During the brief glimpses of the corpse-like figure she portrays, Vianello projects a sense of evil that seems inherent and quite unearthly.

The best performance is by the fine character actor Robert Flemyng in the role of Dr. Hichcock. His deep, rich voice and steely-eyed expression enhance his performance as the man of science who continues to delve into the mysteries of life and death while losing his humanity along the way. Flemyng's other roles included tales of espionage such as *The Man Who Never Was* (1956) and lightweight comedies including the well made *Touch of Larceny* (1959). Flemyng played another mad doctor in the colorful but routine *Blood Beast Terror* (1968). The latter flick cast Peter Cushing as a shrewd police inspector who tracks down Flemyng's murderous daughter — a "were-moth" that feeds on human blood. Flemyng also acted in a tale of alien abduction entitled *The Body Stealers* (1969), starring George Sanders and Maurice Evans, and played a minor role in *The Medusa Touch* (1978), a chiller starring Richard Burton as a man whose psychic powers spell disaster for all who cross his path.

Riccardo Freda went on to direct the passable chiller *The Ghost* which is supposedly a sequel to *The Horrible Dr. Hichcock*. Perhaps Freda's horror credits do not represent his best work, since his spectacle films of the 1950s were generally more successful. Even around the time *The Horrible Dr. Hichcock* was produced, Freda was doing exceptional work for director André De Toth by directing some first-rate action sequences for *The Mongols* (1961) and *Gold for the Caesars* (1962); epics were probably his forte. Freda's chillers are remembered for their startling images if not for their overall quality.

Horror Castle

Original title: *La virgine de Norimberga (The Virgin of Nuremberg)*. A.k.a. *Terror Castle*. Zodiac, AA. 83 minutes. 1965 (ORD: 1963). Eastman Color, CinemaScope. Dir/Spfx: Anthony Dawson (Antonio Margheriti). Prod: Marco Vicario. Writ: Dawson, Richard Palton (Riccardo Pallotini), Edmond Greville. Based on the novel

The Virgin of Nuremberg by Frank Bogart. Ph: Pallotini. Mus: Riz Ortolani. Ed: Angel Colly (Otello Colangeli). Cast: Rossana Podestà, Georges Rivière, Christopher Lee, Mirko Valentin, Jim Dolen, Luciana Milone, Luigi Serverini, Patrick Walton, Lucille Saint-Simon, Rex Vidor, James Borden.

Antonio Margheriti's second "haunted house" flick, following the comparatively restrained *Castle of Blood*, is visually adequate but strikingly grisly. The camera dwells lovingly on bloodied eye sockets and mutilated faces, all of it in vivid Eastman Color. An emphasis on excessive gore and sadism obscures the positive aspects of a potentially creepy, pleasurably scary horror tale.

On a stormy night, an American woman named Mary (Rossana Podestà) awakens from an uneasy sleep in the German castle of her wealthy new husband, Max Hunter (Georges Rivière). It is not the unfamiliar surroundings that disturb her slumber, but the sound of an agonized scream that comes from deep within the castle. Mary cautiously leaves the bedroom after finding that her husband is strangely missing.

A series of moans can still be heard and she follows the ghastly cries to an exhibition room filled with medieval instruments of torture. A puddle of blood is seen at the foot of an Iron Maiden. Mary fearfully opens the door of the torture device and finds the corpse of her maid — eyes pierced by the spikes embedded within the lid. Overcome by horror, Mary faints as the lid of the Iron Maiden slowly swings shut.

Mary regains consciousness in her bedroom where her husband Max and the family physician (Luigi Severini) are present. Unable to detect any disorder that could account for Mary's fainting spell, the doctor concludes it was the result of nervous exhaustion. Max assures his wife that nothing unusual occurred on the previous night. Her story of the maid's mutilated corpse was merely a nightmare. The woman in question, however, has left her position at the castle.

As Max claimed, there is nothing amiss in the torture chamber and the Iron Maiden is free of bloodstains. Mary is still skeptical, but not as frightened. During their quiet conversation, however, Mary is startled by the sudden intrusion of Erich (Christopher Lee), caretaker of the black museum. Max assures Mary that Erich is quite loyal and can be trusted completely. Nevertheless, he remains an imposing figure, clad in black and standing well over six feet tall. Seeing that his services are not presently required, Erich bows and clicks his heels in a military fashion before departing from the room. Max tells Mary that the deep scar near Erich's right eye is the result of a wound suffered during the war.

Mary spends more and more of her time alone in the castle as her husband's absences become more frequent. The dark atmosphere of the gloomy structure and the furtive nature of the mysterious Erich continue to play upon Mary's nerves. Another mystery develops when she sees a nattily dressed stranger lurking on the castle grounds. Although Mr. Selby (Jim Dolen) is soft-spoken and seems quite innocent, his claim to be an American tourist doesn't quite ring true. Perhaps the "tourist" is not as innocent as he appears — but what is the nature of his threat?

The pieces of the frightening puzzle first begin falling into place when the authorities bring the American in for questioning. He is actually an undercover agent for the FBI. The local police are informed by Selby that his mission relates to the search for a Nazi war criminal and that information has established a circle of association with Max Hunter. Such information accounts for his interest in the castle and the questioning of Mary Hunter.

Mary is still on edge as the castle is beset by strange noises, threatening voices and sinister figures moving within the shadows. Another frightening sight is the mannequin of a medieval executioner, on display in the black museum. This fearsome, black hooded figure is both frightening and dramatic, with its tunic, high boots and heavy black gauntlets. One night, the Executioner seems to become endowed with life and pursues Mary through the darkened corridors of the castle. Mary reaches her bedroom and manages to lock the door. When the masked figure reaches through a broken door panel, Mary stabs his arm with a knife.

The assailant flees, making his way to a dimly lit street near the estate. Hiding in the shadows, he spies a buxom brunette who languorously puffs a cigarette while waiting on a street corner. Creeping up from behind, he attacks her; she loses consciousness after a brief struggle. "You thought I wanted to abuse your body!" he cries. "But what I have in store for you is death!"

After carrying her to a stone chamber in the lower levels of the castle, he binds the girl to a chair. After reviving his captive, the hooded fiend begins preparing his deadly instrument of torture. A hungry rat has been placed in a cage designed for attachment to the victim's head. The madman states that this means of punishment has long been forbidden as being too barbaric, but he feels no compunction about utilizing it.

Unknown to the hooded killer, Mary has overcome her terror and begun to search the castle for the fiend. She watches the terrible drama unfold by peering between the iron bars of the madman's chamber door. As the victim begins screaming in agony, Mary seizes a mace from a stone wall and storms into the chamber. The madman flees into a dark passageway while Mary removes the cage from the victim's face and unties her. The girl becomes hysterical as she touches her bloodied nose and cries, "I don't want to live with my face this way!"

Unable to calm the girl, Mary cautiously approaches the shadowy tunnel in search of the hooded fiend. She soon finds the unconscious form of a man clad in the executioner's garb, though the black hood has been removed. Mary sees, to her horror, that the man is Max. A few moments pass before the clicking of boot-heels can be heard emanating from an adjoining tunnel. The footsteps cease, and Erich appears, the terror of this dreadful night finally proves too much for Mary who loses consciousness.

Mary awakens in her bedroom once again as Max attempts to explain the events of the previous night. He denies he is responsible for the recent mayhem. Max assures his wife that the young brunette has been hospitalized and will recover from her wounds. Sadly, he cannot provide satisfactory answers to his wife's questions. Although she still loves Max, Mary decides to leave the castle.

Mary and her maid Trudy (Luciana Milone) prepare to depart, but to leave they must pass through the black museum. Once again the dreadful presence of the Executioner can be felt, although he seems to be hidden from view. As Trudy runs toward the exit, Mary seizes a halberd and turns to face what she believes to be her tormentor. Striking the hooded figure before her, Mary cries out, "I've killed you...you monster!" But it is only a costumed mannequin that she has struck down.

Trudy screams and disappears from sight near the opposite end of the chamber. Mary rushes to her aid, but finds the hapless girl's corpse within the shadows. Out of the dark corners appears the hooded madman, who seizes Mary. In the struggle, she yanks the hood from his head. The fiend backs away slowly as he emerges from the shadows and his grotesque features become illuminated within a pale light. His eyes sunken...head and face hairless — no nose — he resembles a living skull. Hatred gleams in his eyes as he bares his teeth in rage.

In the meantime, Erich attempts to enter the castle and finds all of the doors locked. After climbing a castle wall, he falls and is knocked unconscious. After regaining consciousness, he realizes that the authorities must be alerted.

The Executioner binds Mary to a table and threatens her with a scalpel. There is grim determination in his monstrous face as the blade glistens in his gloved hand. For some reason, he finds himself unable to continue his attack and hurls the scalpel to one side. The madman carries her off to what he considers a more suitable fate... death in the Iron Maiden.

Accompanied by the police, Erich drives furiously back to the Hunter estate. He finally reveals the secret of the castle to a shrewd inspector. The terrible series of events can be traced back to the days of the Third Reich, at a time when Germany was facing defeat. An unsuccessful attempt on Adolf Hitler's life, engineered by a group of renegade generals, brought a swift response from the Nazi regime. The participants were executed with the exception of Gen. Hunter — Max's father. Subjected to experimental surgery, the elder Hunter's skin was completely removed from his face. "They called him their living skull" states Erich with an edge of bitterness in his voice.

The terrified Mary, secured within the Iron Maiden, watches in horror as the mad former general slowly begins pushing the lid shut. Max suddenly appears and calls out to his father, who fails to recognize him. Seizing a battle-axe, the madman squares off for a confrontation with his son. Erich arrives with the authorities just as the killer is poised to strike. Special agent Selby draws his revolver and opens fire, striking the madman in the chest. Fatally wounded, he staggers away and ignites a blaze with a torch in order to block pursuit by the police. Max rescues Mary as the deadly spikes of the Iron Maiden hover just inches away from her face.

Flames spread quickly as Max and the others flee the castle. Erich, still moved by loyalty to the tormented general, rushes headlong into the blaze. He finds the dying man laying in one of the corridors, kneels beside him and softly addresses him as "general." The mind of the murderous yet tragic former soldier returns to normal as he recognizes Erich — a trusted friend and one-time comrade-in-arms. "The war still goes on," mutters the quickly fading Hunter. "We must stop them...Erich." With that, the disfigured victim of Nazi atrocities breathes his last. Oblivious to the fiery destruction around him, Erich remains by the general's side as the weakened ceiling collapses.

Max and Mary embrace one another as the reign of terror comes to an end.

The veneer of anti-war feeling that emerges during the final minutes of *Horror Castle* hardly seems appropriate. Gen. Hunter, an incredibly sadistic killer and torturer, fails to evoke the slightest sympathy for 90 percent of the film. Nevertheless, the political overtones of the closing scenes provide an innovative twist to an eclectic, sensationalized story.

The uninspired script seems even more disappointing when one considers the talent involved. Director Margheriti was joined by cinematographer Riccardo Pallotini and fellow director Edmond Greville in completing the screenplay. Pallotini's visual skills enriched Margheriti's *Castle of Blood* and provided most of what little value existed in Riccardo Freda's *The Witch's Curse* (1964). The prolific Greville directed the eerie remake of *The Hands of Orlac* (1961), starring Mel Ferrer and Christopher Lee. Sadly, the combined skills of Margheriti, Pallotini and Greville only managed to create material that is mediocre at best.

On the positive side, Richard McNamara wrote the English language version of *Horror Castle* and provides basically sensible English dialogue. This is quite surprising when one considers McNamara's past record. He also wrote the English versions of the horrendous "sons of Hercules" series — hacked-up abortions based on films that were no better than second-rate to begin with.

As a director, Antonio Margheriti provides few of the subtle, wonderfully atmospheric moments present in his more successful *Castle of Blood*. Instead, Margheriti prefers to stun the audience with gratuitous gore and graphic tortures that disgust rather than frighten. The more blatant forms of horror had been conveyed far more effectively by Hammer Films in such chillers as *The Curse of Frankenstein* (1957) and *Horror of Dracula* (1958). The latter films used gore and violence strategically to heighten the feeling of tension at appropriate moments. In short, a hint of mayhem is sometimes more frightening than a blood-spattered overdose. However, Margheriti builds some good tension during the last 15 minutes as the hapless heroine seems moments away from a gruesome death and her husband frantically attempts to rescue her.

A few horrific sequences are marred somewhat by the widescreen image that lessens the claustrophobic sense of horror, especially in regard to some nasty business involving the Iron Maiden. Use of color rather than black-and-white is another drawback, with occasionally gaudy excesses destroying the shadowy feeling of horror that should persist throughout the film. Color does provide a few moments of visual beauty in what is obviously an Italian landscape, despite a German setting. One last major flaw, on a technical level, is the use of a blaring jazz score that seems more suitable for a Mickey Spillane thriller than for a tale of Gothic horror.

The film relies heavily upon several competent performances. Rossana Podestà comes off best with her polished portrayal of the frightened but tenacious heroine. Podestà was born to Italian-Argentine parents in Libya in 1934. The olive-skinned beauty seemed perfect for spectacle films set in exotic locales. She acted in such costume dramas as Robert Wise's *Helen of Troy* (1955), *Fury of the Pagans* (1960), *Alone Against Rome* (1962) and *Sodom and Gomorrah* (1963). However, the actress also appeared in several fantasies and portrayed Snow White in *The Seven Dwarfs to the Rescue* (1952). Podestà was later cast as the spell-casting Circe in *Ulysses* (1955) and as a fetching young sorceress in Antonio Margheriti's *The Golden Arrow* (1964). Podestà brings an admirable mixture of strength and vulnerability to her role in *Horror Castle*. Mary Hunter, left to her own resources, emerges as an unusually aggressive heroine in a scenario that could have easily contained the stereotypically helpless, whining female.

Also restrained is Georges Rivière as the troubled Max, who harbors a dark family secret. We really don't see enough of Rivière's character, but he brings a great deal of energy to the last hysterical minutes of the film. Rivière began showing some versatility at this stage in his career, playing heroes and villains with equal competence. Audiences thrilled to his creepy portrayal of the mysterious leader of the corrupt "Black Scorpions" in *Agent 383: Passport to Hell* (1964). He was also the brutal town boss in Sergio Corbucci's *Minnesota Clay* (1965), an Italian western starring Cameron Mitchell.

Christopher Lee delivers a typically fine performance, free of the grimacing and eyeball-rolling that less skilled actors would have brought to their portrayal of the scarred, black-clad Erich. In contrast, Yugoslav actor Mirko Valentin relies more on facial contortions because of the heavy makeup that restricts subtle facial expressions.

There isn't much to recommend *Horror Castle* beyond its few good performances and occasionally striking visuals. The film was in European release for over a year before being distributed in the United States by Allied Artists. Originally, the flick was double-billed with a straight suspense film, *Nightmare in the Sun* starring Ursula Andress and John Derek. Widely released early in 1965, the films earned marginal U.S. profits and attracted little attention from the critics. *Horror Castle* remains a minor credit for both Christopher Lee and Antonio Margheriti, who have done far better.

Isabel, Duchess of the Devils
(Isabella, duchessa dei diavoli)

Cinesecolo/Indief/Hape Film. 86 minutes. 1969. Eastman Color, CinemaScope. Dir: Bruno Corbucci. Writ: Giorgio Cavedon, Mario Amendola, Elisabeth Forster. Ph: Fausto Zuccoli. Cast: Brigitte Skay, Tino Scotti, Mimmo Palmara, Fred Williams, Emina de Witt, Salvatore Borgese, Mario Novelli, Renato Baldini, Enzo Andronica.

In 1968, the influence of the ABC-TV series *Batman* was being seen in low-camp action flicks — efforts in which the subject matter was strictly tongue-in-cheek or merely played for laughs. Sadly, the lightweight approach of the fabled *Barman* series was soon abandoned in favor of lurid, grisly features catering to sadomasochistic tastes and aimed more toward the sexploitation market. Such is the case with *Isabel, Duchess of the Devils*, which is based on an Italian comic strip created in 1966 by Alessandro Angiolini. Thus far, this is the only film production based on the strip.

Isabel (Brigitte Skay) is an aggressive, beautiful noblewoman whose parents are murdered by the evil Baron von Nutter (Fred Williams) and his minions. Although the family castle is seized by the brigands, Isabel fights her way out and escapes into the countryside. During the struggle, she cuts off the nose and one ear of the Baron, who then takes to wearing a leather mask. Not being one to forgive and forget, he sends his men to scour the region for Isabel. Eventually, she is captured and forced back to the castle where the Baron takes sadistic pleasure in degrading and torturing the woman. The torments continue until Isabel finally breaks free and strikes back in all her fury. Both Isabel and the Baron escape the castle, leaving open the possibility of a sequel that never came about.

Brigitte Skay is well-cast physically as Isabel, though her acting ability leaves much to be desired. Actually, the role of Isabel would have been perfect for Martine Beswick, whose sensual, authoritative acting enriched such Hammer thrillers as *One Million Years B.C.* (1966) and *Prehistoric Women* (1966). Skay's other movie credits include *24 Hour Lover* (1970) and Mario Bava's mediocre *Twitch of the Death Nerve* (1971).

In thankless supporting roles, one will find several male co-stars familiar to fans of Italian action and adventure films. Mimmo Palmara acted in the fantasy-adventures *Hercules* (1959), *Hercules Unchained* (1960), *Goliath Against the Giants* (1963) and *Hercules and the Captive Women* (1963). Renato Baldini filled roles in *The White Warrior* (1961), *The Golden Arrow* (1964), *Snow Devils* (1965) and AIP's *Spy in Your Eye* (1966). Cloak and dagger roles were filled by Enzo Andronica in *00-2 Most Secret Agents* (1965) and *Italian Secret Service* (1968) while Salvatore (a.k.a. Sal) Borgese acted in Italian westerns like *The Bounty Hunters* (1970) and *Adios Sabata* (1971).

There is some good color photography provided by Fausto Zuccoli, who also handled the camerawork for the predictable but visually competent *Spy in Your Eye*. Zuccoli's camera emerged as one of the few good things about Antonio Margheriti's *The Young, the Evil and the Savage* (1969), released several months before *Isabel, Duchess of the Devils* reached theaters.

Director Bruno Corbucci is the brother of Sergio Corbucci, whose Italian westerns include at least one cult favorite — *Minnesota Clay* (1965), starring Cameron Mitchell and Georges Rivière (of *Castle of Blood*). Bruno lacks both his brother's imagination and his skill at building and maintaining an atmosphere of tension. Instead, he takes perverse pleasure in concentrating on Isabel's torments which the camera lovingly details. Nevertheless, the Corbucci brothers — much like Roger and Gene Corman — carried on an effective working relationship within the film industry. With Bruno writing and Sergio directing, the Corbuccis collaborated on *The Slave* (1963), starring Steve Reeves, and the fast-moving oater *Django* (1966) with Franco Nero.

Isabel, Duchess of the Devils might have emerged as passable entertainment had it been less mean-spirited and avoided wallowing in its depravity. Bruno Corbucci went on to write and direct the mediocre *Crime at Porta Romana* (1980), proving that an adequate screenwriter doesn't always possess the skills of a competent director.

Kill Baby Kill

Original title: *Operazione Paura (Operation Fear)*. A.k.a. *Curse of the Dead*. A.k.a. *Curse of the Living Dead*. Ful Films, Europix. 83 minutes (ORT: 85 minutes). 1966. Eastman Color, Panoramic. Dir: Mario Bava. Writ: Bava, Roberto Natale, John Hart. Ph: Antonio Rinaldi. Mus: Carlo Rustichelli. Ed: Romano Fortini. Art Dir: Sandro Dell'Orco. Cast: Giacomo Rossi-Stuart, Erika Blanc, Gianna Vivaldi, Fabienne Dali, Piero Lulli, Max Lawrence, Micaela Esdra, Valeria Valeri, Franco Dominici.

This Mario Bava chiller is said by many to be one of his best

Pressbook art for *Kill Baby Kill* (1966).

efforts, possibly even a minor classic of the genre. It is definitely a good looking film, containing the visual beauty of Bava's more familiar efforts plus a few interesting new twists to an unoriginal premise. Surprisingly, the film received little attention upon its original release and remains unseen by many Bava fans.

A number of bizarre suicides have occurred in the Baltic village of Karmingen. A big-city coroner receives a letter from a village girl who pleads for help in dealing with the frightening situation. Dr. Paul Eswai (Giacomo Rossi-Stuart) responds to the desperate plea, but he learns upon his arrival that the young woman is already dead. Eswai and his assistant Monica Shuftan (Erika Blanc) conduct autopsies upon the suicide victims and find that a gold coin has been inserted into the heart of each corpse. Police Chief Kroger (Piero Lulli) is puzzled by the grisly mystery and cannot explain the gruesome tampering with each of the bodies.

Eswai's investigation reveals a circle of association between the suicides and a pair of reclusive old women, the embittered Baroness Graps (Gianni Vivaldi) and a black-robed witch named Ruth (Fabienne Dali). The strange deaths are accompanied by visions of a golden-haired child who is discovered to be the spirit of the Baroness' seven-year-old daughter. Many years earlier, the girl bled to death after a tragic accident. Villagers preoccupied with a celebration ignored the desperate mother's pleas for help. Now, after years of mourning, Baroness Graps enjoys watching the campaign of vengeance unfold. She dwells alone in her villa, hiding behind black lace curtains in dim candlelit rooms. Revenge is her only reason for living as her will to destroy the village evokes the murderous spirit's terrible visitations.

Ironically, the second outcast of the village has become the nemesis of evil by conducting white magic rituals to save the souls of suicide victims. The insertion of a gold coin into the heart of each victim is carried out by the witch Ruth in order to redeem that individual and save the spirit from the clutches of Satan.

Eswai learns that the desperate letter he originally received was written by the sister of his assistant, Monica. It becomes apparent that Monica will soon suffer the fate of her sister unless Ruth intervenes with the proper mystical rites.

Is he a - Madman? Ghoul? Vampire? Werewolf? Take your pick! They're all to be found in abundance in Europix-International Ltd's triple avalanche of grisly horror, ORGY OF THE LIVING DEAD! The three terror features are now playing at the .. .. theatre.

MAT 102 B

Pressbook art and copy for *Kill Baby Kill* (1966) under the alternative title *Orgy of the Living Dead.*

There is a final confrontation between witch and vindictive mother, with the Baroness losing the battle. The spirit of the long-dead child is finally at peace as Karmingen is freed from her reign of terror.

Horrors, both subtle and overt, fill this thriller distinguished by Bava's fine sense of flow. Karmingen is a village that reeks of death and the film's series of striking images reinforces that grim illusion. Trees are black and twisted...narrow streets are covered with cold, swirling mists...buildings are crumbling into ruin... rooms are shrouded in cobwebs and barely illuminated by candles — much like a mortuary. Carlo Rustichelli's haunting musical score effectively enhances the fine visuals and a compelling motion picture experience.

Nevertheless, there are scripting flaws that detract from the visual poetry of the film. Too many rabbits are pulled from the proverbial hat with one revelation after another disrupting the moody scenario. The "murders by suicide" become redundant rather than frightening with each killing punctuated by the mournful tolling of a bell — a gimmick lifted from Camillo Mastrocinque's *Terror in the Crypt* (1963).

However, the film is refreshingly free of the sensationalism that began creeping into Bava's chillers in the mid-60s. The voyeurism evident in "The Telephone" segment of Bava's *Black Sabbath* (1964) became a strong element in his *Blood and Black Lace* (1965), which also contained an inherent theme of sadomasochism. *Kill Baby Kill* lacks even the healthy eroticism of an ordinary male-female relationship as the contact between Dr. Eswai and Monica remains fairly sedate.

Perhaps it is the maternal instinct that the film seems more concerned with. An embittered mother seeks revenge and strikes out at those around her while a spell-casting witch extends her motherly protectiveness to include her entire "brood"—the inhabitants of the village. There is also a neat reversal of stereotypical good-evil images as a clad-in-black witch displays a basic humanity lacking in the child-spirit whose murderous nature betrays the implied innocence of her golden hair and cherubic face.

Kill Baby Kill was not as widely distributed in the United States as other Bava efforts that were probably more salable. The film doesn't explore horrors with deep psychological meanings or concentrate on the mayhem created by vampires, werewolves or other stock horror heavies. Instead, we see a little girl whose sudden appearances instill self-destructive tendencies in those who see her. Such a premise may not offer much promise to die-hard dread addicts. Giacomo Rossi-Stuart, usually a second male lead, delivers a nicely tuned performance as Dr. Eswai. Equally effective is Erika Blanc who gives the role of Monica an air of quiet charm and an undertone of apprehension. Blanc later played a horrific role as a murderous demon in the Italo-Belgian chiller *The Devil's Nightmare* (1971), starring Jean Servais.

Kill Baby Kill may not be Mario Bava's best thriller, but the film offers another opportunity to enjoy the director's bravura cinematics.

The Last Man on Earth
(L'ultimo uomo della terra)

A.k.a. *I Am Legend*. A.k.a. *Naked Terror*. AP Produzione La Regina, AIP. 86 minutes. 1964. B&W, CinemaScope. Dir: Sidney Salkow, Ubaldo Rasona. Prod: Robert L. Lippert. Writ: Logan Swanson (Richard Matheson), William P. Leicester. Ph: Franco Delli Colli. Mus: Paul Sawtell, Bert Shefter. Makeup: Piero Mecaci. Ed: Gene Ruggero. Cast: Vincent Price, Emma Danieli, Franca Bettoia (Bettoja), Giacomo Rossi-Stuart, Umberto Rau (Raho), Christi Courtland, Tony Corevi, Hector (Ettore) Ribotta.

Richard Matheson's chilling 1951 novel *I Am Legend* had the necessary ingredients for what could have been a horror masterpiece. Originally, a screen adaptation was planned by Hammer Films, but the title was dropped from their production slate. The story of one man's quixotic struggle against a horde of vampires after a worldwide plague was finally brought to the screen with Forrest J Ackerman's assessment of the film as a "Dull, uninspired version of an exciting novel." Though not a winner, *The Last Man on Earth* contains some atmospheric sequences and occasional snatches of good dialogue.

The streets of Los Angeles are deserted, covered by a shroud of silence broken only by the howling of the wind. With the coming of dawn, Robert Morgan (Vincent Price) stoically begins his daily routine of the past few years: Eat enough food to function, search the streets for dead bodies to be incinerated and seek out the undead creatures who prowl the night — seeking blood. Morgan fills his shoulder-bag with sharpened wooden stakes, then embarks upon his daily search-and-destroy mission. Vampires hide in the dark corners and shadowy corridors of apartment buildings, decrepit shacks and once-elegant mansions. The social distinctions associated with such structures are no longer significant since any of them may hide reanimated corpses helpless in the daylight. Morgan claims as many as possible, hauling the impaled bodies to a huge pit once designated by the authorities as an incineration dump for plague victims.

As night falls, Morgan takes shelter in his barricaded house while shuffling, pale corpses wander the streets. "Morgan…we're gonna get you, Morgan," drones a vampirized former colleague named Ben Cortman (Giacomo Rossi-Stuart). Morgan's mind reaches back several years to a time when the two men shared a strong bond and expressed equal concern over a fearful plague in Central Europe. As this flashback begins, the terrible new disease claimed many lives and no effective treatment is available. Morgan attempts to dispel Cortman's fears, assuring him that a vaccine will be discovered long before the plague affects North America. The men rejoin their friends and loved ones as they enjoy the orange glow of the sun and gentle breeze that make their backyard barbeque even more enjoyable.

Several months later, the autumn winds howl as dead leaves scatter the yard and cover the now empty picnic table. The plague has ravaged Europe and now exists as a worldwide crisis. Morgan, a brilliant biologist, joins his colleagues in a desperate search for an effective vaccine. Cortman's fears are fanned by terrible new developments. Why are the bodies being burned? What about the rumors of the dead returning to life and seeking blood? Morgan dismisses such talk as hysteria and claims that burning bodies is an effective means of slowing the spread of the bacteria. Cortman is not convinced and barricades himself in his house. A cross and a string of garlic adorn his front door to repel the undead. Morgan contemplates the sad situation, certain that Cortman is now quite insane.

The truth about the plague emerges when Morgan's own child becomes infected. Blindness, the first symptom, affects the girl, who only lives for a short time. Troops take her body for incineration.

Pressbook art for *The Last Man on Earth* (1964).

When Morgan's wife Virginia (Emma Danieli) succumbs to the disease, he swears that her remains will be spared from the flames. After burying her body in a wooded area, Morgan returns home to deal with his grief. Late that night, he hears a low moaning and a scratching sound at the front door. He cautiously approaches the door, opening it to reveal the reanimated, grime-encrusted corpse of Virginia. She shuffles forward with arms outstretched, whispering her husband's name…

These painful memories still fill Morgan's mind on a day when he visits the mausoleum where Virginia rests. Suddenly realizing that darkness has fallen, he rushes out into the night where the thirsty dead stumble and sway grotesquely during attempts to seize him. Morgan makes his way to the car and drives furiously back to his house where there is another encounter with the undead. Finally barricaded in his house, Morgan hears the sound of clubs shattering glass and striking metal surfaces.

The next morning, Morgan views with indifference the vampires' destruction of his car. A brisk walk to an automobile showroom provides a new car that helps prolong his grim, monotonous existence. However, a new development mystifies Morgan as he discovers the remains of vampires impaled with steel stakes. The metal shafts have been forged somewhere by an unknown party. Although the mystery preys upon his mind, Morgan sees the possibility of companionship when he sees a small dog wandering the street. Morgan gives chase but soon loses sight of it.

Morgan returns home to an unexpected surprise: He finds the dog waiting on the doorstep. The animal whimpers and hides in a corner after hearing the nightly thumping and moaning of wandering vampires. "You're afraid of them too, aren't you, boy?" Morgan asks as he pets the trembling creature.

Morgan finds a trace of blood on his hand and wonders if the deadly bacteria might be present. Placing a blood smear on a slide, he finds that his fear is valid. He laughs mirthlessly before hopelessness drains his energy completely. "What's the use?" he mutters.

Morgan buries the impaled dog in an open field and, after completing the grim task, is stunned to see the approaching figure of a young woman. She fails to see him at first, but utters a cry of surprise when Morgan calls out. She turns to run away, but Morgan pursues the girl and finally grasps her arm.

Despite his good intentions, Ruth (Franca Bettoja) continues to resist contact. "It's either them or me!" he curtly states and walks away. Although she balks at first, the girl reluctantly follows him. Tensions ease somewhat as they arrive at Morgan's home, but Morgan is never satisfied with answers concerning her survival of the plague and the nightly vampiric onslaughts.

Morgan leaves the living room briefly and returns with a string of garlic which Ruth regards very negatively. She turns suddenly pale while experiencing nausea and disorientation. The allergic reaction typical of vampires seems to mark Ruth as being one of them. She denies the accusation and withdraws from her pocket a syringe and vials of chemicals. Ruth reveals that this vaccine has been developed by members of her community — a thriving new sub-culture also fighting the vampires. The colony is able to control the disease but not cure it. Morgan is even more startled to learn that many of the "vampires" he impaled were members of her community. Among citizens of the new society, he is thought of as a worse monster than the blood-lusting creatures who walk the night.

Morgan watches as Ruth withdraws a hidden pistol and reveals that the society has decided to eliminate him. She must hold him captive until a party of armed men can arrive to carry out his execution. Sick of struggle, the enraged Morgan taunts her and asks her why she can't carry out the death sentence herself. Ruth breaks into tears as she drops the pistol and admits that she has no stomach for killing.

Now feeling more compassion than anger, Morgan tries an experiment that may cure the girl. The medical apparatus in his home allows Morgan to give Ruth a transfusion of his blood, which is free of bacteria. Miraculously, her pallor is replaced by a healthy complexion as her strength and vigor return. Morgan's blood proves to be an effective vaccine against the plague. The joy of the moment proves to be short-lived as the shambling Cortman finds his way into the house and attacks the girl. Morgan seizes Cortman and hurls him against a wall. Military convoy-type trucks arrive, filled with heavily armed men on a search-and-destroy mission. Ruth pleads with Morgan to flee for his life; the raiders are determined to exact vengeance against him.

Morgan begins his flight, but briefly hides behind a clump of bushes as the raiders form a line and advance on the befuddled vampires. Cries of terror and surprise escape their undead throats as the bloodsuckers are impaled with steel stakes. Cortman climbs to the roof of Morgan's house to escape the massacre, but is brought down by a burst of machine-gun fire. When a searchlight reveals his hiding place, Morgan draws a revolver and fires a wild shot. The raiders pursue him and engage in a running gun battle.

Morgan makes his way to a deserted urban military outpost and drops several of his pursuers with well-aimed bullets before locating the building's armory. He barricades the door from the inside and discovers a supply of tear gas bombs, some of which he places into a pouch. Escaping through an unlocked window, he finds his way to the street as the chase resumes. Twisting, turning and hurling bombs as he runs, Morgan manages to slow the raiders' pursuit.

Despite the swirling clouds of blinding gas, a stray bullet strikes Morgan and he staggers into a church. Painfully making his way between rows of benches, he finally braces himself against the altar. Despite his waning strength, Morgan straightens to face his opponents and shouts his defiance as a steel lance is hurled with deadly accuracy. Morgan collapses, a steel shaft protruding from his middle.

With the battle concluded, women and children enter the church and view the "monster" who once persecuted them. Ruth arrives and rushes to Morgan's side. She tries to comfort the dying man who weakly mutters, "I was a man...and they were afraid of me." As Morgan expires, the weeping girl turns to leave. The onlookers back away from the woman who was once one of them. Her head bowed, she walks away while ignoring those around her. Ruth already seems to accept the lonely life that she must lead with the same stoicism that Morgan once showed.

Shot in 1963, *The Last Man on Earth* was released in the U.S. by AIP in 1964 as the top half of a double-bill with a British science-fiction thriller, *The Unearthly Stranger*. Definitely hurt by its low budget, *The Last Man on Earth* rarely presents an adequate depiction of widespread human devastation. Although there are supposedly multitudes of the undead, Morgan's struggle seems to be against 25 reanimated corpses and an equal number of half-human opponents. Early scenes which depict the discovery of the plague and its emergence as a global threat lack plausibility depiction because of small-scale production. Morgan's recollections provide some sense of the human tragedy and personal loss, though we rarely see the story of mankind on the wane.

Another problem is the miscasting of Price in the lead role. Price is more restrained than usual, but he isn't rugged enough for the character. His death scene, with its elaborate posturing and grand gestures, would have been more appropriate in a Shakespearean tragedy. A more effective portrayal could probably have been achieved by either Jack Palance or Cameron Mitchell, both of whom entered the European action market in the early 1960s. Mitchell especially was no stranger to European horror and delivered competent performances in Mario Bava's *Blood and Black Lace* (1965) and the Spanish chiller, *Man-Eater of Hydra* (1967). His performance in Giacomo Gentilomo's *Last of the Vikings* (1962) contained a mixture of strength, anguish and bitterness with an undercurrent of vulnerability. Such elements are present in the character of Robert Morgan.

The handful of supporting roles are handled effectively by performers who generally remained unfamiliar to American audiences. The only exception is Giacomo Rossi-Stuart, who acted in several low-budget spectacles and, under the pseudonym of Jack Stuart, starred in Antonio Margheriti's science-fiction flick *Planet of the Prowl* (1965). One of the actor's medium-budget credits is the World War II adventure yarn *Hornet's Nest* (1970), starring Rock Hudson.

Sidney Salkow, a one-time director of Broadway plays, switched to the medium of film in the 1930s. He specialized in B movie fare, largely westerns and gangster melodramas. There were exceptions, however, most notably a stirring adaptation of a Jack London tale, *The Adventures of Martin Eden* (1942). Glenn Ford starred in the latter effort, relating the harrowing experiences of a young seaman on a sailing vessel.

Salkow's *The Last Man on Earth* also deals with the struggle of one man against overwhelming forces with somewhat less dramatic effect. The quiet moments are quite acceptable as we see Morgan deal with his sense of loss or feel the claustrophobic terror evoked by the nightly wanderings of vampires who lurk beyond his barricaded door. Action sequences, however, are fairly ordinary as they are handled without imagination and have their participants move in unrealistic, formal patterns. George Romero handled a similar scenario with considerable flair in *Night of the Living Dead* (1968). The Romero cult favorite merged shock and excitement value quite smoothly while presenting violent sequences that contained the believable elements of confusion and spontaneity.

On a positive note, the widescreen black-and-white photography helps the story. The oversized image occasionally de-emphasizes Morgan's claustrophobic horrors, but also conveys the vast emptiness of a once-thriving city. Makeup effects of Piero Mecaci are fairly subtle with applications of greasepaint to whiten faces and provide dark circles beneath the eyes. The walking corpses in this flick are refreshingly free of protruding fangs, bat-like eyebrows or other melodramatic excesses often present in vampire flick. Even the Paul Sawtell-Bert Shefter score seems comparatively restrained when one thinks of their other collaborations, among them the delightfully bombastic scores of such thrillers as *The Black Scorpion* (1957), *It! The Terror from Beyond Space* (1958) and *The Fly* (1958).

Richard Matheson wrote the original screenplay under the pseudonym of Logan Swanson. A New Jersey native born in 1926, the talented Matheson felt that his original screen treatment was more than adequate. The producers didn't agree and hired William P. Leicester to rewrite. The final treatment may not be quite as moody as the novel, but is still faithful to the plot and features a few snatches of stimulating dialogue. Morgan sees his survival of the plague as evidence that he was "chosen" to save the Earth and purify it of the undead abominations. His egotism and brutal crusade finally make him as monstrous as the creatures he attempts to eradicate. The sad fate that befalls men when they lose their humanity is neatly conveyed during the closing sequences.

Salkow and Price were soon teamed again with more effective results in the United Artists thriller *Twice Told Tales* (1963). Price acted in several Italian productions during the 1960s, including a pair of costume dramas, *Queen of the Nile* (1962) and *Rage of the Buccaneers* (1964). His role in Mario Bava's SF-comedy *Dr. Goldfoot and the Girl Bombs* (1966) is the closest thing to a second Italian horror credit.

I Am Legend was remade by director Boris Sagal as *The Omega Man* (1971), starring Charlton Heston as Robert Neville (the character's name in the novel). This film succeeds well on its own terms, but emerges largely as a slick science-fiction adventure with a few horrific touches. Matheson's novel has yet to be properly presented on the silver screen, but *The Last Man on Earth* occasionally captures the essence of the work.

Libido

Nucleo Film. 85 minutes. 1966. B&W. Dir: Julian Berry (Ernesto Gastaldi). Writ: Berry, Victor Storff (Vittorio Salerno). Ph: Ramón Garrón (Romolo Garroni). Cast: Dominique Boschero, John Charlie Johns (Giancarlo Giannini), Mara Maryl (Maria Chianetta), Alan Collins (Luciano Pigozzi).

After writing such tripe as *Werewolf in a Girl's Dormitory* (1963), Ernesto Gastaldi tried directing his mediocre material as well with this routine thriller based on a screenplay by Gastaldi and Vittorio Salerno. The cliché-ridden story has a youth named Christian secretly watching his mentally deranged father murder his mistress. After the terrible deed is completed, the father takes his own life by leaping off a cliff. Years later, Christian (Giancarlo Giannini) is now a young man who has learned to live with his psychological scars and decides to return to his late father's country home. Christian is accompanied by a lovely young wife, Helene (Dominique Boschero), and another married couple who are his closest friends, Paul (Luciano Pigozzi) and Brigitte (Maria Chianetta).

At first, it seems Christian will be able to settle in the long-deserted family home without being tormented by dreadful memories. However, the villa is soon beset by nocturnal disturbances and other strange incidents that seem to indicate his father's furtive presence. Has the crazed killer been hiding in the isolated house for these many years? Or is it his malevolent spirit that has returned to torment his innocent son? The creepy occurrences continue until the sensitive Christian, dwarfed by the memories of his father's cruel acts, is finally pushed past the breaking point.

The "haunting" of the villa is actually a ruse devised by Helene and Brigitte to drive Christian insane and seize his inheritance. They succeed all too well as Christian becomes convinced that he is now his own father. He repeats the murderous acts that are now directed toward women who are greedy and manipulative — much like the father's mistress. After the climax of the killing spree, the mad Christian leaps from the same cliff where his father committed suicide years earlier.

Libido borrows the game-playing scenario of the classic *Diabolique* (1955) while rehashing the structure and some character relations of Roger Corman's *Pit and the Pendulum* (1961). Basic elements lifted from the latter film are transposed to a modern-day setting in Italy. Fans of the Corman-Poe film will recall that Richard Matheson's script had a nobleman (Vincent Price) tormented by the memory of his monstrous father (as a child, he witnessed the murder of his mother by his father, who accused her of adultery). Years later, the Price character is tormented by supposedly supernatural occurrences that are orchestrated by his own wife (Barbara Steele), whom he believes to be dead. Price becomes convinced that he is his own father and embarks on a killing spree before falling to his death in a deep pit.

Although imitation is the sincerest form of flattery, director Gastaldi lacks Corman's fine sense of flow. A preoccupation with Cormanesque Freudian gimmicks and needlessly arty touches destroy the atmosphere of tension that might have helped the film to emerge as a halfway decent thriller. Gastaldi later fared even worse with his hackneyed script for the suspenser *The Sweet Body of Deborah* (1969), a Carroll Baker vehicle with elements of sexploitation. However, *Libido* is helped by the striking black-and-white photography of Romolo Garroni whose fine camera previously enriched *Caesar the Conqueror* (1961), a handsome spectacle starring Cameron Mitchell.

The comparatively small cast of *Libido* features a couple of familiar faces that should be recognized by fans of Italian horror films and fantasies. Female lead Dominique Boschero played a supporting role in Antonio Margheriti's fantasy-adventure *The Golden Arrow* (1964) before turning to sex farce with roles in *Paris When It Sizzles* (1964) and *The Double Bed* (1965). Boschero also played Richard Harrison's love interest in AIP's *Secret Agent Fireball* (1966), a James Bond-like tale filled with hi-tech gadgets. The second male lead, Luciano Pigozzi, is a familiar genre figure who appeared in many Mario Bava and Antonio Margheriti thrillers of the 1960s.

However, *Libido* is worth noting mainly for an early screen appearance by Giancarlo Giannini, who hides behind the awkward English translation of his name — John Charlie Johns. The actor soon filled minor roles in such major films as the World War II melodramas *Anzio* (1968) and *The Secret of Santa Vittoria* (1969). Giannini (born 1942) displayed his softer side in a fairly amusing black comedy entitled *Arabella* (1969), with minxy Virna Lisi. It was in the films of Lina Wertmüller that Giannini became known for his enigmatic portrayals of hard-bitten men given to violent rages, while intermittently displaying a core of vulnerability that is otherwise carefully hidden. The actor began doing theater work for Wertmüller in 1966.

Wertmüller's *Swept Away by an Unusual Destiny in the Blue Sea of August* (1975) first brought Giannini to the attention of critics who admired his strangely compelling portrayal of a world-weary, embittered proletarian who forms a love-hate attachment to a wealthy female employer. The actor later delivered another fine performance in a Wertmüller romantic comedy entitled *Blood Feud* (1979), starring Sophia Loren.

Giannini, despite his slim but muscular build and rugged good looks, displays the wistful qualities that were once attributed to Peter Lorre. Much like Lorre, the sad eyes and pouting expression of Giannini help to project a child-like torment that evokes sympathy for violent but troubled characters. *Libido* may not be much of a film, but fans of Lina Wertmüller's work will enjoy seeing a competent early performance by one of the director's favorite actors.

The Long Hair of Death
(I lunghi capelli della morte)

Cinegai. 100 minutes. 1964. B&W. Dir: Anthony Dawson (Antonio Margheriti). Prod: Felice Testa Gay. Writ: Robert Bohr (Bruno Valeri), Julian Berry (Ernesto Gastaldi). Ph: Richard Thierry (Riccardo Pallotini). Cast: Barbara Steele, Giorgio Ardisson, Halina Zalewska, Robert Rains, Jean Rafferty (Giuliano Raffaelli), Laureen Nuyen (Laura Nucci), John Carey, Jeffrey Darcy.

A clichéd tale of vengeance from beyond the grave, *The Long*

Pressbook art for *The Long Hair of Death* (1964).

Hair of Death owes part of its premise to Riccardo Freda's *The Witch's Curse* (shot in 1961) and also borrows considerably from Mario Bava's *Black Sunday* (1961). Horror queen Barbara Steele's presence helps to save the film from utter mediocrity. It was her second thriller for director Antonio Margheriti, following the more effective *Castle of Blood* (shot in 1962).

Set in the 16th century, the story deals with the horrific series of events set into motion by the ruthless Count Humbolt (Giuliano Raffaelli), whose wife is burned at the stake for a murder committed by the Count's decadent son Kurt (Giorgio Ardisson). The condemned woman leaves behind two grown daughters, Helen (Barbara Steele) and Lizabeth (Halina Zalewska). Torn by anguish after watching the terrible injustice that is perpetrated by the authorities, the more aggressive Helen proves to be as much a threat to the Count as the nobleman's late wife was. Count Humbolt's ruthlessness emerges once again as he decides to eliminate Helen as well.

It is then that *The Long Hair of Death* becomes distinguished mainly by its striking images rather than by the unimaginative story of the undead Helen's revenge against the Count and his son. On a stormy night, the dank and musty tomb of Helen is opened in a startling fashion by a sudden bolt of lightning. Helen's return from the dead proves too horrifying for Count Humbolt, who dies of a heart attack. A close-up of Steele's worm-infested face is reminiscent of a similar scene in *Black Sunday* that had the grisly countenance of the undead witch Asa (Steele) being revealed after the removal of her death mask. Director Mario Bava provided us with a close-up of the ravaged, ashen-white face of Asa — scorpions scurrying from out of the empty eye sockets.

Much as in Margheriti's *Castle of Blood*, there is an abundance of visual beauty in *The Long Hair of Death*. Atmospheric landscapes, large baroque rooms and striking black-and-white photography provide a treat for the eyes. There are also many eerie scenes of silent figures who lurk in shadows or wander through dimly lit rooms. Die-hard horror movie addicts are sure to enjoy such genre trappings, but one often wonders why producers fail to devote as much time and energy to finding a good script.

Beyond Steele's usual polished performance, there are several fine portrayals in supporting roles. Giorgio Ardisson played the impulsive, womanizing yet brave and devoted sidekick of Reg Park in Mario Bava's *Hercules in the Haunted World*, shot in 1961. He was also cast as the courageous, fiery-tempered brother of Cameron Mitchell in *Last of the Vikings* (1962). Evil Kurt Humbolt allows Ardisson to fill the role of an out-and-out villain, which he does with great relish.

Other fine characterizations are achieved by Giuliano Raffaelli as the Malevolent Count and Halina Zalewska as the winsome Lizabeth. Raffaelli later appeared in Mario Bava's *Blood and Black Lace* (1965) and another Margheriti thriller, *The Wild, Wild Planet* (1966). Zalewska acted in a pair of Margheriti science-fiction flicks, *Snow Devils* (1965) and *The War Between the Planets* (1971). As "Alina" Zalewska, she joined the cast of Luchino Visconti's *The Leopard* (1963), a handsomely produced historical epic starring Burt Lancaster and Alain Delon.

Long Hair of Death producer Felice Testa Gay later made some straight action flicks; he produced a slick rehash of gangster film clichés entitled *The Hired Killer* (1967), starring Robert Webber and Franco Nero. Cinematographer Riccardo Pallotini ("Richard Thierry") often used pseudonyms as he applied his talents to additional thrillers by Mario Bava and Antonio Margheriti. Pallotini again used the alias of Richard Thierry for AIP's *Secret Agent Fireball* (1966), starring Richard Harrison.

Screenwriter Ernesto Gastaldi improved remarkably with his complex, skillful treatment for Mario Bava's *La frusta e il corpo (The Whip and the Body)*, released in the United States as *What!* in 1964. Sadly, Gastaldi's work reverted to the level of such incompetent, hackneyed yarns as *Libido* (1966) and *The Murder Clinic* (1967). The latter two efforts were no different from any one of a dozen or more psychological thrillers released in the early to mid–1960s.

Barbara Steele and Antonio Margheriti continued to work separately within the field, though neither was associated with another horror credit that was quite worth seeing. These two unique talents jointly scored a triumph with *Castle of Blood*, the echoes of which provide occasional moments of interest in the otherwise longwinded *The Long Hair of Death*.

Mill of the Stone Women
(Il mulino della donne di pietra)

A.k.a. *Horror of the Stone Women*. A.k.a. *The Horrible Mill Women*. A.k.a. *Le Moulin des supplices (The Mill of Torments)*. A.k.a.

Pressbook art for *Mill of the Stone Women* (1963).

Mill of the Stone Maidens. A.k.a. *Drips of Blood.* Vanguard/Faro/Explorer/CEC, Parade. 94 minutes (ORT: 95 minutes). 1963 (ORD: 1961). Eastman Color, Dyaliscope. Dir: Giorgio Ferroni. Prod: Gianpaolo Bigazzi, Lucien Vittet. Writ: Ferroni, Remìgio del Grosso, Ugo Libatore, Giorgio Stegani. Based on a short story by Peter Van Weigen. Ph: Pier Ludovico Pavoni. Mus: Carlo Innocenzi. Ed: Antonietta Zita. Art Dir: Arrigo Equini. Cast: Pierre Brice, Wolfgang Preiss, Scilla Gabel, Dany Carrel, Herbert Boehm, Marco Guglielmi, Liana Orfei, Olga Solbelli.

This grim chiller has earned the praise of a small cult of fans who compare it to Mario Bava's *Black Sunday* (1961) and Antonio Margheriti's *Castle of Blood* (1964) as a landmark genre effort. *Mill of the Stone Women* is an odd film — offbeat and quite atmospheric — but is doesn't quite equal the best of Bava or Margheriti.

Set in Amsterdam around 1912, the story deals with art student Hans Von Arnim (Pierre Brice), who feels drawn to the strangely beautiful statues decorating an old mill. Prof. Wahl (Wolfgang Preiss) uses the mill as a cover for the horrendous secret treatments of his ailing daughter, Helfy (Scilla Gabel). Her strange illness requires frequent blood transfusions and the professor obtains the vital fluids by adducting young women and draining them of blood. The process utilized by Wahl petrifies the bodies, thus creating the sculptures that have drawn admiration within artistic circles.

Wahl himself is unable to see the full horror of his acts as he devotes his time to attempts at saving his dying daughter from an inevitable fate. Helfy cannot be cured, but the terrible cycle continues as more lives are claimed and each succeeding treatment proves to have only temporary success. Hans finally becomes aware of the horror that lingers beneath the surface of the mill and within the soul of Prof. Wahl. Art is the product of man's humanity, and it is the loss of Wahl's humanity that has resulted in a horrendous series of events. Wahl must face this terrible reality as Hans brings the truth to light and the grisly conflict is concluded.

Though well-produced, this film adaptation of a Flemish tale becomes quite exhausting despite a pleasurably ghastly scenario. There are times when we are watching a routine "mad doctor" thriller — and a rather slow-paced one at that. In certain respects, plotting and character relations resemble those of Georges Franju's

Mill of the Stone Women 153

Yeux sans visage (Eyes Without a Face), a 1960 production also known as *Horror Chamber of Dr. Faustus* in its 1963 American release. The Franju classic dealt with the doomed attempts by a plastic surgeon to restore the face of his daughter, who was disfigured in a traffic accident. Skin grafts are provided by hapless young women who are kidnapped and subjected to grisly experimental surgery—until the daughter finally rebels. Franju combines poetic imagery with overt physical horrors and achieves compelling results. In *Mill of the Stone Women*, director Giorgio Ferroni creates some striking images with little substance to reinforce them. However, the film's images were borrowed by other filmmakers, including (Jack Hill's, *Blood Bath* [1966] and similar sculptures of women decorating the shadowy studio of vampire-artist William Campbell.)

Ferroni later turned to directing Italian westerns after handling a halfway decent spectacle, the visually excellent *The Trojan Horse* (1962), starring Steve Reeves and John Drew Barrymore. *Wanted* (1969) is a spaghetti western directed by Ferroni, who used the pseudonym of Kelvin Jackson Padget for most of his other ersatz oaters. His typical credits, under the name Padget, include *Blood for a Silver Dollar* (1965), *One Silver Dollar* (1967) and *Fort Yuma Gold* (1969).

Pierre Brice, who excels as the art student, also turned to European westerns like *Apache Gold* (1963), *Last of the Renegades* (1964), the West German *Among Vultures* (1964) and *A Place Called Glory* (1965).

Wolfgang Preiss delivers a restrained performance as Prof. Wahl, which is one of the actor's lesser known villainous characterizations. Preiss became more familiar for his subtly chilling portrayal of the arch-criminal Dr. Mabuse in the early 1960s revival of the popular villain from the silent film era. He played the role in *The Invisible Dr. Mabuse* (1960), *The Return of Dr. Mabuse* (1963) and *The Thousand Eyes of Dr. Mabuse* (1963). Other Preiss credits include *The Mad Executioners* (a.k.a. *The Hangman of London*, 1965), plus such major films as *The Train* (1965), starring Burt Lancaster, and the Frank Sinatra war drama *Von Ryan's Express* (1966).

Giorgio Ferroni made a brief return to the genre with a gory chiller entitled *The Devil's Night* (*La notte dei diavoli*, 1972). This effort was based (very loosely) on "The Wurdulak," a vampire story by Leo Tolstoy which received a more atmospheric treatment in

Mario Bava's *Black Sabbath* (1964). *The Devil's Night*, with its graphic bloodletting and frequent use of the zoom lens, comes off as a superficial tribute to Bava before we reach a climax that implies the hero has imagined the vampiric onslaught — a reference to the twist ending of *The Cabinet of Dr. Caligari* (1919). Ferroni's chillers are derivative, borrowing considerably from Bava, Franju, Robert Weine and Terence Fisher — the latter being especially lionized by Ferroni, since *Mill of the Stone Women* was intended as a tribute to Fisher.

The Minotaur, Wild Beast of Crete

Original title: *Teseo contro il minotauro (Theseus Against the Minotaur)*. A.k.a. *Warlord of Crete*. United Artists. 96 minutes. 1963 (ORD: 1961). Technicolor, Totalscope. Dir: Silvio Amadio. Prod: Giorgio Agliani, Dino Mordini, Rudolphe Bolmengen. Writ: Sandro Continenza, Gian Paolo Callegari, Daniel Mainwaring. Ph: Aldo Giordani. Mus: Carlo Rustichelli. Ed: Nella Mannuzzi. Art Dir: Piero Polleto. Cast: Bob Mathias, Rosanna Schiaffino, Alberto Lupo, Rik Battaglia, Nico Pepe, Susanne Loret, Vittorio Vaser, Carlo Tamberlani, Nerio Bernardi, Tina Lattanzi, Paul Muller, Tiziana Casetti, Alberto Plebani, Andrea Scotti, Milo Malagoli.

A familiar tale of a mythological hero and his struggle against a cave-dwelling monster forms the core of this fantasy-epic spiced with elements of horror. Though occasionally atmospheric and fitfully exciting, the film is largely lacking in visual horrors, and the final confrontation between man and monster is disappointingly brief.

Political turmoil on the island of Crete has taken its toll in lives as the power-mad Queen Phaedra (Rosanna Schiaffino) dispatches raiding parties on brutal purges of peasant villages. One raid reveals the existence of a peasant girl named Ariadne (also Schiaffino), the exact image of Phaedra. The queen's general, a shrewd fellow named Chrysone (Alberto Lupo), notices the resemblance while his men are preoccupied with their murderous tasks. Amid the confusion and fiery turmoil, Chrysone has the girl taken prisoner, and she is quickly removed from the scene of carnage. Ariadne fails to resist in the slightest way, being overcome by grief and horror at witnessing the slaughter of her parents.

Theseus (Bob Mathias), the courageous Prince of Athens and a respected war hero, opposes the savage exploitation of the kingdom's peasant population. Phaedra has an amorous eye for Theseus, but he is a man of the people despite his noble birth. The prince is determined to seek social justice for all of the people and constantly interferes with the oppressive policies of the monarchy. A fearsome and furtive creature called the Minotaur has become a symbol of the government's ruthlessness. This monster, purportedly half-man and half-bull, dwells in a cold, dark labyrinth that has become the scene of intermittent sacrifices. Innocent young maidens have been sent into the twisting series of tunnels, never to be seen again.

The hapless Ariadne is kept in chains, languishing in the dank lower level of the palace. Chrysone sees some definite potential for exploitability in the girl's incredible resemblance to the queen, though Phaedra is less interested in the girl.

A frantic confrontation with hostile forces nearly results in Theseus being drowned. He is saved through the intervention of supernatural forces as Aphrodite herself rescues him from certain death. The exquisitely beautiful goddess brings Theseus to her divine abode — an astral plane in which he will be safe. Although the love of Aphrodite is indeed tempting, Theseus confesses that his heart belongs to the fetching Ariadne. He gently explains his love for the girl while expressing his gratitude to Aphrodite for her circle of protection. The goddess complies with the prince's wishes and Theseus finds himself magically transported to the shores of Crete.

Phaedra decides that Ariadne presents a threat to her and orders that the girl's face be seared with a red-hot blade, thus destroying any resemblance. A burly man-at-arms prepares the blade, but the arrival of Theseus prevents the deed from being perpetrated. Theseus and the Queen's torturer engage in a tense struggle. During the fight, the servant hurls the heated blade at Theseus, accidentally striking the Queen's face. Severely burned, she turns to run madly from the dungeon and falls into a pit filled with ferocious felines. Theseus slays the servant with a quick thrust of his sword.

Chrysone arrives, but he makes no hostile moves toward Theseus. The death of the Queen may instead serve his purpose. "Phaedra was beautiful…but evil," states Chrysone in a matter-of-fact tone. Ariadne could easily take her place as a more humane ruler. It would be a peaceful transition, rather than change produced through revolutionary struggle. Theseus decides that the offer should be accepted, since refusal could prove to have dire consequences.

The masquerade goes smoothly, but the ambitious Chrysone attempts to use Ariadne as a figurehead while becoming the actual political force in Crete. Ariadne soon outlives her usefulness and is doomed to perish in the dreaded labyrinth of the Minotaur. Theseus takes up the sword again, backed by a bold insurgent named Demetrius (Rik Battaglia) and his dedicated followers. A furious battle rages in the throne room as the sword-wielding Chrysone is finally pierced by many blades in a mass attack. Theseus enters the labyrinth in search of Ariadne.

The prince moves cautiously through the series of twisting, torch-lit tunnels. Theseus soon comes upon a stone chamber that he carefully enters. A fierce roar is heard from behind as the Minotaur (Milo Malagoli) emerges from an adjoining tunnel.

Theseus turns to face the monster, who stands at least seven feet tall. Its massive bulk equals that of a grizzly bear with powerful arms and claw-like hands. The prince thrusts his blade into the creature's flesh, backs away and thrusts a second time with little effect. Forced against a stone wall, Theseus realizes that there is no escape. This is a fight to the death. As the monster approaches its hideous face can be seen as a mockery of a human's, endowed with a row of sharp teeth. Seized by the beast, Theseus is lifted and slammed against the chamber wall.

Torn and bloodied, Theseus grasps a torch from the wall and thrusts it into the monster's eye-sockets. The beast staggers away, howling in pain and rage. Theseus ignores his own injuries and takes advantage of the Minotaur's sudden vulnerability. Seizing a large rock, the stalwart prince makes his way to a ledge above the monster and hurls the massive stone upon its hideous head. The half-human corpse lies still as Theseus emerges victorious. Reunited with Ariadne, they emerge from the shadowy labyrinth into the bright sunlight.

A fan looking for sword-and-sandal entertainment could do far worse than *The Minotaur, Wild Beast of Crete*. Action sequences are frenetic and well choreographed, effectively enhanced by a rousing Carlo Rustichelli score. Sumptuous sets and elegant costumes, combined with the widescreen color photography of Aldo Giordani, all provide great visual appeal.

Unfortunately, the film leaves much to be desired as a chiller. The title menace is seen for less than two of the film's 96 minutes. There is a brief glimpse of the monster's arm in the opening scene as a terrified female sacrifice screams in terror before a taloned hand covers her face. The final confrontation is fairly entertaining, with the Minotaur resembling a cross between a bear and the marauding mutant of Roger Corman's *Day the World Ended* (1956). As the highlight of the film, however, the duel is a bit of a disappointment. Most of the film is devoted to mildly diverting but predictable displays of villainy and heroism. A prolonged cat-and-mouse chase within the labyrinth could have created a proper atmosphere of tension before the final confrontation with the monster.

Several members of the supporting cast were familiar for their appearances in historical epics before earning solid horror credits. Alberto Lupo acted in *Esther and the King* (1960) and *Ursus in the Valley of Lions* (1961) before playing the mad scientist in *Atom Age Vampire* (1963), Susanne Loret, who makes a striking Aphrodite, played Lupo's terrified victim in the latter flick. Rik Battaglia acted in such costume dramas as *Prisoner of the Volga* (1960) and *Sodom and Gomorrah* (1963) before playing an undead assassin in *Nightmare Castle* (1966). Rosanna Schiaffino, who is more than adequate in her dual role, later played the evil title character in Damiano Damiani's *The Witch* (1967).

However, *The Minotaur, Wild Beast of Crete* was intended mainly as a vehicle for one-time Olympic Star Bob Mathias. The actor was almost as beefy as Steve Reeves and possessed competent acting ability. Mathias, born in 1930 in Tulare, California, won the 1948 Olympic decathlon at age 17 — the youngest competitor to accomplish such a feat. He scored a second victory in the same competition during the 1952 Olympics in Helsinki, Finland. Mathias continued to amaze people with his athletic prowess by winning all ten decathlons that he entered between 1948 and 1956.

Mathias portrayed himself energetically and congenially in *The Bob Mathias Story* (1954). He later played a major supporting role in the weak *China Doll* (1958) before accepting the lead in the Silvio Amadio effort. Mathias seemed like a natural for rugged costume dramas, though he failed to enjoy a long career as a leading man. He also acted in a very silly comedy entitled *It Happened in Athens* (1962). In this flick, Jayne Mansfield starred as a woman who offers herself to be the bride of the man who wins the 1896 Olympics. Bob Mathias was billed fourth in a role that exploited his Olympic achievements.

Director Silvio Amadio handled other period adventure films, including *White Slave Ship* (1962), starring Pier Angeli and Edmund Purdom. Amadio later directed a mediocre Italian thriller entitled *Maniac Mansion* (1978). *The Minotaur, Wild Beast of Crete* remains his most successful effort, mainly as an exhilarating, mythical ballet of male violence and not as a chiller. It's too bad that Amadio couldn't get his genres straight.

The Murder Clinic

Original title: *La lama nel corpo (The Knife in the Body)*. A.k.a. *The Blade in the Body*. A.k.a. *The Night of Terror*. A.k.a. *Revenge of the Living Dead*. A.k.a. *The Murder Society*. Leone/Orphée, Europix. 86 minutes (ORT: 87 minutes). 1967 (ORD: 1966). Technicolor, Techniscope. Dir/Prod: Michael Hamilton (Elio Scardamaglia). Writ: Julian Berry (Ernesto Gastaldi), Martin Hardy (Luciano Martino). Ph: Mark Lane (Marcello Masciocchi). Mus: Frank Mason (Franco De Masi). Makeup: Massimo Giustini. Ed: Richard Hartley (Alberto Gallitti). Art Dir: Alberto Salvatore. Cast: William Berger, Françoise Prévost, Mary Young, Barbara Wilson, Max Dean (Massimo Righi), Delphine Maurin, Harriet White, Philippe Hersent, Anne Sherman, Patricia Carr, William Gold, Anne Field.

A thoroughly predictable horror-suspenser, *The Murder Clinic* is based on a novel by Robert Williams entitled *The Knife in the Body*. Photography and editing are a cut above the average, but the rest is exceedingly ordinary on every level.

In England of the 1890s, a clinic operated by skilled surgeon Dr. Robert Vance (William Berger) has become the scene of a series of grisly killings. A maniac, hooded and armed with a straight razor, has embarked on a nightly murder spree that claims the lives of several women. Dr. Vance is suspected, though several other suspects are paraded in front of the camera from time to time. A blackmailer and a winsome young woman named Claudine (Françoise Prévost) fall victim to the blood-spattered blade. A creepy, wild-eyed inmate named Fred (Massimo Righi) also seems a likely choice as a psychotic killer — but he becomes a victim as well.

Dr. Vance has been conducting experiments in skin grafts for his sister-in-law Laura (Delphine Maurin), who was disfigured by a fall into a lime pit some years earlier. There is some question as

The Murder Clinic (1967) was also released under the title *Revenge of the Living Dead* and billed with other "Living Dead" pictures.

to whether Laura actually fell into the pit...or was pushed by some unknown party. Laura leads a sad, reclusive life in the attic of the Vance home. Her sister Elizabeth Vance (Mary Young) is herself confined to the house as an invalid. Obviously, the home life of the doctor is far from pleasant as he must spend much of his free time caring for the two sick women. A sympathetic nurse named Mary (Barbara Wilson) provides the moral support and positive reinforcement that Dr. Vance lacks. Mary remains loyal to him, despite the horrendous situation that has entrapped them.

We finally learn that the crazed killer is Elizabeth, whose insane jealousy drove her to kill any woman who was attractive and had some link socially with her husband. Mary nearly falls victim to the razor-wielding madwoman but manages to escape. Elizabeth and her disfigured sister perish in a frantic climax. Dr. Vance is absolved of any wrongdoing and must start a new life — with the winsome Mary ready to assist him.

Ernesto Gastaldi provides a typically hackneyed script for this flick, borrowing from well-known genre efforts. His basic premise, which has a doctor being suspected of murdering deaf-mutes at a clinic, is taken from the atmospheric Edgar Wallace adaptation *The Dark Eyes of London* (1940), starring Bela Lugosi. A doctor performing a series of unsuccessful skin grafts on the disfigured face of a reclusive woman closely resembles the premise of Georges Franju's *Yeux sans visage* (1960), released in the U.S. as *Horror Chamber of Dr. Faustus* in 1963. The imitative nature of Gastaldi's works marked his entire career. He already hit rock bottom with the inept hodgepodge of clichés in the Paolo Heusch thriller *Werewolf in a Girl's Dormitory* (1963). Skillful direction partially salvaged two other Gastaldi scripts, *The Horrible Dr. Hichcock* (1964) and *Blood and Black Lace* (1965). Gastaldi did write a sensible, generally intriguing screenplay for the original, untampered *La frusta e il corpo (The Whip and the Body)*. The Mario Bava effort was more widely known to American audiences in its truncated form as *What!* (1964). Sadly, Gastaldi's flashes of creativity and Bava-like brilliance have been few and far between.

There is a certain degree of visual flair that helps *The Murder Clinic* maintain some level of interest lacking in the mediocre script. Rooms are dimly lit and haunted by shadows and mysterious shapes. A claustrophobic atmosphere is created by these sequences, which alternate with shots of blue skies and green landscapes. The juxtaposition of images has an exhilarating effect upon the viewer that the routine episodes of horror-suspense fail to generate. The striking photography by Marcello Masciocchi is a definite asset to the film, with the skillful editing of Alberto Gallitti providing good continuity. The cast is generally adequate and includes such talents as Harriet White and Massimo Righi, who are familiar from their appearances in some of Mario Bava's horror films.

Despite a story that consists of little more than ordinary programmer material, *The Murder Clinic* contains enough elements of interest to qualify as a passable time-killer.

My Friend, Jekyll
(Mio amico, Jekyll)

A.k.a. *My Pal, Jekyll*. Cinematografica Marino Girolami/Cei Incom. 100 minutes. 1964 (ORD: 1960). B&W. Dir/Prod: Marino Girolami. Writ: Girolami, Giulio Scarnicci, Carlo Veo. Ph: Luciano Trasatti. Cast: Ugo Tognazzi, Raimondo Vianello, Abbe Lane, Carlo Croccolo.

This lurid, silly and rarely amusing sex-farce supposedly found its origins in the classic Robert Louis Stevenson SF-horror novel *The Strange Case of Dr. Jekyll and Mr. Hyde*.

The film introduces us to a homely, sexually repressed fellow named Prof. Fabius (Raimondo Vianello), who finds a scientific means of satisfying his libidinal instincts while protecting his spotless reputation. He devises a method of projecting his consciousness into the body of a young man named Giacinto (Ugo Tognazzi), a teacher at a school for girls. The befuddled Giacinto, while possessed by the professor's personality, becomes a good-natured lecher who takes great pleasure in organizing sex parties with the voluptuous young ladies in his classes. Giacinto must eventually track down the culprit responsible for his schizophrenic behavior. Unable to continue with his naughty escapades via "astral projection," Fabius is forced to make a fateful decision. He transfers his personality into the body of a chimp at the local zoo!

The comic scenario avoids the chemically induced means of transformation depicted in the Stevenson novel and in its various screen adaptations. Instead, the script bases its premise on the concept of metapsychosis—the transmigration of the soul from one body to another. This concept might have provided the framework for a decent straight horror flick, rather than for a heavy-handed spoof. The sex-teasing, poorly written dialogue and unimaginative direction of Marino Girolami prevent the film from succeeding on its own crude terms. Girolami soon embarked on a series of softcore adult features that were just as badly written and directed as *My Friend, Jekyll*.

However, there is some good black-and-white photography by

Luciano Trasatti, whose visual skills also distinguished the otherwise vapid *The Bloody Pit of Horror* (1966). Raimondo Vianello delivers an amusing performance as the lecherous Prof. Fabius. Vianello later turned up in such spicy comedies as *Any Wife's Enemy* (1967) and *Kiss the Other Sheik* (1967). One of the many beautiful women featured in *My Friend, Jekyll* is minxy Abbe Lane as the female lead. Lane previously acted in such second-rate American productions as William Castle's *The Americano* (1955) starring Glenn Ford, a low-budgeter entitled *Chicago Syndicate* (1955) and Cornel Wilde's halfway decent *Maracaibo* (1958). More recently, she filled a supporting role in the extravagant, star-studded *Twilight Zone — The Movie* (1983).

The best (yet probably saddest) thing about *My Friend, Jekyll* is the competent performance of Ugo Tognazzi, a former accountant who distinguished himself in the theater before turning to the medium of film. During the 1950s, he played minor roles in a great many efforts as he worked at a feverish pace. In 1959 alone, Tognazzi appeared in a total of 12 films. He also starred in his own 1950s TV series *One, Two, Three*. Tognazzi later played the male lead in the exceptional comedy-drama *The Fascist* (*Il federale*, 1961) and also starred in the fine drama *The Terrace* (*Il terrazza*, 1963).

When *My Friend, Jekyll* made its rounds of American theaters in 1964, critics ridiculed the film while the public largely ignored it. That same year, Tognazzi redeemed himself by starring in an effective mixture of fantasy, comedy and bitter-sweet romance, Marco Ferreri's *The Ape Woman (La donna scimmia)*. The Italo-French co-production cast him as a money-hungry promoter who exploits as a freak a woman (Annie Girardot) whose body is completely covered with hair. A spark of decency is finally aroused within the shrewd businessman as he comes to love the she-freak. Tognazzi later played one of Jane Fonda's many lovers in Roger Vadim's campy *Barbarella* (1968), based on the famous comic strip.

My Friend, Jekyll can only be remembered as a less than fair time-killer that fails both as satire and as sexploitation. American audiences had already seen a far more effective Jekyll-Hyde spoof in 1963 when Jerry Lewis directed and starred in the often hilarious *The Nutty Professor*.

Nightmare Castle

Original title: *Amanti d'oltretomba (Lovers Beyond the Tomb)*. A.k.a. *The Faceless Monster*. A.k.a. *Orgasmo*. A.k.a. *Night of the Doomed*. Cinematografica Emmeci, Allied Artists. 90 minutes (ORT: 100 minutes). 1966 (ORD: 1965). B&W. Dir: Allan Grunewald (Mario Caiano). Prod: Carlo Caiano. Writ: Mario Caiano, Fabio de Agostini. Ph: Enzo Barboni. Mus: Ennio Giorsi. Cast: Barbara Steele, Paul Miller (Muller), Helga Liné, Lawrence Clift, Rik Battaglia, John McDouglas (Giuseppe Addobbati).

This bit of hokey "horrorama" merges science-fiction in a Victorian setting with grisly shock sequences, horror-mystery clichés and the supernatural. All that, and we also get to see Barbara Steele with blond hair. The film as a whole isn't very good, but it's still a must for Steele fans.

The isolated castle of the brilliant but deranged Dr. Stephen Arrowsmith (Paul Muller) becomes the scene of torture and mayhem one terrible night. Arrowsmith, who suspects his wife of infidelity, finds his suspicions verified when he catches spouse Muriel (Barbara Steele) in the act with her lover, David (Rik Battaglia). Both lover and unfaithful wife are subjected to prolonged torture and mutilation before they finally expire.

Some time passes before Arrowsmith links himself with softspoken, blond Jenny (Steele again), the half-sister of lustful, raven-haired Muriel. Jenny is unaware of her sister's fate and is puzzled by her disappearance. Arrowsmith's intellect, affluence and cultured ways manage to charm Jenny into accepting his proposal of marriage. However, it is the girl's inheritance that interests Arrowsmith, whose housekeeper Solange (Helga Liné) is secretly his lover.

Jenny is tormented by terrible nightmares as well as the daily cruelties of her husband, whose inexplicable callousness has its desired effect. The girl suffers from nervous exhaustion, a condition that her husband wishes to use as a rationale to have her declared insane. With Jenny committed to an insane asylum, Arrowsmith would be able to claim her fortune.

However, Jenny's doctor will not declare the girl insane and

Pressbook art for *Nightmare Castle* (1966).

suspects foul play by Dr. Arrowsmith. The young Dr. Derek Joyce (Lawrence Clift) believes that Jenny's husband is motivated by greed and may have eliminated Muriel. Derek and Jenny form an alliance in their struggle to uncover the truth.

Dr. Arrowsmith has also been conducting experiments involving the regeneration of blood through electrical impulses. Such electrically charged blood is necessary for the survival of Solange, who suffers from a strange malady. On the night that Arrowsmith plans another treatment for his mistress, supernatural forces intervene in a terrifying and deadly manner.

The vindictive spirits of Muriel and David return to take vengeance upon the murderous doctor. Also doomed to suffer the wrath of the undead is Solange, who rests on an operating table in the laboratory. Blood coursing through her veins is electrically revitalized by Arrowsmith's specially designed generator. The undead David enters the laboratory, coldly eyes the terrified Solange and slowly approaches the girl. His hand tears savagely at the delicate tangle of wires and slender tubes linking Solange to life-prolonging equipment. Blood splatters the walls of the laboratory as Solange breathes her last.

Dr. Arrowsmith becomes the victim of Muriel. Her return from the grave is greeted with stunned disbelief by the man of science. In a dazed delirium, his terror turns to a sudden fascination for the nearly forgotten beauty of Muriel. Her delicate features, high cheekbones and dark, piercing eyes are quite seductive. The unreality of the situation works its spell on Arrowsmith, who pushes the lustrous black hair away from her face — the right side of which has been ravaged by acid. Muriel laughs maniacally as her murderous husband cries out in terror. Arrowsmith passes out, then revives and finds himself bound to a chair which is set ablaze by Muriel. The mad doctor suffers a grisly demise, engulfed in flames.

Derek and Jenny attempt to flee the castle, but find themselves trapped by the avenging spirits. The two terrified innocents realize what must be done. Knowing that the surgically removed hearts of the spirits have been placed in an urn hidden in the parlor, they frantically locate and remove the disembodied organs. The hearts are burned in the fireplace as the approaching undead forms of Muriel and David suddenly vanish.

Nightmare Castle is a complicated mishmash that merges clichés from a number of horror subgenres without generating any interest in the basically muddled story. Rather, this is a well-mounted tribute to the screen presence of Barbara Steele as horror queen of the 1960s. She is at one moment a predatory temptress (*à la Pit and the Pendulum*), the next a tormented wraith (*à la Castle of Blood*) and vengeance-seeking monster (*à la Black Sunday*). She also emerging as the paragon of cultured innocence and aristocratic beauty (*à la The Horrible Dr. Hichcock*). Steele projects all of these images with the verve and charisma fans expect of her.

The supporting cast is generally adequate, with Paul Muller doing his villainous bit and Helga Liné making a fetching villainess. Liné has acted in a number of European horror films, including such offbeat thrillers as *The Saint vs. Dr. Death* (*Santo Contra el Doctor Muerte*, 1974) and *Saga of Dracula* (1975). Lawrence Clift makes a pensive yet energetic hero while the more familiar Rik Battaglia is given far less to do as the lover of Muriel. Fans of Italian epics and costume dramas will remember Battaglia from such efforts as *The Minotaur, Wild Beast of Crete* (1963) and *Sandokan the Great* (1965).

Director Mario Caiano, previously known for such sword-and-sandal efforts as *The Terror of Rome Against the Son of Hercules* (1961), emerges as a competent horror director in the Grand Guignol vein. The film is grisly at times, but not to the point that the gore and mayhem have a numbing or nauseating effect upon the audience. The graphic violence is used strategically in the early sequences and closing moments of the film, with the rest being a showcase for Barbara Steele's considerable talent. In one great scene (the most shocking in the film), the murderous Dr. Arrowsmith falls victim to the exotic charm and supreme beauty of the undead Muriel. He languorously brushes the hair away from her face, unexpectedly revealing her decaying physiognomy. This highly effective moment is more frightening than the film's blood-spattered torments.

Nightmare Castle is one of Barbara Steele's lesser efforts and is of interest mainly for its examination of the many faces that the actress has presented to movie audiences. This chiller does little to further her career, but emerges as an effective summary of it.

Planet of the Vampires

Original title: *Terrore nello spazio (Terror in Space)*. A.k.a. *Demon Planet*. A.k.a. *Planet of Terror*. A.k.a. *Outlaw Planet*. A.k.a. *The Planet of the Damned*. Italiana International/Castilla Cinematografica/AIP. 86 minutes. 1966. Pathe Color, Colorscope. Dir: Mario Bava. Prod: Fulvio Lucisano. Writ: Bava, Ib Melchior, Louis Heyward, Callisto Cosulich, Alberto Bevilacqua, Antonio Roman, Rafael J. Salvia. Based on the short story "Night of Twenty-One Hours" by Renato Pestiniero. Ph: Antonio Rinaldi. Mus: Gino Marinuzzi, Jr., Antonio Perez Olca. Ed: Antonio Gimead. Cast: Barry Sullivan, Norma Bengell, Angel Aranda, Evi Marandi, Fernando Villena, Ivan Rassimov, Rico Boido, Massimo Righi, Stelio Candelli, Mario Morales, Alberto Cevenini.

Planet of the Vampires

The fourth Mario Bava thriller to be released in the United States by AIP is this eerie Italo-U.S.-Spanish co-production shot in Rome. *Planet of the Vampires* is a largely familiar but highly atmospheric tale of Gothic horror told within a science-fiction framework. Despite budget limitations, it is handled with considerable horrific flair.

A pair of spaceships have embarked upon a journey to a new solar system where a strange distress signal is originating from an unknown world. Mark Markary (Barry Sullivan), commander of the *Argos*, contacts the sister ship as their destination approaches. The commander's younger brother Toby (Alberto Cevenini) is a crew member of the second vessel, the *Galliot*. The men share positive contact for a brief time as they view one another on the telescreens of ship communications. Toby is in good spirits and seems to be adjusting well to interplanetary space flight.

As Mark's ship approaches the new world, the gravitational force proves stronger than expected. While the others are left helpless by the tremendous G-force, Mark reaches the instrument panel and flips an automatic control switch, enabling the *Argos* to make a safe landing. Mark is the only crew member who has avoided losing consciousness.

Cosmic disturbances suddenly cease and conditions apparently return to normal — until crew members begin to regain consciousness. A fetching brunette named Sanya (Norma Bengell) is the first to awaken, her face cold and expressionless. She suddenly attacks Mark for no apparent reason. Mark reluctantly fights back and knocks Sanya to the ground. She then regains her senses and is bewildered by the situation. Mark tangles briefly with an astronaut named Wess (Angel Aranda) before having to rescue Sanya from yet another "possessed" crew member. The conflict is repeated throughout the vessel as men furiously fight one another before being "knocked" to their senses.

Mark and his friends discuss the strange, frightening mass insanity that afflicted them before realizing that aging scientist Karan (Fernando Villena) is still affected by such behavior. Before the others can stop him, he enters the air-lock and soon emerges on the surface of the planet. Karan stumbles and falls heavily in his mad flight, with the physical jolt bringing him to his senses.

Pressbook art for *Planet of the Vampires* (1965).

Mark decides that the first order of business should be to establish contact with the sister ship. An expedition locates the landing site of the *Galliot* and finds the vessel to be badly damaged; the crash has left no apparent survivors. Crew members apparently fought and killed one another after being seized by the same mania that affected Mark's crew. The dead astronauts are buried beneath the planet's surface — but soon after the burial detail departs, the corpses are revived by unknown forces and begin to unearth themselves.

One of the *Argos* sentries is mysteriously killed, his face horribly mutilated. As the body lies on a slab in the ship's sick bay, a female astronaut named Tiona (Evi Marandi) examines files. As she closes the door of a steel cabinet, she comes face to face with the dead man, who stares mutely at her. Tiona screams before losing consciousness. When she is revived by fellow crew members, her hysterical description of the incident seems quite implausible. But just what has happened to the body of their late comrade?

Two members of the sister ship's crew arrive, claiming that they fled from the self-destructive rampage that affected their comrades. The story seems acceptable, but it is actually a subterfuge used to cover an alien conspiracy. One of the newcomers steals a vital piece of equipment and escapes the *Argos*. His companion is captured and the truth about the mysterious series of events is revealed. This planet, known as Aura, is occupied by the disembodied intellects of a long-dead race. These are creatures who seek to escape their barren world by possessing the bodies of humanoid interlopers. These are symbiotic relationships: human and alien co-exist while sharing the information possessed by each personality. Mark and the others refuse to accept such parasitism. The undead captive suddenly "dies" a second time as the alien entity leaves his body.

Mark decides that a raid on the sister ship is necessary if they are to recover the stolen device and escape the planet. The otherworldly zombies have grown stronger, claiming two more of Mark's men. His crew has been reduced to six and the assault on their enemies must be carried out while they are still strong enough. Mark and Sanya furtively make their way into the ghostly vessel while space soldier Eldon (Mario Morales) hides behind a rock formation, ready to give cover with ray-gun fire. Evading the cold eyes of enemy sentries, they manage to recover the piece of equipment. But Mark must now fight the reactivated body of his brother Toby. After grappling with him briefly, Mark seizes a fallen ray-gun and reluctantly fires bolts of energy into Toby's legs. With its host disabled, the parasitic entity flees the body and Toby is at rest.

Sanya joins Mark in fleeing the spacecraft as their zombie opponents pursue them. Eldon leaves his concealed position and rushes into the clearing where the ship is located. He joins his two companions as they engage in hand-to-hand combat with the walking corpses. Eldon is killed in the confrontation, though Mark and Sanya resume their flight across the bleak landscape. As they approach the *Galliot*, Karan and Tiona position themselves behind a ridge and open fire. Although they slow the attack with sporadic ray-blasts, both fall victim to the energy beams fired by a zombie who approaches from behind.

With the three surviving astronauts safely aboard the vessel, and the recovered piece of equipment in its proper place, the ship makes a hasty departure. Wess sadly reflects on the innocent lives that have been lost. Mankind has been saved, but the struggle has claimed the lives of many brave comrades. Mark seems suddenly detached, though he denies that any new problem is preying on his mind.

Wess retires to a brief rest period, but is disturbed by a strange sound at the entrance to his quarters. He asks the possible intruder to speak out and be recognized, but receives no response. Wess is startled to see a slightly distorted reflection of Mark's face on a smooth metal surface. The commander remains silent and soon disappears from view.

Wess heads for the control room where Sanya is seated behind an instrument panel. He relates the strange story to her and expresses his fear that Mark has been possessed by an alien lifeforce. Sanya is skeptical at first, but then arms herself and accompanies Wess to another chamber where Mark is seated behind a telescreen. "Mark," she states unemotionally. "Wess knows about us." Wess is stunned. He refuses to accept the parasitic domination by the aliens and vows to stop the coming invasion of the world. He rushes madly to the chamber containing sensitive equipment vital to the ship's propulsion system. Seizing a metal lever, he strikes out at one intricate device and releases a burst of energy that courses through his body. An anguished cry escapes his throat as he collapses, lifeless.

Mark and Sanya decide to land on the nearest inhabited world. As they approach their chosen planet, an image of a large community comes into focus on the telescreen. It is the skyline of a major American city. Mark laughs softly as he comments on the "primitive" nature of this strange world. Sanya expresses curiosity over how the inhabitants will greet them. Mark responds, "Well, I hope...for their sake."

The unsurprising "surprise" ending, in which a crew of astronauts is revealed as an alien expedition heading for Earth, was all too familiar. SF-horror buffs had seen it done before on television's original *The Twilight Zone* as well as the Czech-made *Voyage to the End of the Universe* (a.k.a. *Ikaria XB-l*, 1964). *Planet of the Vampires* definitely owes a great deal to Edward L. Cahn's *Invisible Invaders* (1959). The latter flick had alien intellects possessing the bodies of dead men in an attempt to conquer our world with hordes of murderous zombies. One must also recognize the influence of the infamous *The Brain from Planet Arous* (1957), which had a large, disembodied alien brain possessing Earthling John Agar.

The rejuggling of SF-horror clichés was nothing new for writer Ib Melchior, who previously wrote the screenplays for the predictable *The Angry Red Planet* (1960), *Reptilicus* (1963), *Journey to the 7th Planet* (1963) and the occasionally interesting *The Time Trav-

elers (1964). Such programmers were endowed with colorful touches and occasional plot twists that brought a certain freshness to shopworn scenarios.

Melchior, born in Denmark on September 17, 1917, was also an old hand at dealing effectively with the time and budget restraints of a B-grade feature. Previously, he was active in early television's science-fiction romps, working as technical director for *Tom Corbett, Space Cadet* (NBC, 1950–1956), which was produced on a limited amount of money and on a short schedule. Melchior later worked on the *Men in Space* series, writing two episodes "Water Tank Rescue" (aired October 28, 1959) and "Voice of Infinity" (April 20, 1960). His great energy and ingenuity helped low-budgeters to look more expensive than they actually were.

Fans of AIP horror films were excited by the announcement that Melchior's screenplay *Outlaw Planet* went before the cameras in Rome on March 10, 1965. The completed feature, widely known as *Planet of the Vampires*, utilized a final screen treatment by Melchior that represented the work of seven writers — including director Mario Bava and long-time associate Alberto Bevilacqua. Melchior supervised the English language version of the film, which was shortened by about two minutes. Several brief nude scenes were deleted from the American prints.

As a director, Bava provides some highly atmospheric moments plus several mildly thrilling action sequences. The best single scene, prolonged by slow motion, has dead astronauts rising from their graves on the mist-covered alien landscape and discarding their polythene shrouds. Other scenes feature the fine visuals for which Bava is well admired. An abundance of colored mists, ghostly reflections and scenes of strange figures moving silently through darkened rooms manage to hold our interest when the underdeveloped story and two-dimensional characters fail to do so. One eerie, quietly effective moment has the astronauts attempting to unearth a corpse and finding the grave empty. Instead, they are greeted by the low moaning of a gust of wind that sweeps the polythene shroud from the empty grave. Such points of reference from Bava's period chillers are quite intriguing.

There is an international flavor to the cast, headed by American screen veteran Barry Sullivan (1914–1995). Two years earlier,

Sullivan played the lead role in another AIP thriller, *Pyro*. The latter flick had the actor displaying a near-manic energy in the role of a fire-scarred madman who relentlessly stalks a former lover (Martha Hyer). Previously, Sullivan either starred or played second male leads in such films as *The Bad and the Beautiful* (1952), *Forty Guns* (1957) and *The Purple Gang* (1960). His career declined somewhat in the mid-1960s, but Sullivan still sought leading man roles in B features and mediocre medium-budget films like *My Blood Runs Cold* (1965) and *This Savage Land* (1966). Still rugged at 51, Sullivan competently handles the strenuous action sequences of *Planet of the Vampires*.

The supporting cast includes Brazilian actress Norma Bengell, who previously acted in *Mafioso* (1962) and *The Myth* (*El Mito*, 1965). Sultry and olive-skinned, she adequately fills the role of Sanya, which was originally intended for AIP starlet Susan Hart. Greek actress Evi Marandi previously appeared in *Francis of Assisi* (1961) and *Paris When It Sizzles* (1964). At the time, she was more familiar for being the girlfriend of George Hamilton than for her film appearances. Angel Aranda, as the courageous Wess, hails from Spain. The young actor played vigorous supporting roles in such epics as *The Last Days of Pompeii* (1960), *The Colossus of Rhodes* (1962) and *Goliath Against the Giants* (1963).

Despite cheap sets and familiar situations, *Planet of the Vampires* successfully merges two genres. Costumes and weapons help to generate a 1930s sci-fi pulp flavor, while swirling mists and streaks of color provide a dazzling visual display that helps to disguise the inadequate sets. Mario Bava returned to a conventional setting for his next tale of Gothic horror, *Kill Baby Kill* (1966).

The Planets Against Us
(I pianeti contro di noi)

A.k.a. *The Man with the Yellow Eyes*. A.k.a. *The Monster with Yellow Eyes*. Vanguard/Teleworld. 85 minutes. 1964 (ORD: 1961). B&W. Dir: Romano Ferrara. Prod: Alberto Chimenz, Vico Pavoni. Wit: Ferrara, Piero Pierotti. Ph: Pier Ludovico Pavoni. Cast: Michael

(Michel) Lemoine, Maria Luz, Jany Clair, Otello Toso, Peter Dane, Marco Guglielmi.

A familiar premise is explored in this Italo-French SF-horror distinguished by good photography and an occasional atmospheric sequence somewhat out of context with the rest of the film. Aliens invade the earth with a force of androids — automatons covered with artificial flesh and outwardly normal. Such a scenario formed the basis of many stories found in the science-fiction pulps as well as the SF-horror comics of the 1950s and early 1960s. Nevertheless, one can detect a few good scenes sandwiched between long stretches of tedium.

Mysterious events have occurred at missile bases and space exploration centers around the world. Technological mishaps, apparently acts of sabotage, have been taking place and causing delays in the space programs conducted by the super-powers. Into this strange and dangerous scenario comes a tall, silent stranger named Branko (Michel Lemoine). There is sadness about the fellow that seems to attract women within Parisian social circles. One such female admirer is a voluptuous brunette (Jany Clair) whose endeavors, social and artistic, have left her feeling unfulfilled.

Branko continues to establish contact with young women as he indulges in the bawdy night life of Paris. He soon meets an attractive girl who is married to a rocket scientist. The woman (Maria Luz) shares casual contact with him at first, as she apparently attempts to alleviate the feeling of emptiness in her life. However, Branko is not the mild-mannered introvert that he seems to be. One day, as they are sitting together in the girl's car, they discuss his strange detachment from mainstream society and his lack of any open emotional responses. "I'm not human," states Branko in a matter-of-fact tone. The woman is stunned by the statement and seems determined to evoke an emotional response from Branko. Placing her arms around his neck, she draws close to Branko and kisses him deeply, but suddenly recoils with a startled cry. "Your lips are like ice!" she exclaims.

Still expressionless and apparently unaffected, Branko makes a casual statement about her show of emotion. Perhaps he should appreciate such positive intentions, though human feelings mean nothing to him. His eyes glow with an unearthly energy as he begins to wield a mesmeric control over the girl. She is now about to become an accomplice in alien attempts to sabotage the French space program.

The girl's kidnapping puts the police and federal agents on Branko's trail. One night, as Branko and the woman are being pursued by the authorities, she stops her car while Branko uses his deadly powers against the pursuing agents. Removing the leather gloves that he normally wears, Branko touches the hand of one agent. A flash of white light erupts at the point of contact as the agent cries out and collapses. The car speeds away before remaining agents are able to intervene. Moments later, the men view with horror the corpse of their colleague, which has been reduced to mummified remains by the radioactive touch of Branko.

French secret agents and police officials correlate information concerning Branko. The secret services of other countries have provided relevant documentary footage recording the possibly sinister activities at missile bases. Unexplained mishaps at foreign bases may be linked to the mayhem currently afflicting Paris. Special attention is paid to film clips in which an individual resembling Branko can be seen wearing various uniforms and performing specialized tasks.

The investigators draw a disturbing conclusion: Branko is only one member of a team of identical saboteurs spread across the globe. The conspiracy to destroy all attempts at space exploration has its origin in a world beyond our solar system.

Branko visits the apartment of the lonely artist, who suspects nothing about the true nature of the deadly stranger. As he enters her bedroom, the elated woman embraces Branko and falls victim to his deadly touch. She lies still, sprawled across the bed as her body turns into a pile of radioactive dust.

Branko's winsome captive is beginning to suffer the effects of radiation sickness. Apprehended by the authorities, she has been hospitalized while Branko wanders the streets alone. Something strange happens to the alien android, who suddenly feels compelled to seek out the girl. While passing a group of schoolboys, he raises his hands high above his head in order to avoid inflicting his lethal touch upon any of them.

Agents armed with specially designed guns are prepared to confront the deadly alien. Branko approaches a car occupied by one agent, who fires the weapon. A brilliant flash of light is emitted from its bulbous glass end piece. Branko responds by slaying his opponent with a lethal touch of his hand. However, the light beam has damaged the vital mechanisms within the android's torso.

Branko seizes the car, which is occupied by a trio of schoolboys. Positioning himself uncertainly behind the steering wheel, the now disoriented invader begins driving. Darkness falls as Branko arrives in a rural area where he stiffly motions at the three youngsters to leave the car. He quickly dons a silver pressure suit in preparation for a rendezvous with fellow androids at a specified departure point. Branko wages a battle against time as his decaying physiognomy makes the desperate flight from the authorities even more strenuous.

Teams of armed agents continue to pursue Branko, whose artificial flesh gradually melts into putrescence. The alien saucer lifts off shortly before his arrival, avoiding any possible confrontation with the Earthmen. Branko finally loses consciousness as his car veers off the road and comes to an abrupt stop. The hovering spacecraft discharges a ball of pure energy which hurtles toward the car and envelops Branko's remains in a white-hot flash.

Government vehicles screech to a halt and men pour from the cars and approach the wreck. One of the men pans over the car's interior with a TV camera, transmitting the ghastly scene to his superiors in a government building. All that remains of Branko is a framework of metal wires attached to a few metal cudgels. The alien has been destroyed by his own kind, but one can only wonder how many other alien intruders may still be lurking among us.

The Planets Against Us is routine alien invasion stuff fashioned after the sort of thrillers that inundated American movie screens during the 1950s. Clichéd characters become involved in predictable situations until the world is saved by "man's humanity" as a passive alien discovers the meaning of love — which results in his own destruction. We've seen variations on this premise in such thrillers as *Beast With a Million Eyes* (1956), *I Married a Monster from Outer Space* (1958), *War of the Satellites* (1958) and *12 to the Moon* (1960), just to name a few.

Michel Lemoine spends much of his screen time as the great stone face, though his glassy-eyed projection may provoke more laughs than chills. During the film's final moments, he manages to evoke some interest in a sickly sort of way. Lemoine soon fared somewhat better with his emotionally charged portrayal of Marco, the tormented nobleman held captive by an evil duke in *Prisoner of the Iron Mask* (1962). The actor's other screen credits include *Conquest of Mycene* (1965), *Night of Lust* (1965) and a comparatively small role in Antonio Margheriti's *The Wild, Wild Planet* (1966). The rest of the cast is merely adequate with the exception of Jany Clair, who delivers a sensual portrayal of the sexually repressed young artist. Clair later excelled as the ruthless Queen Agar in *Hercules Against the Moon Men* (1965).

Although Romano Ferrara's direction fails to generate much excitement value, he provides several eerie, highly atmospheric sequences. Scenes of the murderous Branko wandering darkened streets or bleak landscapes are handled in a subtle manner and evoke a few pleasurable chills. These creepy sequences are strikingly photographed by Pier Ludovico Pavoni, whose visual skills also provided some fine moments in *Mill of the Stone Women* (1963). Pavoni's other credits include some elaborate historical epics: the *Pharaoh's Woman* (1961), *The Centurion* (1962) and *Invasion 1700* (1965). Director Ferrara went on to write the screenplay for the AIP secret agent thriller *Spy in Your Eye* (1966).

Many fans found *The Planets Against Us* disappointing compared to other "spaghetti" science-fiction/horror flicks. The sense of adventure and excellent special effects of Antonio Margheriti's best genre efforts (such as *Battle of the Worlds*, 1961) are absent. Also lacking is the intensity of Mario Bava's *Planet of the Vampires* (1965) with its mist-filled landscapes and admirable Gothic trappings that help to maintain a sense of foreboding. *The Planets Against Us* occasionally manages a dark, dream-like quality, but such atmospheric moments are few and far between the clichés of ordinary programmer material.

The Playgirls and the Vampire

Original title" *L'ultima preda del vampiro (The Last Prey of the Vampire)*. A.k.a. *The Last Victim of the Vampire*. A.k.a. *The Vam-*

pire's Last Victim. A.k.a. *Desires of the Vampire*. A.k.a. *Curse of the Vampire*. Nord Film Italiana, Fanfare. 76 minutes (ORT: 85 minutes). 1964 (ORD: 1960). B&W. Dir/Writ: Piero Regnoli. Prod: Tiziano Longo. Ph: Ugo Brunelli. Mus: Aldo Piga. Ed: Mario Arditi. Art Dir: Giuseppe Ranieri. Cast: Walter Brandi, Lyla Rocca, Maria Giovannini, Alfredo Rizzo, Tilde Damiani, Corinne Fontaine, Erika di Centa, Marisa Quattrini, Antoine Nicos, Leonardo Botta, Ivy Holzer.

Hot on the heels of Renato Polselli's *The Vampire and the Ballerina* (1962) came this blatant rehash starring Walter Brandi, who filled a major supporting role in the earlier flick. This time out, Brandi plays a dual role as hero and heavy. Quality-wise, the results are about the same as those of the Polselli film.

One night, a troupe of burlesque performers take shelter in the eerie castle of Count Gabor Kernassy (Walter Brandi). The five well-proportioned chorus girls, the piano player and their manager are made welcome by the lonely Count, who is quite explicit about one necessary rule: None of the guests are to leave their rooms after dark. Predictably, some of the girls are unable to follow this simple request and they encounter another member of the Kernassy family. This one has been dead — or rather undead — for centuries. The elder Kernassy (Brandi again) is a vampire.

A sensual brunette named Katia (Maria Giovannini) is claimed by the vampire and joins him in stalking further victims. Several other visitors fall prey to the bloodlust of the vampiric Kernassy before his good descendant Gabor courageously intervenes and saves the terrified heroine, Vera (Lyla Rocco), from being claimed by the vampire. In a final confrontation, the abrupt opening of curtains manages to bathe the vampire in the sunlight that he dreads. The sanguinary fiend crumbles into dust — a sequence obviously inspired by Terence Fisher's *Horror of Dracula* (1958).

Beyond pilfering the climax of the Fisher classic and borrowing the basic scenario of *The Vampire and the Ballerina*, writer-director Piero Regnoli's effort seems to continue its imitative nature with the story of the two Kernassys, one good and one evil. Earlier that year (1960), a Mexican chiller, Fernando Cortes' *La marca del muerto* (*The Mark of the Dead*), told the story of the brilliant Dr. Malthus (Fernando Casanova), who conducts bizarre experiments in his

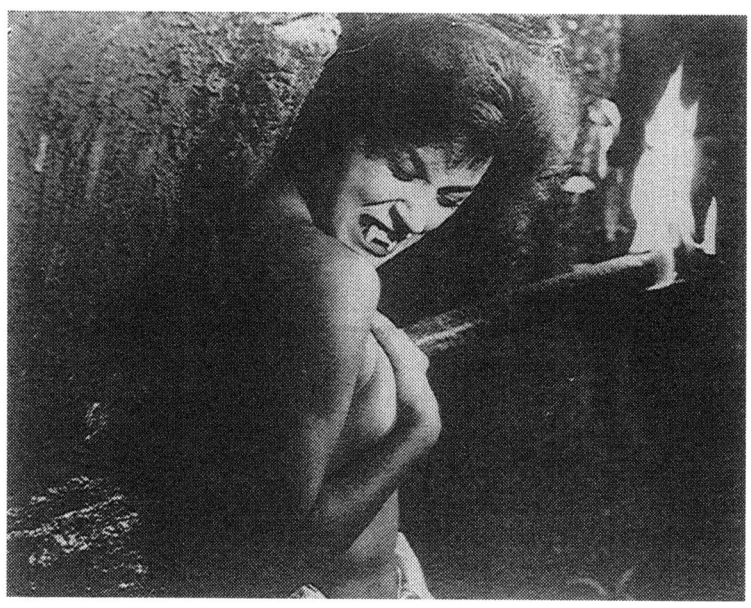

The vampire Maria Giovannini in *The Playgirls and the Vampire* (1964).

isolated mansion. Malthus revives his long-dead grandfather, also a gifted chemist (and also played by Casanova), with his rejuvenation formula. The revitalized ancestor preys upon women in attempts to maintain his renewed strength and youth. The elixir of youth requires the blood of young women, and this scientific vampire continues his reign of terror until perishing in a tense struggle with his grandson. American producer-director Jerry Warren restructured the Cortes film, which was retitled *Creature of the Walking Dead* for a 1966 U.S. release.

The premise of the Fernando Cortes thriller seemed to have been reworked with a vampiric slant for *The Playgirls and the Vampire*, even casting the male lead in a dual role as hero and fiendish ancestor. Though imitative and marred by unimaginative direction, the film doesn't really need to rely on fresh concepts or an atmosphere of tension. Titillation is the key word in this flick, which is more about voyeurism than vampirism. We are treated to intermittent peep shows as the women appear in various states of undress before Kernassy sinks his teeth into their necks. The most lurid scenes were deleted for American release, with nearly ten minutes of footage being trimmed from the original length.

Beyond the presence of horror regulars Brandi and Alfredo Rizzo, the film features several beautiful women who exhibit wildly divergent acting styles. Most of the girls never drew much attentions and filled minor roles in horror films and costume dramas. Lyla Rocca, who plays the heroine, was the second female lead in *The Red Cloak* (*Il mantello rosso*), an elaborate adventure film set in 16th century Italy. This was probably the highlight of Ms. Rocca's career.

The genre achievements of other talents involved in the film are few indeed. Producer Tiziano Longo was later responsible for a routine mad slasher flick entitled *Slaughter Hotel*. Ugo Brunelli's black-and-white photography, easily the best thing about *The Playgirls and the Vampire*, helped to relieve the boredom of the lethargic 1961 thriller *Slaughter of the Vampires*.

Piero Regnoli first began his association with the horror field by co-authoring the screenplay of Riccardo Freda's *I vampiri* (*The Vampires*) a 1956 chiller released in the United States as *The Devil's Commandment*. Formerly a film journalist, his preoccupation with the female anatomy in *The Playgirls and the Vampire* soon became his main focus as Regnoli settled into directing sexploitation films.

The Possessed

Original title: *La donna del lago* (*The Woman of the Lake*). BCR Produzione/Institute Luce. 90 minutes. 1965. B&W. Dir: Luigi Bazzoni, Franco Rossellini. Prod: Manolo Bolognini. Writ: Bazzoni, Rossellini, Giulio Questi. Ph: Leonida Barboni. Cast: Peter Baldwin, Virna Lisi, Salvo Randone, Valentina Cortese, Pia Lindstrom, Philippe Leroy, Piero Anchisi.

Despite a potentially creepy premise, this routine psychological horror film fails due to mixed intentions. The story opens with Peter Baldwin arriving in a small Italian town to conduct a search for the woman he loves (Virna Lisi), who has mysteriously disappeared. The inhabitants of the town seem quite indifferent to Baldwin's plight. In fact, the people who reside in the community are extremely isolated and drained of their vitality, as though they have given up on life completely.

Other disappearances have also occurred locally and Baldwin's investigation soon leads to a middle-aged spinster (Valentina Cortese). The loneliness and emptiness experienced by the tormented woman have resulted in long-suppressed hostilities that finally erupt in periodic, murderous rages. She previously murdered her father and brothers, as well as her father's lovers, before the winsome Lisi met a similar fate. As the film closes, Cortese meets her end in the same lake where her victims rest.

One of the inherent problems with *The Possessed* is its schizophrenic nature, as the film attempts to thrill viewers with a tale of terror while preaching to them at the same time. We are supposed to be viewing a serious statement on the curse of emptiness, man's desperate need for companionship and the sad fate that befalls those whose will to live has been crushed by life's many trials and defeats. Sadly, the attempts at significance consist mainly of a few major characters staring silently off into the distance with a faraway look on their faces. Apparently, such scenes are intended to portray the torment of people who must deal with deeply rooted aggressions and spend much of their time pondering "the meaning of it all." These pensive moments quickly become redundant and destroy any atmosphere of tension that may have existed early in the film.

Plot twists borrow from such Hammer psychological thrillers as *Maniac* (1962), *Paranoiac* (1963) and *Nightmare* (9164), as well as Mario Bava's *The Evil Eye* (1962). In fact, Valentina Cortese portrays a character who is quite similar to that of her charming but murderous shopkeeper in the latter effort. The actress delivers a surprisingly wooden performance with remaining cast members delineating their roles in a trance-like fashion. Several of the performers exhibited more than adequate acting ability in previous roles; for example, Pia Lindstrom was effective as the second female lead in *Marriage Italian Style* (1964), starring Sophia Loren. Horror buffs will remember Philippe Leroy as the dashing hero of *Castle of the Living Dead* (1964). The French actor also delivered rugged portrayals in such action films as *Alone Against Rome* (1960) and *55 Days at Peking* (1963). Peter Baldwin competently portrayed Barbara Steele's lover in Riccardo Freda's *The Ghost* (1965). Baldwin soon tried his hand at being a screenwriter, co-authoring the script of a maudlin soaper called *A Place for Lovers* (1969). The latter effort was panned by most critics and is undoubtedly the worst film of both director Vittorio De Sica and star Marcello Mastroianni.

However, there is some good black-and-white photography provided by Leonida Barboni, whose camerawork enriched Pietro Germi's hilarious *Divorce Italian Style* (1962), the Oscar-winning comedy starring Marcello Mastroianni and Daniela Rocca. Other talents who redeemed themselves after the release of *The Possessed* include Franco Rossellini and Giulio Questi, who co-wrote the film's screenplay and originally worked together on Fellini's *La dolce vita* (1960). Rossellini later produced two fine dramas directed by Pier Paolo Pasolini: *Teorama* (1969), which cast Terence Stamp as a young man who might be Satan, and *Medea* (1970), an intriguing and well-played tale of the legendary sorceress. Rossellini also produced an awful film entitled *The Driver's Seat* (1973), which had Elizabeth Taylor playing a mentally ill woman who journeys to Rome to find a murderer who will end her miserable existence.

The Possessed might have emerged as good entertainment had it been played as a straight horror-suspenser and dispensed with an arty sub-text that belonged more in a Fellini-esque fantasy like *Juliet of the Spirits*.

Satanik

A.k.a. *Satanic*. Rodiacines/Copernices, Governor. 1968. Eastman Color, totalscope. Dir: Piero Vivarelli. Prod: Romano Mussolini. Writ: Eduardo M. Brochero. Ph: Silvano Ippoliti. Cast: Madge (Magda) Konopka, Julio Pena, Armando Calvo, Umi (Umberto) Raho, Luigi Montini, Mimma Ippoliti, Antonio Pica, Isarco Ravaioli, Luis de Tejada.

This routine Italo-Spanish horror film is based on a comic strip much like the colorful "Diabolik," which provided the basis for Mario Bava's vibrant fantasy-adventure *Danger: Diabolik* (1968), starring John Phillip Law in the title role. However, *Satanik* lacks

Pressbook art for *Satanik* (1968).

the good-natured silliness of the Bava effort and fails either to frighten or excite the audience with its horrific images.

The story deals with the experiments conducted by an eccentric but brilliant scientist who discovers a serum that will cure physical impediments and restore youthful vigor to those who receive regular treatments. When the aging, incredibly ugly female lab assistant learns of the formula's development, she demands an immediate treatment. Due to the experimental nature of the serum, her superior decides that it may not be prudent to submit to such a demand. The woman is not to be dissuaded. She kills her employer and seizes the formula, which quickly achieves the desired results: The once hideous creature is transformed into a ravishing beauty (Magda Konopka) determined to live life to the hilt. She seeks luxury and excitement while craving the admiration of men.

Konopka becomes a deadly seductress, draining men of their money and vitality. She coldly destroys the lives of the innocent as well, after finding that further treatments are necessary to maintain her youth and beauty. Despite horrendous acts, the woman continues to pursue her passions and nocturnal pastimes as she settles into the night life as a cabaret performer. Her victims grow in number and police finally trace the trail of bodies to this strange woman. The authorities finally close in as Konopka reverts to her deformed state in full view of a nightclub audience.

The basic scenario of *Satanik* comes off as a rehash of the somewhat more effective *The Face of Terror* (*La cara del terror*, 1964), a Spanish thriller that was more skillfully directed and featured good performances by Lisa Gaye and Fernando Rey. Another variation of the same premise was the Azteca/Columbia co-production *Madame Death* (*La señora muerte*), starring John Carradine. This flick cast the popular actor as a mad doctor who transforms Regina Torn into a crazed killer with a desperate need for the blood-based serum that will maintain a normal appearance. Kurt Neumann's *She-Devil* (1957) preceded all of these efforts and told the story of a terminally ill woman (Mari Blanchard) who is transformed into a murderous beauty by the formula of well-meaning scientists Albert Dekkar and Jack Kelly. Neumann's film certainly had some influence in forming the basic scenario of *Satanik*.

Horror buffs will enjoy the presence of a few familiar genre faces in the supporting cast of *Satanik*. Fans of Mexican chillers will recognize Armando Calvo in a major supporting role. Calvo was adept at playing both heroes and heavies in south-of-the-border productions. He was a murderous doctor in *The Witch's Mirror* (*El espejo de la bruja*, 1960) and a courageous police detective in *Orlak, the Hell of Frankenstein* (*Orlak, el Infierno de Frankenstein*, 1960). Two very familiar actors in Italian horror and science-fiction films are also featured. Umberto Raho acted in *Castle of Blood* (1964) and *The Ghost* (1965) while Isarco Ravaioli was included in the casts of *The Vampire and the Ballerina* (1962) and *Snow Devils* (1965). Raho and Ravaioli appeared together in Margheriti's *The Wild, Wild Planet* (1966).

The best thing about the film is Silvano Ippoliti's impressive widescreen color photography. Ippoliti's previous credits included *Sodom and Gomorrah* (1962), *Hercules, Samson and Ulysses* (1966) and the Italian oater *Navajo Joe* (1968), starring Burt Reynolds. The 1971 release *Sacco and Vanzetti* also made use of Ippoliti's visual skills. It is sad to see his talent wasted on such trivia as *Satanik*.

Sex Party

Original title: *Delitto allo specchio* (*Criminal in the Mirror*). PI Cinematografica/Roc. 77 minutes. 1963. B&W. Dir: Jean Josipovici. 2nd Unit Dir: Ambroglio Molteni. Prod: Josipovici, Pasquale Tagliaferri. Writ: Josipovici, Giorgio Stegani. Ph: Raffaelle Masciocchi. Cast: John Drew Barrymore, Antonella Lualdi, Gloria Milland, Michel Lemoine, Mario Valdemarin, Luisa Rivelli.

Despite its ridiculous English language title, *Sex Party* is a horror film of sorts — and a horrible film. The clichéd scenario of this Italo-French effort has all the ingredients for an enjoyable tale of hokey horror melodrama. There is an old castle, an arrogant and beautiful mistress of the estate (Antonella Lualdi), a sinister family servant and a creepy mystic (John Drew Barrymore) whose gloomy predictions are realized on one dark night. Also on hand are a number of two-dimensional party guests who do the expected cowering and screaming as the family servant goes berserk and threatens everyone. Everybody "does his thing" in *Sex Party*, but the only one who does it with any flair is cinematographer Raffaele Masciocchi. His fine camera also enlivened the period chillers *Mill of the Stone Women* (1963), *The Horrible Dr. Hichcock* (1964) and *The Ghost* (1965).

The cast members deliver uniformly inadequate performances, with the most surprisingly inept portrayal being delivered by the usually intense and polished actor John Drew Barrymore. His typical manic energy is missing from this flick as he is required to do little more than stand passively in the background while everyone else erupts into a state of hysteria. Barrymore, a promising young leading man of the 1950s, was given more to work with in Giuseppe Vari's *War of the Zombies*, a 1965 AIP release originally titled *Roma contro Roma* (*Rome Against Rome*). The latter flick starred Barrymore as a spell-casting religious zealot and allowed the actor to display his ham while reciting some suitably eloquent pseudo-Shakespearean dialogue.

Female lead Antonella Lualdi, cast in the role of the doomed Serena, lacks the sensual charm that she previously displayed in her typically seductive roles. Even her mildly erotic dance sequence generates little in the way of interest or excitement value. Lualdi, the daughter of an Italian father and a Greek mother, was born in Beirut, Lebanon, on July 6, 1931. Her previous film credits include *The Overcoat* (*Il cappotto*, 1952), *The Red and the Black* (1954), *End of Desire* (1962) and — perhaps her best effort — Claude Chabrol's *Web of Passion* (1961). The latter film cast the actress as an exotic beauty who becomes a murder victim. Lualdi also appeared in the bawdy *Tre storio proibite* (*Three Forbidden Stories*), the dramatic *Disorder* (*Il disordine*, 1964), the adventure films *The Mongols* (1966) and *The Sea Pirate* (1967) and a fairly amusing sex farce entitled *How to Seduce a Playboy* (1968).

There is some additional visual appeal provided by two other beautiful women who usually exhibit competent acting ability. Gloria Milland acted in such fantasy epics as *Atlas Against the Czar* (1964) and *Goliath Against the Giants* (1963). Luisa Rivelli filled roles in Jules Dassin's steamy *Where the Hot Wind Blows* (1960), the star-studded TV feature *The Poppy Is Also a Flower* (1966) and the Italian oater *The Big Gundown* (1968).

Male co-stars include Michel Lemoine, a sad-eyed and often monotone actor who previously starred in *The Planets Against Us* (*I pianeti contro di noi*), an Italo-French SF-horror shot in 1961 and released in the United States about three years later. Mario Valdemarin concentrated mainly on rugged adventure films that either cast him as an armor-clad warrior (*Hercules and the Captive Women*, 1963) or as a modern day military man (*Sandokan the Great*, 1964).

Giorgio Stagani, who co-authored the script for *Sex Party*, previously achieved more success by writing potentially interesting material for such spotty efforts as *The Trojan Horse* and *Mill of the Stone Women* (1963). Stegani later wrote the screenplay for the rough-and-tumble western *Beyond the Law* (1967), starring Lee Van Cleef. Co-producer Pasquale Tagliaferri later scored a triumph when he produced Mario Bava's *Knives of the Avenger* (1967), an exciting tale of Viking vengeance starring Cameron Mitchell.

Sex Party remains the only directorial effort of Jean Josipovici; co-director Ambrogio Molteni enjoyed more success as a screenwriter. Molteni excelled at weaving tales of adventure told with a lavish period setting (*David and Goliath*, 1961, *The Tartars*, 1962, *The*

Seven Tasks of Ali Baba, 1963). Molteni's screenplay for *The Giant of Metropolis* (1964) mixed science-fiction and adventure with sporadically effective horrific touches.

Josipovici and Molteni fail to exhibit a comprehensive grasp of the horror genre in *Sex Party* as they miss the opportunity to fully exploit a creepy setting. We have seen a number of chillers in which a claustrophobic sense of horror is generated by similar circumstances as a handful of people find themselves trapped in a gloomy old mansion. Hysteria alone is no substitute for the gradual building of tension seen in such admirable chillers as James Whale's *The Old Dark House* (1932) and William Castle's silly but amusing *House on Haunted Hill* (1959). The script by Josipovici and Giorgio Stegani borrows from both of the previously mentioned chillers as well as from Ford Beebe's *Night Monster* (1942), another tale of mysticism and murder in an isolated mansion. Sadly, *Sex Party* is lacking in both the subtle horrors of Whale and the creepy fun of William Castle at his best.

She Beast

Original title: *La sorella di Satana* (*The Sister of Satan*). A.k.a. *Il lago di Satana* (*The Lake of Satan*). A.k.a. *Revenge of the Blood Beast*. Leith Films, Europix. 76 minutes. 1966 (ORD: 1965). Eastman Color, CinemaScope. Dir: Michael Reeves. Prod: Paul Maslansky. Writ: Michael Byron (Reeves). Ph: Amerigo Gengarelli. Mus: Ralph Ferraro. Ed: Nira Omri. Cast: Barbara Steele, Ian Ogilvy, Mel Welles, John Karlsen, Jay Riley, Richard Watson, Ed Randolph.

Barbara Steele's seventh horror film remains her least successful. *She Beast*, an Italo-British co-production shot in Yugoslavia, is distinguished mainly by the invigorating presence of Steele, who is merely adequate in a thankless role. The film is also worth mentioning as the first solo effort of director Michael Reeves (1944-1969), whose brief career indicated the presence of great talent and unrealized potential.

The routine tale of supernatural horror is set in a modern-day Transylvanian village where a young woman becomes an unwilling

Pressbook art for *She Beast* (1966).

participant in the reign of terror waged by an 18th century witch. The seemingly sedate village was the scene of mayhem and madness, some 200 years earlier. At that time, an outcast named Vardella became the victim of local witch-hunters who sought her out for practicing black magic. Many villagers assisted in the capture of the hideous, cave-dwelling witch before watching her prolonged torture and eventual execution.

In the more peaceful present, a British couple, Veronica (Steele) and her husband Philip (Ian Ogilvy), arrive in the village for a vacation. They find modest but adequate lodging in an establishment run by a congenial innkeeper (Mel Welles). This idyllic vacation becomes a nightmare, however, when during a leisurely drive Philip's car veers off the road and plunges into a lake. The young man makes it to the shore safely, but Veronica vanishes — as the monstrous Vardella emerges from beneath the lake in her place. The undead witch causes mayhem until Philip allies himself with the local intellectual, Count Van Helsing (John Karlsen). An expert on local lore and psychic phenomena, Van Helsing is aware of Vardella's existence. The Count also understands the mystical rites necessary to vanquish the evil entity and save Veronica from a terrible fate.

Philip and Van Helsing capture Vardella and subject her to the ritual of "dunking" in the lake from which she first emerged. The rites and incantations have the desired effect as Vardella disappears from sight and Veronica emerges in her place. Van Helsing, a descendant of a famous witch-hunter, has fulfilled a long-awaited destiny and saved the village from destruction. Philip leaves the region with Veronica, who has no knowledge of the frightening events of recent days. Although her husband is relieved to depart from the village, Veronica smiles and remarks, "I'll be back."

The final twist, a direct steal from Roger Corman's *The Haunted Palace* (1963), seemed to leave open the possibility of a sequel that never came about. Much of the story borrows from the chillers of Mario Bava and Antonio Margheriti while lacking the technical slickness and consistently dark atmosphere of either director's best works. However, Michael Reeves cannot bear all the blame for creating a tedious, often crude effort. He was paid very little money for handling this rush job and also saw fit to rewrite much of the original script under a pseudonym, "Michael Byron." Judging from the mediocre results, one can only wonder how bad the original treatment was.

She Beast producer Paul Maslansky was quite impressed with the talent and great energy exhibited by Reeves when he directed a few action sequences for Maslansky's *Castle of the Living Dead* (1964). The producer entrusted *She Beast* (originally titled *La sorella di Satana* [*The Sister of Satan*]) to the 21-year-old, providing him with a completed script and a shoestring budget. Steele was hired for only four days work and her actual role in the film is very small.

There are two good performances by actors who manage to rise well above their material. Ian Ogilvy delivers a nicely tuned portrayal of Philip, the young husband who struggles against dark forces. Ogilvy went on to act in Reeves' two remaining directorial efforts. *The Sorcerers* (1967), starring Boris Karloff, and *Conqueror Worm* (1968), which featured Ogilvy as a young soldier who takes a stand against the murderous Witchfinder General (Vincent Price) of Oliver Cromwell. Ogilvy has gone on to play many TV and movie roles, becoming best known as Simon Templar — television's *The Saint* — several years after Roger Moore left the role.

Another fine portrayal is delivered by Mel Welles as the local innkeeper. Welles, a native of New York born in 1930, made his film debut in director Jacques Tourneur's *Appointment in Honduras* (1953). The actor soon became familiar to horror fans as one of Roger Corman's most talented and dependable stock players. He played a major supporting role in Corman's *The Undead* (1957), hailed by some as Corman's best early chiller. Corman's *Attack of the Crab Monsters* (1957) cast Welles as a pompous scientist who falls victim to a giant crustacean. However, the actor's most famous role, and probably his best performance, is that of flower shop owner Gravis Mushnik in Corman's hilarious *The Little Shop of Horrors* (1960).

Reeves' anti-establishment attitude was not only expressed artistically in his films, but also within his personal lifestyle. He was an uncompromising man who refused to tolerate any attempts by co-workers and fellow artists to alter his original concepts. Conflicts over artistic differences and character interpretation occurred frequently between Reeves and Vincent Price during the filming of *Conqueror Worm*. "Reeves hated me!" Price once exclaimed in an interview. Perhaps there were times when Reeves hated himself.

A lethal combination of pills and alcohol took the life of Reeves at age 24. The fatal overdose was apparently intentional as the sensitive Reeves was crushed by the abrupt end of a love affair. Director Gordon Hessler was assigned by AIP to handle the film originally intended as Reeves' next effort, *The Oblong Box* (1969), starring Vincent Price. One can only imagine what sociological implications would have been injected by Reeves into the story of plantation owners who suffer the ravages of a deadly curse enacted by victims of their exploitation.

As it is, the full body of Reeves' work consists of four films, with *She Beast* being his least successful effort. Nevertheless, the film contains occasionally fierce and intriguing images plus the crude beginnings of philosophical framework present in the director's other films. Reeves' efforts concerned the struggle of one individual rejected and persecuted by mainstream society. Apparently, Reeves himself experienced a similar conflict — one that he failed to overcome.

Slaughter of the Vampires

Original title: *La strega dei vampiri* (*The Witch of Vampires*). A.k.a. *Curse of the Blood Ghouls*. A.k.a. *Curse of the Ghouls*. Mercury Film International, Pacemaker. 84 minutes. 1961. Eastman Color, Totalscope. Dir/Writ: Roberto Mauri. Prod: Dino Sant'Ambrogio. Ph: Ugo Brunelli. Mus: Aldo Piga. Ed: Jenner Menghi. Cast: Dieter Eppler, Walter Brandi, Graziella Granata, Paolo Solvay, Gena Gimmy, Alfredo Rizzo, Edda Ferronao, Carla Foscari, Marietta Prucaccini.

During the early to mid-1960s—Italian vampire flicks made their rounds of theaters in the United States—some of them very good, like Mario Bava's *Black Sunday* (1961). Few were as slow-paced and boring as *Slaughter of the Vampires*. Though visually competent, the film is distinguished mainly by its remarkable lack of vitality.

In a castle on the outskirts of Vienna during the 19th century, a wealthy young couple (Walter Brandi and Graziella Granati) plan to begin a quiet, comfortable life together. They are unaware that the castle's former occupant, a vampiric count (Dieter Eppler), still lurks in the region waiting for the arrival of new victims. Years earlier, Eppler was driven from the castle when it was stormed by a mob of vampire-hunters from the nearby village. One of his bloodlusting brides was claimed by the villagers, but the Count managed to escape the melee. The presence of the furtive Count is soon felt by the voluptuous, raven-haired Graziella, whom he chooses to be his new female companion.

As Brandi sees his wife grow weaker, the local doctor concludes that the evil Count is responsible for her condition. Precautions against further vampiric assaults prove futile as the woman is claimed by the Count and begins to prowl the night as one of the undead. Brandi himself seems to be in danger of being claimed by the nocturnal bloodsuckers and he is suspected of having been tainted by the curse of vampirism. The village doctor, backed by torch-bearing locals, eliminates the Count's two brides—including Graziella. Within the ruins of a stone chamber, Brandi confronts the sanguinary nobleman and dispatches him by driving a great steel stake through his heart.

Despite a potentially creepy premise, *Slaughter of the Vampires* lacks the great virility, exciting action sequences and brisk pace possessed by Hammer's Dracula thrillers and by the efforts of Bava and Antonio Margheriti. Roberto Mauri's unimaginative direction does little to thrill the audience or to create an atmosphere of tension. The opening sequence, in which Eppler and his vampire brides are pursued by torch-bearing villagers, is less thrilling than a typical New York City rush hour. Mauri's flat, uninspired approach to his subject matter was also evident in his hostage-suspense drama *Lost Souls* (*Vite perdite*), a 1961 release starring Virna Lisi.

Performances are equally uninspired, even by genre regulars Brandi and dependable Alfredo Rizzo. Graziella Granata, a buxom actress with a languorous expression, was good at breathing heavily. This is something she did very well in a number of films dealing with mature themes, most notable the bawdy *White Voices* (1965) featuring Barbara Steele, the queen of Italian horror. Granata also delineated lustful roles in *Run for Your Wife* (1966) and *Taste for Women* (1966) while making an attractively packaged "prop" in the spaghetti western *Beyond the Law* (1967).

Dieter Eppler, as the evil Count, is good at glaring, though he doesn't bare his fangs as well as Christopher Lee. Eppler later played a minor supporting role in a Christopher Lee chiller, West Germany's *The Torture Chamber of Dr. Sadism* (1967). Other roles for Eppler have included a part in the West German SF-horror *The Head* (1963), plus appearances in the adventure films *Under Ten Flags* (1960), *I Deal with Danger* (1966) and *Dead End* (1970).

Eppler's vampiric assaults on Granata provide a few mildly erotic moments, though the film's sexual overtones lack the intensity of Christopher Lee's seductions in the Hammer Dracula films. Ugo Brunelli's camera makes the most of some atmospheric sets and enhances the sense of foreboding present within a few eerie clusters of trees. Aldo Piga's heavy-handed score seems more appropriate for a tearjerker than for a vampire flick. Piga improved somewhat with his atmospheric scores for *The Vampire and the Ballerina* (1962), *The Playgirls and the Vampire* (1964) and *Terror-Creatures from the Grave* (1966).

In 1969, *Slaughter of the Vampires* was reissued by Pacemaker as *Curse of the Blood-Ghouls*; the distributor removed 12 minutes from the film. (The original, longer version had already been playing on television for several years.) Predictably, the re-release failed to draw much of an audience.

Snow Devils

A.k.a. *Snow Demons*. Mercury Film International/Southern Cross, MGM. 92 minutes. 1965. Eastman Color. Dir: Anthony Dawson (Antonio Margheriti). Prod: Margheriti, Joseph Fryd. Writ: Charles Sinclair, William Finger, Ivan Reiner. Original Story: Audrey Wisberg. Ph: Riccardo Pallotini. Mus: A. Francesco Lavagnino. Spfx: Victor Sortolda. Ed: Otello Colangeli. Cast: Jack Stuart (Giacomo Rossi-Stuart), Amber Collins (Ombretta Colli), Renato Baldini, Archie Savage, Wilbert Bradley, Halina Zalewska, Furio Meniconi, Peter Martell, Isarco Ravaioli, Enzo Fiermonti, Freddy Hagar (Goffredo Unger).

Although Antonio Margheriti is known mainly for his period horror films, he also directed a pair of halfway decent science-fiction adventures in the early 1960s. His *Battle of the Worlds* (1961) pitted scientist Claude Rains and his friends against a rogue planet on a collision course with Earth. The film was released in Italy as *Il planeta degli uomini spenti* (*The Planet of Extinguished Men*). Margheriti's visually striking *Assignment: Outer Space* (1963) has astronauts attempting to destroy an unmanned spacecraft that radiates a deadly force-field. Both efforts are distinguished by very good special effects sequences and excellent color photography. Unfortunately Margheriti's cut-rate science-fiction films originally done for the small screen are very disappointing. *Snow Devils* is one such tailored-for-TV effort and it is very likely the director's worst film.

The basic premise has good potential: the invasion from space scenario is juxtaposed with the popular Abominable Snowman myth. As the story opens, we find Earth threatened by a sudden series of terrible natural disasters. The greatest scientific minds of the world are unable to identify the cause of the devastating occurrences. An international expedition to the Arctic finally reveals the source of worldwide destruction as the malevolent super-technology of furtive alien invaders. These other-worldly intruders, burly humanoid types covered with a thick layer of fur, are the creatures known as the Yeti. The aggressive "snowmen" use their science to upset the ecological balance of our world, unleashing the fury of nature. This means of warfare is difficult for mankind to counter with effective defensive measures. A counter-offensive, however, would not be considered by world leaders who are not even aware that the disasters taking place are actually strategic assaults staged by invaders. However, the intervention of stalwart Giacomo Rossi-Stuart and his team of trouble-shooters make the invading snowmen from the planet Aytia shiver in their boots. After a series of routine encounters with the aliens, our heroes emerge triumphant while Earth's ecological balance is restored.

The film's basic premise could have provided good entertainment had it been handled with skill and polish — not to mention a decent budget. Margheriti is capable of far more than the dreary, dull direction he exhibits here; he fails to generate even the lowest level of excitement value. Cheap sets and inept special effects hardly add to the film's aesthetic value. The fine color photography of Riccardo Pallotini is the film's only bright spot. Acting is fair at best with adequate performances being delivered by such Margheriti regulars as Isarco Ravaioli, Goffredo Unger and Ombretta Colli, all cast, however, in stereotypical, two-dimensional roles. Giacomo Rossi-Stuart, who plays the male lead, also stars in Margheriti's *War Between the Planets* (1965) with the actor using the pseudonym of Jack Stuart.

Four films were constructed from the TV serials shot for *Fantascienza*, a popular Italian program aimed mainly at juvenile science-fiction fans. *Snow Devils* and *The Wild, Wild Planet* (1966) contain elements of horror while *War Between the Planets* (a.k.a. *Planet on the Prowl*) and *War of the Planets* (1971) are basically straight science-fiction adventures. The films were picked up for American release by MGM, but they drew little attention and remain unfamiliar to many fans. Margheriti later stated in an interview that he never expected the TV serials to be released to theaters as feature films.

Spirits of the Dead

Original title: *Histoires extraodinaires (Extraordinary Stories)*. A.k.a. *Tales of Mystery and Imagination*. Les Films Mareau/Cocinor/AIP. 117 minutes (ORT: 120 minutes). 1969. Eastman Color. "Metzengerstein": Dir: Roger Vadim. Writ: Vadim, Pascal Cousin, Clement Biddlewood. Ph: Claude Renoir. Mus: Jean Prodromides. Ed: Helene Plemiannikov. Cast: Jane Fonda, Peter Fonda, Françoise Prévost, James Robertson Justice. "William Wilson": Dir: Louis Malle. Writ: Malle, Clement Biddlewood. Ph: Tonino Delli Colli. Mus: Diego Masson. Ed: Franco Arcalli, Susanne Baron. Cast: Alain Delon, Brigitte Bardot, Katia Christina. "Toby Dammit": Dir: Federico Fellini. Writ: Fellini, Bernardo Zapponi. Ph: Giuseppe Rotundo. Mus: Nino Rota. Ed: Ruggero Mastroianni. Art Dir: Fabrizio Clerici. Cast: Terence Stamp, Salvo Randone. MPAA rating R

Here is a thriller that is one-third Italian and brilliant, two-thirds French and ordinary. *Spirits of the Dead* is the sort of international production that might inspire confusion in the United States, while earning the admiration of French critics. The merger of acting and directorial styles is quite intriguing, though the film sometimes suffers from other failings.

Fans of AIP horror films were generally satisfied with this effort since the quality of AIP's Poe thrillers had been declining after the release of Roger Corman's triumphant *The Tomb of Ligeia* (1965). Such films as Michael Reeves' *Conqueror Worm* (1968) and Gordon Hessler's *The Oblong Box* (1969) were spotty but basically disappointing Poe adaptations that contained graphic physical violence but depicted little of the emotional violence present in Corman's psychological thrillers. A welcome digression from this pattern came via *Spirits of the Dead*, released by AIP in the summer of 1969.

The first story, Roger Vadim's "Metzengerstein," is a visually striking and sometimes intriguing chiller that finally emerges as a routine soft-core tale of debauchery. Jane Fonda portrays a decadent baroness who causes the death by fire of her cousin (Peter Fonda), a man for whom she feels a love-hate attachment. Her victim returns from the dead in the form of a great black stallion that

Pressbook art for *Spirits of the Dead* (1969).

eventually carries the Baroness to her own fiery death. During the course of the story, director Vadim provides us with well-photographed glimpses of voyeurism, lesbianism, sadomasochism and even a hint of bestiality. There is also a dollop of incest by casting Jane Fonda's brother Peter in the male lead. All of this adult material is enough to establish the decadence of the Baroness several times over.

Nevertheless, the basic scenario established in "Metzengerstein" still generates considerable interest. When the Baroness begins to hate her own corrupt nature, she becomes obsessed with the black stallion — a strong, proud creature that represents the purity of nature. Vadim makes extensive use of the color red which, within the context of the story, is symbolic of death. For example, we see many shots of a tapestry bearing the image of the horse, which has fiery, crimson eyes. The final scene, depicting the death of the Baroness, has her being "purified" when she is enveloped by a sheet of red flames. Fluid camerawork by Claude Renoir, atmospheric sets and a fine performance by Ms. Fonda help "Metzengerstein" emerge as a halfway decent thriller, but not as the classic it might have been.

"William Wilson," the second segment, begins with an intense running-in-terror sequence as the title character (Alain Delon) escapes from the scene of a fatal duel that he fought with a diabolical twin. This "doppelganger" is Wilson's own conscience that emerges as a separate physical entity. The twin relentlessly hounds the ruthless Wilson from his demented childhood until a final confrontation as an equally twisted military man. The series of encounters is revealed through flashbacks as Wilson confesses the killing of his twin to a priest. Unable to convince the priest that this strange story of life-long persecution is anything more than a drunken delusion, the despairing Wilson leaps to his death from the belltower of the church. His body is found impaled with the same dagger that he used to slay his twin.

Although director Louis Malle fails to maintain the sheer terror of the opening scene, "William Wilson" moves smoothly and features a monotone but well-cast performance by Alain Delon. The best sequence is a thoroughly engrossing card game between Wilson and the cold-eyed, cigar-puffing Josephine (Brigitte Bardot), during which Wilson (predictably) cheats like hell. After he is exposed by the intruding twin, the two Wilsons engage in some well-directed, fitfully exciting swordplay. The mixture of chills, fast action and intriguing deceptions depicted in "William Wilson" amount to a competent but ordinary thriller. Some dialogue between the two Wilsons could have added considerable interest to this tale about a man's evil nature.

Federico Fellini's "Toby Dammit" is the film's final segment, based on Poe's "Never Bet the Devil Your Head." This sequence stars Terence Stamp in the title role, a Shakespearean actor who agrees to star in the first "Catholic" western. Much of the story portrays the devaluation of art through crass commercialism as we see a once respected artist trade his integrity for the hollow comforts of newly acquired wealth. The shallow nature of Toby's life becomes obvious when he does a TV interview designed to promote his new image as an eccentric but exciting screen personality. Toby answers one flippant question after another while technicians provide a series of artificial responses in the form of canned laughter or applause. The silly discourse turns abruptly serious when Toby is asked about his belief in supernatural forces. Although he rejects the existence of God, Toby firmly believes in the Devil, whom he sees as a madly grinning little girl. This strange child, a corrupt demon from Hell, constantly fondles a white ball and beckons at Toby to join in her game. Toby finally does embrace the game and suffers the consequences of his decision.

Clint Eastwood was originally considered for the role of Toby Dammit, a decision that would have provided clever points of reference to the actor's previous roles. The casting of Eastwood, known for his Italian westerns, would have been a clever in-joke with the actor playing a character who stars in a western produced by the Roman Catholic church. This is the sort of humor that Fellini previously employed in *La dolce vita* (1960). The latter film featured Lex Barker as an alcohol-soaked Hollywood has-been who turns to roles in the European action market. One scene has the drunken Barker lying unconscious in a parked car and being spied by a pair of photographers. "Snap a picture of that guy!" states one photographer. "He used to play Tarzan."

Although Eastwood's presence might have provided an interesting touch of neo-realism, the dynamic Terence Stamp is more than competent as Toby Dammit. Stamp is superb as the typical Poe hero—a sensitive aesthete tortured by his own acute senses and overwhelmed by forces beyond his control. Fellini, however, smoothly merges his own favorite themes with the universe of Poe. We see a stylish, incisive study of decadence conflicting with positive human values as the search for wealth and pleasure leaves only emptiness where there was once a life filled with meaning.

Toby attempts to find consolation in his material state, racing furiously along dark and narrow streets in a sleek new sports car. These streets are peopled with costumed mannequins—a chef here …a waiter there…and many other socially defined roles in which men are trapped. Toby, the tragic individualist, still attempts to follow his own path after betraying his ideals. His doomed struggle concludes after a last encounter with the child-demon. She still tempts him with the white ball, which is just as flawless as the dreams and ideals he once pursued. Still unaware that you can't bet the devil your head and win, Toby races toward his fate. He fails to notice the razor-sharp wire strung along the road...

"Toby Dammit" was subjected to some changes in the soundtrack by American-International. Most notably, there was the insertion of the pop song "Ruby," performed by Ray Charles. The song fits perfectly into a nightclub atmosphere as the drunken Toby languorously ponders the flirtation of a young woman sitting next to him.

Beyond its thought-provoking subtext, "Toby Dammit" features some of the trappings associated with the mass-produced Italian horror film. Narrow streets, eerie mists and an imaginative use of color create images that are quite familiar from Mario Bava's thrillers. In fact, the child-demon has often been compared to a similar entity in Bava's *Kill Baby Kill* (1966). The grotesque, staring faces that populate the darkened rooms and landscapes of "Toby Dammit" could easily be found in the average Riccardo Freda horror flick.

However, the lofty intentions of Fellini's first-rate mixture of horror and social commentary are usually absent from the efforts of less distinguished Italian directors. Although the thrillers of Bava and Freda succeed on their own modest terms, it is good to appreciate an Italian horror tale that frightens its audience while leaving people with something to think about afterwards.

Terror-Creatures from the Grave

Original title: *Cinque tombe per un medium* (*Five Graves for a Medium*). A.k.a. *Coffin of Terror*. MBS Cinematografica/International Entertainment, Pacemaker. 85 minutes (ORT: 90 minutes). 1966. B&W, Panoramic. Dir: Ralph Zucker (Massimo Pupillo). Prod: Frank Merle (Francesco Merli). Writ: Roberto Natale, Romano Migliorine. Ph: Charles Brown (Carlo Di Palma). Mus: Aldo Piga. Ed: Robert

Pressbook art for *Terror-Creatures from the Grave* (1966).

Ardes (Ardis). Cast: Barbara Steele, Walter Brandt (Brandi), Richard Garret (Riccardo Garrone), Marilyn Mitchell (Mirella Maravidi), Alfred Rice (Alfredo Rizzo), Alan Collins (Luciano Pigozzi), Tilde Till, Ennio Balbo, Steve Robinson, Edward Bell, Rene Wolfe.

A routine tale of murder, revenge and the living dead is helped mainly by excellent camerawork that partially compensates for an eclectic, unimaginative script.

Set in the 1890s, the story deals with events in a gloomy castle after the master of the household — the eccentric Dr. Hauff— meets an untimely end. His mysterious widow Cleo (Barbara Steele) secretly orchestrated the murder of her husband with the help of servants and the initial involvement of businessman Joseph Morgan (Riccardo Garrone). The family lawyer, Albert Kovaks (Walter Brandi), is an employee of the sly Morgan and becomes aware of the circumstances behind the death of Dr. Hauff. Kovaks establishes a link with Corinne Hauff (Mirella Maravidi), innocent daughter of the murdered man.

However, the dangers posed to the inhabitants of the castle involve more than the repercussions of an ordinary murder plot. Dr. Hauff was secretly a warlock whose dark powers have reactivated the medieval victims of the Black Plague buried on castle grounds. Ravaged bodies rise out of the darkness to claim their victims. The squadron of the undead returns nightly with each new victim joining their ranks.

Cleo and Morgan are finally claimed with the only survivors being Corinne and the young lawyer. The undead predators pursue the young couple as a thunderstorm erupts — with nature's fury providing unexpected results. Rain immunizes the survivors while destroying the zombies with the cleansing power of white magic.

Barbara Steele has done worse thrillers than this quickie, probably hitting rock-bottom with Michael Reeves' *She Beast* (1966). Ignored by many critics and panned by the few who bothered to review it, *Terror-Creatures from the Grave* was quickly dismissed as mere drive-in trivia. Steele reminds us, in her portrayal of Cleo Hauff, that she is quite adept at being cold-eyed, furtive and treacherous. Unfortunately, the film requires her to do little else beyond the two-dimensional confines of the Roberto Natale-Romano Migliorine script. Such a role is largely a waste of talent in light of the wide range of emotions that the actress skillfully display in *Black Sunday* (1961) and *Castle of Blood* (1964).

The film features several other competent performances. In fine form are genre regulars Walter Brandi as crusading lawyer Albert Kovaks and Luciano Pigozzi as the family servant, Kurt. Riccardo Garrone, who portrays the double-dealing Joseph Morgan, was previously known for a number of non-horror roles. He acted in such major films as *La dolce vita* (1960) and *The Swordsman of Siena* (1962), starring Stewart Granger. Mirella Maravidi, who is third-billed as Corinne Hauff, later joined Riccardo Garrone as part of the supporting cast for a lightweight comedy entitled *Three Bites of the Apple* (1967), starring David McCallum.

Massimo Pupillo's lack of imagination is obvious in his direction, which fails to create a proper mood of tension. Far more effective is the crisp black-and-white photography of Carlo Di Palma, who later handled the camerawork for Bernardo Bertolucci's *Tragedy of a Ridiculous Man* (1981) and Disney's *The Black Stallion Returns* (1983). However, some fine photography and a few good performances are unable to compensate for the direction and hackneyed script. Writer Roberto Natale provided a halfway decent screenplay for Mario Bava's *Kill Baby Kill* (1966), then began concentrating on Italian westerns, most notably *A Long Ride from Hell* (1970), which was originally titled *Vivo per la tua morte*. The latter effort was co-authored by the film's star, Steve Reeves.

Terror-Creatures from the Grave may be seen as ordinary Saturday matinee schlock of the type that satisfied hordes of blood-thirsty kids. As in many of its type, some semblance of quality managed to emerge in spite of slipshod origins and the lack of any lofty intentions. The film features several talented individuals who soon went on to bigger things, but honed their skills by helping to turn out attractively mounted tripe.

Terror in the Crypt

Original title: *La cripta de l'incubo* (*The Crypt of the Demon*). A.k.a. *La maldición de los Karnsteins* (*The Curse of the Karnsteins*).

A.k.a. *The Karnstein Curse*. A.k.a. *The Crypt of the Vampire*. A.k.a. *The Vampire's Crypt*. A.k.a. *Karnstein*. A.k.a. *The Crypt and the Nightmare*. A.k.a. *Carmilla*. A.k.a. *Crypt of Horror*. MES Cinematografica/ Hispamer Films, AIP. 84 minutes. 1963. B&W. Dir: Thomas Miller (Camillo Mastrocinque). Prod: William Mulligan. Writ: Julian Berry (Ernesto Gastaldi), Robert Bohr (Bruno Valeri), Mario Del Carmen, Ramón Martínez, José L. Montes. Ph: Julio Ortas, Giuseppe Acquari. Cast: Christopher Lee, Audrey Amber (Adriana Ambessi), Ursula Davis (Pier Ana Quaglia), José Campos, Nela Conjiu, Vera Valmont, José Villasanti, Angel Milland (Angela Minervini).

This admittedly atmospheric but otherwise fairly ordinary chiller is based on Joseph Sheridan Le Fanu's 1871 vampire tale "Carmilla." It is the third screen adaptation of the work, following Carl Dreyer's restrained *Vampyr* (1931) and Roger Vadim's far more graphic, updated *Blood and Roses* (1961). *Terror in the Crypt* dispenses with the tale's more volatile portrayal of vampire-lesbianism, portraying the admirable Gothic trappings of the story while failing to convey its spirit.

The Karnstein estate surrounds the castle of an affluent and aristocratic family. Count Karnstein (Christopher Lee), a dignified 19th century gentleman, has led a decent life with few regrets over past misdeeds. However, there is a terrible legacy that the Karnstein family has had to bear — the legend of Sheena. Bizarre, frightening tales of the evil ancestor have haunted the family for many years. Sheena was thought to have been a witch whose practice of black magic caused misery and destruction for those around her.

The Count has become concerned about the morose state of his daughter Laura (Adriana Ambessi), who believes that she has become the recipient of a family curse. Perhaps she is even the reincarnation of the evil Sheena. Strange nightly disturbances, as well as Laura's decaying emotional state, have led to Count Karnstein to appeal for outside help.

Several guests arrive, including a pair of doctors and a charming young woman named Lyuba (Pier Ana Quaglia) who becomes Laura's closest friend. The two women share their fears and hopes, often comforting each other with the touching of hands and with soft embraces. For a time, the positive contact works wonders in relieving Laura's severe depressions. Sadly, the nocturnal disturbances at Castle Karnstein now move from being mysterious to becoming terrifying and ultimately deadly.

The occupants of the castle dread the coming of darkness. Storms seem to occur more frequently, while the tolling of a chapel bell marks the start of murderous events. An eccentric housekeeper meets a grisly end after attempting to help Laura by performing mystical rites intended to dispel the evil spirits. Another victim is a harmless beggar given to philosophical ramblings. One night, the uninterrupted tolling of the bell is found to be caused by the beggar's corpse, which hangs limply from the bell rope, noose around his broken neck.

Laura feels she is unconsciously responsible for these horrors, but the faithful Lyuba still seeks to be her friend. One night, the two women flee the castle at the insistence of Lyuba, who claims to be interested in saving Laura from the family curse. Laura discovers to her horror that Lyuba is the reincarnation of the evil Sheena. During the terrifying confrontation, Laura finds the strength to resist the spell-casting female fiend. The Count and his friends arrive as Lyuba-Sheena is cheated of her last victim. In the final scene, Sheena fades quickly into a gray mist.

Le Fanu's "Carmilla" was originally published in a London Magazine called *The Dark Blue* in 1871. More than a spook tale about a female vampire, "Carmilla" tells the story of a character obsessed with attempts to preserve beauty. This obsession leads to an uncontrollable attraction to a beautiful woman and the emergence of a bizarre love affair. We are finally taught that narcissism and an uncompromising passion for life will destroy both ourselves and those around us.

An Italo-Spanish co-production, *Terror in the Crypt* borrows a few epigrams from Le Fanu's original story. There are several pensive moments in which one character (the strange beggar) reflects on the fleeting nature of man's happiness and on his very existence. However, the full potential of Ernesto Gastaldi's script remains unrealized. Gastaldi injects a "surprise" ending of the type that he used previously for *Werewolf in a Girl's Dormitory* (1963). The latter flick, claimed that the monstrous killer was the one person whom the audience would never suspect. *Terror in the Crypt* generates little in the way of suspense when it comes to guessing the identity of

Sheena. The fetching Lyuba, as upstanding as a girl scout, is too much the paragon of virtue for her not to be hiding evil behind a ubiquitous smile.

Director Camillo Mastrocinque handles his material in a visually appealing style and creates an occasionally eerie scene. The most effective sequence involves a séance in which the corpse of the murdered housekeeper sits upright and points an accusing finger at Laura. This terrifying accusation from beyond death's door is seen in brief glimpses as lightning illuminates the darkened room. Such scenes of horror are few and far between in what is basically a routine haunted house thriller — and a rather slow-paced one at that.

Christopher Lee, though more than adequate as Count Ludwig von Karnstein, was at least ten years too young for the role in 1963. A somewhat older genre figure like Andre Morell would have been appropriately cast as the Count, but the producers wanted a more familiar horror actor whose name would increase the box office potential. Nevertheless, Lee's performance overshadows an ordinary supporting cast that is largely unknown in the United States.

Terror in the Crypt was rarely seen in U.S. theaters but began receiving considerable TV exposure in 1967 as an "American-International Television" release. Other film versions of Le Fanu's work soon reached the silver screen, including a low-budget Spanish chiller entitled *The Blood-Spattered Bride* (1969). American-International entered into a co-production deal with Hammer Films for an ambitious new adaptation — Roy Ward Baker's *The Vampire Lovers* (1970). The latter effort presented the vampiric Carmilla as both a horrifying and a tragic figure rather than a two-dimensional movie menace. Bisexuality was prevalent as Carmilla's erotic exploits involved the conquest of men and women. *Terror in the Crypt* only contains vague implications of lesbianism in two or three scenes.

Hammer also produced *Lust for a Vampire* 91971) and *Twins of Evil* (1972), both of which borrowed substantial parts and portions of the Le Fanu tale. The Karnstein Trilogy helped to inspire semi-versions like *The Velvet Vampire* (1971) and the pretentiously arty *Daughters of Darkness* (1972).

"Carmilla" has yet to be given the screen treatment it deserves. Originally, this tale so impressed Bram Stoker that he was inspired to write *Dracula* as a sequel of sorts to the Le Fanu work. Le Fanu made a thought-provoking statement on human needs and passions, the love of beauty and the fear of its loss, the horror of loneliness and the all-consuming fear of death.

Terror in the Crypt only hints at some of these ideas in a production that might have been a winner had it been handled by Mario Bava or Antonio Margheriti. However, horror buffs may want to see the film for what it could have been, then read Le Fanu's original "Carmilla" to see what a film adaptation should be like.

The Thief of Baghdad
(Il ladro di Bagdad)

A.k.a. *Le voleur de Bagdad*. Titanus/Lux, MGM. 90 minutes (ORT: 100 minutes). 1961 (ORD: 1960). Eastman Color, CinemaScope. Dir: Arthur Lubin. Prod: Bruno Vialati. Writ: Vialati, Augusto Frassineti, Filippo Sanjust. Ph: Tenino Delli Colli. Mus: Carlo Rustichelli. Ed: Gene Ruggiero. Art Dir: Flavio Magherini. Cos: Georges Benda. Spfx: Tom Howard. Makeup: Romolo De Martino. Cast: Steve Reeves, Giorgia Moll, Arturo Dominici, Edy Vessel, Georges Chamarat, Luigi Visconti, Gina Mascetti, Antonio Battistella, Daniele Vargas, Giancarlo Zarfati, Rosario Borelli, Antonio Rasmino, Anita Todesco.

This is the third screen version of the famous story, the first being released in 1924 and starring Douglas Fairbanks with direction by Raoul Walsh; the second was released in 1940, starring Sabu and Conrad Veidt. The Italian version lacks the massive sets of the Walsh film and the eye-popping visuals of the Sabu version. Steve Reeves may not possess the charisma and wit of Fairbanks, but he brings a great amount of energy to his portrayal of the title role.

In the Baghdad of many centuries ago, the likable rogue Karim (Steve Reeves) struggles to survive in a kingdom consisting of a very few rich men and great many poor. He spends much of his time pilfering fruit or lifting the purses of wealthy merchants and dignitaries. Karim often gives the stolen money to hungry children or poverty-stricken friends. Karim's benevolence toward the common man has made him a folk hero among the destitute.

The Sultan of Baghdad must deal with many eager suitors who wish to wed his daughter, the lovely Princess Amina (Giorgia Moll). One such suitor is the sly and ambitious Prince Osman (Arturo Dominici), who secretly administers a love potion to Amina in order to win the girl for himself. Since the potion has been consumed through trickery and its use motivated by the desire for power, the spell turns deadly. Amina is poisoned by the brew and only the curative powers of a fabled blossom — the Blue Rose — can save her life.

Karim learns of the dire situation and decides to embark on the quest for the mystical plant along with several noblemen. The man who obtains the Blue Rose will win the hand of Princess Amina. Karim introduces himself to the Sultan as the prince of another city-state and offers his services. The Sultan graciously accepts and Karim prepares to leave on the dangerous search. Palace guards later discover the bound and gagged dignitary whose royal garb was stolen by Karim.

Traveling by horseback, Karim and the others reach the first of The Seven Gates — enchanted portals bearing the image of the Blue Rose. The men must pass through each of the seven portals to obtain the precious flower. They settle in an eerie forest and prepare a campfire as darkness falls. Karim manages to hold his own with allies of "high birth" and he finally manages to earn a grudging acceptance within the group. However, the sly Prince Osman uses his dagger to puncture the waterskins of his companions before leaving furtively in the dead of night. Only Karim's water rations remain intact since he rests apart from the main group in order not to strain their shaky alliance.

Later, the surrounding trees suddenly become imbued with life, their limbs writhing and reaching out to grasp unsuspecting victims. Karim and the others awaken to confront the monster-trees, one of which seizes a man about the waist and lifts him above the ground. The stalwart Karim draws his sword and hacks at the tentacle-like tree limb, finally severing it and freeing its victim.

Karim and the others flee for their lives as the entire forest becomes alive and dangerous with the predatory trees. Another of the Seven Gates is discovered by Karim, who rushes through the portal, thus escaping from the monster-trees. He continues on his journey under the protection of a strange but charming fellow whose mastery of white magic helps Karim out of one desperate situation after another. The benevolent influence of the magician (Georges Chamarat) assists the quixotic crusader in surmounting such deadly obstacles as boiling lava and the deadly waters of a flood.

Another ordeal places Karim in the sands of a burning desert, where he is briefly reunited with his fellow searchers. The reunion is short-lived as Karim follows a different path and finally enters another of the mystical gates, beyond which lies the temple-like dwelling of a beautiful but evil sorceress. Kadeejah (Edy Vessel) possesses magical potions that turn men into stone. Karim learns of the woman's powers when he examines the statues decorating the dwelling. He sees, to his horror, the petrified forms of his comrades whose search for the Blue Rose has come to a sad end. Karim pretends to accept the hospitality of Kadeejah, who offers him a goblet of wine. He manages to switch goblets with the witch, who falls victim to her own deadly potions. As her body turns to stone, the temple crumbles and Karim barely escapes with his life.

Karim finds the Blue Rose, but must escape from a small army of faceless men clad in black and armed with razor-sharp weapons. Karim gets away through the mystical intervention of his magician-friend, who provides a flying carpet. The thief of Baghdad returns home with the Blue Rose and saves the life of Princess Amina. The Sultan keeps his promise and joyously announces the betrothal of Amina and Karim.

The ambitious Prince Osman still plans to claim Baghdad for himself, if not by marriage then through military means. His legion of mercenaries surround the city and a massive attack is launched upon Baghdad, but Karim's faithful magician intervenes once again. A spell is cast, creating a troop of mystical warriors who descend upon the invaders and make short work of them. Osman is brought to justice as he attempts to flee the battle. With their task completed, the warriors ride off into the desert, vanishing as suddenly as they appeared.

The marriage of Karim and Amina takes place in the palace. Karim scans the throne room for the benevolent magician, but he seems to have missed the festivities. Karim finally glances at the intricately carved figures that decorate the walls. One familiar-looking carving looks in his direction and playfully winks an eye. Karim's secret ally has attended the ceremony after all, as the princess marries a thief who will one day become the benevolent ruler of Baghdad.

This *Thief of Baghdad* probably contains the most horrific images of any of the film versions, especially during the creepy encounters with trees animated by black magic. There is also lightweight Arabian Nights-type adventure laced with some fair visual humor of the style that director Arthur Lubin was known for. Many fans will remember the slapstick and visual gags of such Lubin comedies as his six entries in the "Francis the Talking Mule" series, the charming *The Incredible Mr. Limpet* (1964) and all 143 episodes of the *Mr. Ed* TV series (CBS, 1958-64). Some of these efforts are very foolish, but fun to watch anyway.

Lubin also directed a pair of exceptional thrillers, the first being the creepy *Black Friday* (1940) which juxtaposed gangster melodrama with SF-horror. Just as effective is Lubin's *Phantom of the Opera* (1943), a remake of the 1925 classic that makes excellent use of elaborate sets, elegant costumes and striking Technicolor photography. Lubin brings the same color texture and overall sense of artistry to *The Thief of Baghdad*.

Luckily, the humor contained in *The Thief of Baghdad* is more subtle and far less incongruous than that found in the Lubin *Phantom*. Comic touches are introduced in early sequences by depicting the daily escapades of Karim. Once we settle down to straight adventure with occasional horrific interludes, it is the rascally charm of Karim that provides relief from tension rather than the blatant intrusion of slapstick. Even after our hero escapes from the encounter with the faceless men, we see the return of a soft smile and carefree attitude of a colorful outlaw. The occasional appearances of the helpful magician are equally amusing, but brief enough so as not to damage the atmosphere of tensions in certain sequences.

Steve Reeves is only a fair actor, but he portrays Karim with a casual style befitting a character who seeks happiness rather than wealth or power. There's something in his smile that charms an audience, much like the typical projection of Jack Nicholson in many roles. Reeves (born 1926) was reared in Glasgow, Montana, where an interest in body-building led to his participation in a number of competitions. He earned the titles of Mr. World (in 1947), Mr. America and Mr. Universe. Reeves made an impressive "prop" in early screen appearances, filling a minor role in the romantic comedy *Athena* (1954) before playing a detective in Ed Wood's *Jail Bait* (1954). The latter flick was Reeves' first speaking role. His portrayal of the son of Zeus in Pietro Francisci's *Hercules* (1959) was a major turning point as Reeves settled into doing a series of epics in which he was a muscular yet noble icon defending the weak and the oppressed. He portrayed such characters in *Goliath and the Barbarians* (1960), *The White Warrior* (1960), *The Giant of Marathon* (1961) and *Sandokan the Great* (1964).

The Thief of Baghdad features sporadically effective Tom Howard special effects, excellent photography and a rousing score by Carlo Rustichelli, whose music enriched such Mario Bava chillers as *What!* (1964) and *Blood and Black Lace* (1965). The film features a fine performance by Arturo Dominici, who excelled as the undead Javutich in *Black Sunday* (1961). In the role of Prince Osman, Dominici generates a negative energy that almost takes on a personality of its own.

Like many other Steve Reeves epics, *The Thief of Baghdad* did a respectable business in the United States and was usually booked at showcase theaters in the major cities. There was a fourth film version of the story, done as a 1978 TV feature starring Roddy McDowall and Peter Ustinov. It lacked both a sense of mysticism and excitement value. Arthur Lubin's effort provided polished entertainment for horror addicts *and* fans of colorful costume dramas. More importantly, the film features Steve Reeves' most interesting characterization as he is able to portray an individual who is not only heroic but also possessed with a sly sense of humor. *The Thief of Baghdad* is probably the only one of Reeves' 16 screen credits that is quite worth seeing—and that alone is something.

Uncle Was a Vampire

Original title: *I tempi duri per vampiri* (*Hard Time for Vampires*). Maxim Film/Cei Incom/Monflour Film, Embassy. 95 minutes. 1961 (ORD: 1959). B&W, Totalscope. Dir: Stefano Steno (Vanzina).

Prod: Mario Cechi Gori. Writ: Edoardo Anton, Dino Verde, Alessandro Continenza. Ph: Marco Scarpelli. Cast: Renato Rascel, Christopher Lee, Sylva Koscina, Kay Fisher, Lia Zoppelli, Susanna (Susanne) Loret, Antie Geerk, Franco Scondurra.

Although it was originally intended as a vehicle for the popular Italian comedian Renato Rascel, *Uncle Was a Vampire* is worth noting mainly for the presence of several fine talents. Christopher Lee, familiar from his portrayal of Bram Stoker's infamous Count in Hammer's *Horror of Dracula* (1958), began to emerge as a continental horror star in this flick.

The story is basically routine spook spoof with occasional good moments provided by Rascel, Lee and cinematographer Marco Scarpelli. A down-on-his-luck nobleman, Count Osvaldo (Rascel), has reluctantly sold his castle to a businessman who transforms the aging structure into a hotel. Osvaldo decides to stay on as the caretaker and porter since he has nowhere else to go and will need to earn his keep. A diminutive fellow whose noble birth means little without the reinforcement of wealth and property, Osvaldo finds it difficult to accept such an obscure existence. His lowly new station is especially humiliating since the castle is now inhabited by a number of attractive female houseguests. Winsome hotel worker Lilliana (Sylva Koscina) is the most attractive to Osvaldo, but he can see no way to win her heart with little to offer beyond his love. Perhaps the arrival of Osvaldo's eccentric and (possibly) wealthy uncle, the Baron Rodrigo (Christopher Lee), will revitalize the castle and imbue the family name with the respect that it deserves.

Baron Rodrigo arrives and begins to display a few nocturnal habits that are strange to say the least. Rodrigo's thirst for blood is quenched nightly as he finds a number of desirable young women to choose from within the castle's "stable" of potential victims. Worse yet, the bumbling Osvaldo is tainted with the vampiric legacy of his uncle — an "inheritance" that Osvaldo certainly didn't expect. Life as a vampire isn't easy as our hero must become accustomed to the daily (rather, the *nightly*) grind of rising at dusk and seeking fresh victims to feast upon. All seems hopeless until Osvaldo realized that both escape from the family curse and the possibility for happiness with Lilliana are within reach. Osvaldo's quiet charm and admirable sincerity move Lilliana to the point that she imparts a gentle kiss to the Count. Lilliana's compassion and sense of decency bring Osvaldo's bout with vampirism to an end. Love conquers all — including the malevolent influence of Baron Rodrigo. Osvaldo and Lilliana may now share a happy life together.

Much of the humor in *Uncle Was a Vampire* is derived from some silly, fairly mild sex-teasing in addition to Renato Rascel's attempts to deal with the dusk-to-dawn routine of a hard-working vampire. Rascel (born 1912 in Turin, Italy) can be seen as a sort of predecessor to the American comic actor Don Knotts — a shrill little man out to show the world what he's made of. However, Rascel was always able to play comedy and tragedy with equal flair. His sensitive performance in *The Overcoat* (1954) expresses the daily frustrations and anxieties felt by small, frail men who are dwarfed by society. An actor in films since the mid-1930s, Rascel's other familiar screen credits include *The Monte Carlo Story* (1956), *Arrivederci Roma* (1959) and *The Secret of Santa Vittoria* (1969).

More interesting to horror fans is the appearance of Christopher Lee, who is billed second as the vampire. The son of a British army officer and an Italian mother, Lee (born 1922 in London) began his film career in 1948 with a supporting role in *Corridor of Mirrors*. Over a decade passed before his mastery of eight languages made him a welcome addition to the stable of actors who applied their talents to the European action and horror market that emerged near the end of the 1950s. Lee's fluent Italian, French and German allowed him to recite his own dialogue in foreign-language productions while dubbing his own voice in the English-language versions. *Uncle Was a Vampire* allows Lee to spoof his own image created in Terence Fisher's masterful *Horror of Dracula*, shot in November—December of 1957.

Despite the satirical nature of the Baron Rodrigo role, Lee's characterization is restrained. The actor has always taken all of his roles very seriously, even those casting him in black comedies and (as in *Uncle Was a Vampire*) "Draculampoons." This sober approach to horror-comedy is quite effective since the character being spoofed should never be presented as a buffoon. Such a character doesn't realize that he is ridiculous and should be played as a straight man in a ridiculous situation.

Actually, one may wonder just how effective the film might have been if played as a straight horror yarn. Lee's subtle villainy, his deep, rich voice and tall, black clad frame help him to emerge as quite an imposing figure. There are a number of eerie sequences in which he strides down shadowy corridors and staircases, walks along darkened castle battlements and coldly stalks victims in his own inimitable fashion. His highly atmospheric scenes are generally more amusing than the comic episodes, with the fine black-and-white photography of Marco Scarpelli neatly enhancing the films' Gothic trappings. *Uncle Was a Vampire* was shot in an actual 16th century castle of the outskirts of Rome.

The supporting cast includes Sylva Koscina in the role of Lilliana. At the time, Koscina (born 1934 in Zagreb, Yugoslavia) was best known as Steve Reeves' leading lady in *Hercules* (1959) and *Hercules Unchained* (1960). One of her earliest roles was in an Italian science-fiction comedy entitled *Toto in the Moon* (1957), starring comic actor Antonio de Cortes (more commonly known as "Toto"). The latter flick also featured the talents of director Stefano Vanzina (a.k.a. Stefano Steno) and cinematographer Marco Scarpelli, two years before they teamed again for *Uncle Was a Vampire*. Koscina went on to do bigger things with major roles in such films as *Deadlier Than the Male* (1967), *A Lovely Way to Die* (1968) with Kirk Douglas and *The Secret War of Harry Frigg* (1968), starring Paul Newman. *Uncle Was a Vampire* also features an appearance by Susanne Loret as one of the shapely young ladies residing in Rascel's castle and Kay Fisher is fairly amusing in one of her scatterbrained female roles. Several years later, she played a similar role — a "dizzy" American tourist who falls victim to a vampire-tree in the Spanish *Man-Eater of Hydra* (1967).

Although it received considerable coverage in fanzines of the early 1960s, *Uncle Was a Vampire* received little attention from theater patrons upon its American release in 1961. The film ran at a handful of neighborhood theaters with little or no promotion. Nevertheless, the film is remembered as Christopher Lee's third horror credit, following his success in *The Curse of Frankenstein* (1957) and *Horror of Dracula*. Lee then became a major figure in Italian horror of the 1960s, either starring or playing second male leads.

The Unnaturals
(Contronatura)

A.k.a. *Schrei in der Nacht* (*Scream in the Night*). CCC/Edo Cinematografica/Super International Pictures. 84 minutes. 1969. Color, widescreen. Dir: Anthony Dawson (Antonio Margheriti). Writ: Dawson, Hannes Dahlberg. Ph: Riccardo Pallotini. Cast: Joachim Fuchsberger, Marianne Koch, Dominique Boschero, Claudio Camaso, Alan Collins (Luciano Pigozzi), Marianne Leibl, Marco Morelli, Helga Anders.

There is absolutely no reason to sit through this 84-minute study in sheer boredom directed by Antonio Margheriti, whose genre efforts continued to decline in quality. The story is based on an admittedly creepy scenario involving an isolated estate in 1940s England where a handful of people encounter supernatural forces during a horror-filled night. We are introduced to a mixed bag of travelers, each of whom harbors a dark secret to seek shelter in the mansion of an elderly woman and her eccentric son. The two occupants welcome the strangers into their home.

As the evening wears on, the old woman reveals herself to be a spiritualist and — ostensibly as an entertainment — she psychically delves into the past experiences of her guests. One by one, the visitors are visibly shaken by the woman's revelations that strip away the veneer of civility to reveal sinister, long-buried secrets. Murder, sexual perversion and other immoral acts are revealed in startling detail as the travelers finally come to realize that their hosts are more than mere eccentrics. The woman and her son are actually the ghosts of the mansion's long-dead inhabitants, sent to punish the wicked interlopers. They use their supernatural powers to release the destructive fury of a flash-flood that brings watery death to the mansion's hapless visitors.

Director/co-author Margheriti endows the cliché-ridden *The Unnaturals* with some typical late-1960s nihilism by having a sudden final conflagration polish off the major characters. Before the destructive finale, a story unfolds that is basically a rehash of two classic thrillers. The early scenes borrow considerably from James

Whale's *The Old Dark House* (1932), which had an assorted group of travelers taking refuge in an isolated mansion during a storm and encountering some very strange residents who act as their hosts. *The Unnaturals* late reveals some plot twists that closely resemble substantial portions of an atmospheric, suspenseful thriller entitled *The Phantom of the Convent* (*El fantasma del convento*, 1934). This supernatural melodrama, directed by Fernando de Fuentes, had three travelers seeking shelter in an old monastery where one of the monks tells them of a strange parable that relates directly to the immoral actions of the visitors. When they awaken the following morning, the visitors find the monastery deserted. Their experiences of the night before entailed the revelations of long-dead holy men who appeared before them as apparitions warning of possible tragedies to come.

Beyond its unimaginative script, *The Unnaturals* features uniformly uninspired performances, even by genre favorite Luciano Pigozzi. However, the two real victims of this mess are a pair of fine performers whose talents are wasted—Joachim Fuchsberger and Marianne Koch. The dynamic Fuchsberger (born 1927 in Stuttgart, Germany) became a major leading man in West German mysteries and adventure films of the 1950s and early 1960s. An unlikely cross between James Mason and Brian Donlevy (with streaks of prematurely gray hair), Fuchsberger also acted in a number of war movies as well as several European westerns. Fuchsberger is best known for his roles in a series of atmospheric low-budget adaptations of Edgar Wallace mysteries, produced in West Germany during the 1960s. Some typical credits include *The Dead Eyes of London* (1960), *The Terrible People* (1960), *The White Spider* (1963) and *Carpet of Horror* (1964).

Female lead Marianne (a.k.a. Marianna) Koch acted in over 50 films before accepting a role in *The Unnaturals*. Koch (born August 19, 1930, in Munich, Germany) was the beautiful but wholesome peasant girl who arouses gunslinger Clint Eastwood's sense of decency in Sergio Leone's *A Fistful of Dollars* (1966). The actress also appeared in such American productions as *Night People* (1954), starring Gregory Peck, and the lightweight *Four Girls in Town* (1957). Her science-fiction and horror credits include *Monster of London City* (1964), *Frozen Alive* (1966) and a cloak-and-dagger thriller with science-fiction overtones entitled *Trunk to Cairo* (1966), starring George Sanders and Audie Murphy.

As is often the case with such efforts, the fine photography of Riccardo Pallotini is the best thing about *The Unnaturals*. Director Margheriti continues doing basically mundane thrillers such as the spotty *Web of the Spider* (1970) while also directing such mediocre action flicks as *Killer Fish* (1979) and *Code Name: Wild Geese* (1986). Margheriti never again found the proper mixture of elements that made *Castle of Blood* (1964) so effective.

The Vampire and the Ballerina

Original title: *L'ámante del vampiro* (*The Vampire's Lover*). A.k.a. *The Dancer and the Vampire*. Consorzio Italiano, United Artists. 86 minutes. 1962 (ORD: 1960). B&W. Dir: Renato Polselli. Prod: Bruno Bolognesi. Writ: Polselli, Giuseppe Pellegrini, Ernesto Gastaldi. Ph: Angelo Balstrocchi. Mus: Aldo Piga. Spfx: Leopoldo Rosi, Raffaele del Monte. Art Dir: Amedeo Mellone. Chor: Marissa Ciampaglia. Cast: Hélène Rémy, Tina Gloriani, Maria Luisa Rolando, Walter Brandi, Isarco Ravaioli, John Turner, Pierugo Gragnani, Stefania Sabatini, Ugo Gragnani.

Riccardo Freda's *I vampiri* (*The Vampires*, 1956) and Terence Fisher's *Horror of Dracula* (1958) provided some of the images and character relations in this chiller. Basically a potboiler with a few atmospheric sequences, *The Vampire and the Ballerina* emerges as a mediocre film. On a stormy night, a troupe of actors takes refuge in the castle of a seemingly hospitable Countess (Maria Luisa Rolando) who turns out to be a vampire. She is aided in her sanguinary activities by a repulsive, blood-lusting servant named Luca (Walter Brandi). The predatory pair feed upon their visitors, who gradually become aware of the true nature of their hosts. It is mainly the fetching ballerinas Luisa (Hélène Rémy) and Francesca (Tina Gloriana) who are the intended prey of the vampires. After a number of creepy encounters with the undead, the hunted turn the tables on the hunters. One of the girls holds the Countess at bay with a small cross until the arrival of dawn. The orange glow of the rising

The hideous Luca (Walter Brandi) attacks ballerina Luisa (Hélène Rémy) in *The Vampire and the Ballerina* (1962).

sun then cleanses the castle of its unholy inhabitants, leaving only a few piles of dust.

The sexual implications of the vampire myth are more graphically presented in this flick than in most of its predecessors. Vampires become the most aggressive of love-makers, taking further the covert theme of sexuality present in *Horror of Dracula*. One remembers the brief, strangely compelling foreplay between Christopher Lee and a completely submissive Melissa Stribling before Lee bares his fangs and satisfies his thirst for blood. Unfortunately, the lurid excesses of *The Vampire and the Ballerina* border on soft-core pornography. Walter Brandi's vampire comes off as a crude, sexually repressed fellow who happens to require blood as nourishment. However, Brandi does fairly well when one considers the poor quality of the material. It is interesting to see the actor play a grimy, barbaric individual rather than the impeccably groomed heroes of high moral fiber that he usually portrayed in European thrillers of the 1960s.

Hélène Rémy performs well as the resourceful Luisa, who is a bit more aggressive than the average genre heroine in search of protection from a level-headed male. Fans of Italian adventure films will remember Rémy as the leading lady of Giacomo Gentilomo's brutally exciting *Last of the Vikings* (1962). There is another competent performance by John Turner, a forceful leading man who strongly resembles Richard Greene — or perhaps a slender Orson Welles. Turner soon acted in a far better chiller, *The Black Torment* (1965), starring Heather Sears. Beyond the three good performances, there is some curiously absorbing black-and-white photography by Angelo Balstrocchi.

Co-author Ernesto Gastaldi wrote the screenplays for a number of Italian or international productions of the 1960s, usually hiding behind the pseudonym of Julian Berry. It is interesting to note that this United Artists release retains the original names of cast and crew members. Such American distributors as MGM and Allied Artists usually "Americanized" the credits for the sake of increased salability with English-speaking audiences.

Director Renato Polselli later handled the mediocre *The Vampire of the Opera* (1964), another derivative thriller that is almost as sensationalized and contains a precious few good scenes. Both of Polselli's vampiric thrillers are minor efforts that drew little attention in the United States.

The Vampire of the Opera

Original title: *Il mostro dell'opera* (*The Monster of the Opera*). NIF. 90 minutes. 1964. B&W. Dir: Renato Polselli. Prod: Bruno Bolognesi. Writ: Polselli, Ernesto Gastaldi. Ph: Ugo Brunelli. Mus: Aldo Piga. Cast: John McDouglas (Giuseppe Addobbati), Vittoria Prado, Marc Marian (Marco Mariani), Barbara Howard (Howerd), Catla Cavelli.

As one may assume from its title, *The Vampire of the Opera* borrows its basic scenario from the 1907 Gaston Leroux novel *Phan-*

tom of the Opera. Leroux's work dealt with the plight of the pitifully ugly Erik, who haunts the Paris Opera House and forms an attachment to a beautiful opera singer. Rather than have a disfigured outcast provide the chills, *The Vampire of the Opera* has the mysterious bloodsucker of the title lurking in an old deserted theater and preying upon unsuspecting visitors in a most grisly fashion.

A group of actors come upon an eerie, decrepit opera house which seems to be infected with a sense of foreboding. Shortly before their arrival, the actors were warned by a ghostly figure that the theater is haunted by a vampire, and to enter it would mean their inevitable destruction. Although they scoff at the dark admonition, there is a presence of evil in the structure that makes the actors fearful.

One of the women, a talented but relatively unknown young opera singer (Vittoria Prado), begins to see glimpses of a man (Giuseppe Addobbati) lurking in the shadows. Despite her fear, the girl becomes fascinated with the furtive stranger, a nobleman named Stefano who is devoted to the art form of the opera. Stefano is enamored of the girl, who seems to be the exact image of a long-dead lover. She follows him into the lower levels of the structure where Stefano—a vampire—is unable to control his sanguinary urges. The lust for blood drives him to attack the singer and transform her into one of the undead.

As the other performers continue their rehearsal of a new play, Stefano and his new "bride" begin to prey upon them. Several victims are claimed until hero Marco Mariani fights back against the vampiric onslaught. He attempts to use sympathetic magic at first, burning a portrait of Stefano in order to destroy the vampire through mystical means. Stefano survives the ritualistic assault, only suffering some superficial burns. However, his rage and lust for blood have hardly been cooled. The surviving actors set the vampire on fire before fleeing the opera house in a frantic, Hammer-like ending.

A very weak supernatural thriller, *The Vampire of the Opera* suffers from the unimaginative direction of Renato Polselli, who also collaborated with Ernesto Gastaldi in writing the mediocre screenplay of *The Vampires and the Ballerina*. Although Polselli fared somewhat better with his *The Vampire of the Opera*, elements of sensationalism emerge frequently in both thrillers. The erotic overtones of the vampire myth are delineated in a rather crude, awkward fashion. Not surprisingly, Polselli soon switched to sexploitation features which he directed under the pseudonym of Ralph Brown.

Most of the cast members never became known in the United States with the only familiar name being that of Giuseppe Addobbati ("John McDouglas"), who later played a major role in Mario Bava's *Kill Baby Kill* (1966). The actor was also featured in the colorful science-fiction adventure *Mission Stardust* (1968), which was based on one of the Perry Rhodan novels and starred adult movie actress Essy (*I Am Woman*) Persson. Among his straight dramatic roles, Addobbati acted in *To Commit a Murder* (1970), a tale of espionage starring Louis Jourdan. Addobbati also portrayed the father of Jean-Louis Trintignant in the searing Bernardo Bertolucci drama, *The Conformist* (1971).

The Vampire of the Opera first went into production in 1961, and the shooting was interrupted by serious financial difficulties. Consequently, the feature was not completed until 1964. The film has rarely been seen in the United States. Upon its release in Western Europe, most critics decided that the slipshod effort wasn't worth such a long wait. Many horror buffs displayed a preference for the vampiric chillers of Mario Bava, whose highly effective *Black Sabbath*, released the same year, featured a creepy vampire segment that generated a level of tension missing from Polselli's disappointing efforts.

Venus in Furs
(Venus im Pelz)

A.k.a. *Black Angel*. A.k.a. *Può una morta rivivere per amore? (Can a Dead Girl Revive Through Love?)*. Cineproduzioni Associati/Terra Film Kunst/Towers of London/AIP. 86 minutes. 1969. Movielab Color. Dir: Jess (Jesús) Franco. Prod: Harry Alan Towers. Writ: Franco, Marvin Wald, Carlo Fadda, Milo G. Cuccia. Based on "Venus im Pelz" by Leopold von Sacher-Masoch. Ph: Angelo Lotti. Mus: Manfred Mann, Mike Hugg. Songs: "Let's Get Together" by Robert B. Sherman, "Venus in Furs" by Richard M. Sherman. Vocals by Barbara McNair. Spfx: Howard A. Anderson. Ed: Henry Batista, Mike Pozen, Nicholas Wentworth. Cast: James Darren, Barbara McNair, Maria Rohm, Klaus Kinski, Dennis Price, Margaret Lee, Paul Muller, Adolfo Lastretti, Mirella Pamphili. MPAA rating: R.

American-International's promotional campaign described this flick as "a masterpiece of supernatural love and hate." Poster art depicted James Darren in the embrace of minxy Barbara McNair, implying that the depiction of interracial love would add to the mood of excitement created by the main story concerning murder, lust and vengeance from beyond the grave. Audiences were disappointed on all counts.

The opening scene is on a sunny morning at a Turkish seaside location, where musician Jimmy Logan (James Darren) finds the corpse of a beautiful woman whom he recognizes as Wanda Reed (Maria Rohm). Logan's mind races back several days. A flashback shows him playing trumpet in a jazz combo in a local club. During a break, the voluptuous Wanda captures his attention and he follows her to a nearby location. Wanda, apparently the promiscuous sort, seems to have expected an evening filled with erotic diversions. But the woman is set upon by the homosexual Kapp (Dennis Price), the whip-wielding lesbian Olga (Margaret Lee) and the sadomasochist Steiner (Klaus Kinski). Logan is startled by the savage exhibition, but won't intervene as other people are "just doing their thing."

Logan is understandably shaken after discovering her corpse, but he still indulges in his affair with a slinky, seductive singer named Rita (Barbara McNair). His evening performances at the local club manage to draw typical crowds in which one familiar face stands out — the face of Wanda. Logan establishes contact with the girl and the two young people seem to share a great passion — an inexplicable fascination for each other. Rita attempts to compete with Wanda in the area of love-making, but she realizes that her struggle is useless and bows out.

Wanda desires more than love — she craves revenge against the three degenerates who tortured and killed her. Although she is little more than a vindictive spirit, Logan is entrapped by his desire for Wanda. The girl appears to him before embarking on each of her nightly missions of vengeance. Logan follows her along the narrow, deserted streets until they arrive at the site of each killing. The darkened apartment of the burly Kapp comes alive with the eerie, devilishly erotic projection of Wanda, who tantalizes the sexually frustrated killer until he dies of heart failure. The girl's seduction of Olga concludes with Wanda transforming herself into the mutilated corpse that was her physical shell. Overcome by feelings of guilt, Olga slashes her wrists.

The killing of Steiner plays upon the bizarre fantasies of the sexually twisted loner. Steiner somehow identifies with the story of a Middle East potentate named Ahmed whose unfaithful wife tormented him by binding his limbs to a rope suspended from a ceiling. The husband was forced to watch the girl's passionate encounter with her lover — an encounter in which Steiner sees himself as Ahmed with Wanda in the role of the unfaithful wife. As the lovemaking reaches a feverish pitch, Steiner suffers the fate of the previously murdered Kapp.

With Wanda's thirst for revenge now quenched, the girl suddenly vanishes. Logan finds himself at the same beach house where the story began. There is a body washed ashore in the distance and Logan runs along the shoreline until he reaches it. As he turns the corpse onto its back, he sees that the face is his own. "My God," he mutters. "It's me...I've been dead all this time!"

Venus in Furs looks like a bad dream occurring in slow motion. In fact, this flick is probably the first slow motion horror film, with endless shots of James Darren running along a beach or fur-clad Maria Rohm walking down narrow streets. Even closeups of Rohm (as she mutters inaudible words) are slowed down somewhat, apparently to give the film a sense of mysticism. But the story is so thin and the direction so artless that the film fails to project a dreamlike quality and leaves the audience with a feeling of lethargy.

Director Jesús Franco proved himself quite adequate at handling programmer material with such mildly diverting thrillers as *The Awful Dr. Orloff* (1964), *The Diabolical Dr. Z* (1966) and *Attack of the Robots* (1967). *Venus in Furs*, however, lacks the atmosphere and suspense value of his previous efforts and is handled in a pretentious fashion. The final screen treatment is based on Franco's story which, in turn, was based on a literary work entitled "Venus im Pelz" by Leopold von Sacher-Masoch — the author from whose name the word "masochist" was derived.

The trance-like acting by most of the cast members hardly helps to generate any interest. Darren, a rather dull actor, looks as though he is suffering from a migraine headache from beginning to end. Darren (born in 1936 as James Ercolani) previously specialized in boy-next-door roles with such screen credits as *Gidget* (1959), *Gidget Goes Hawaiian* (1961), *Gidget Goes to Rome* (1963) and *For Those Who Think Young* (1964). Although *Venus in Furs* marked his horror debut, Darren had previously starred in the short-lived ABC-TV series entitled *The Time Tunnel* (1966-1967) which had him fighting alien monsters or other menaces in horror-related episodes. At 33, he wanted to change his screen image with *Venus in Furs* since his appeal in the youth market was waning.

Klaus Kinski (1926–1991) looks stoned to oblivion in the role of Steiner as script and direction prevent him from displaying his famous near-manic energy. Kinski, born in Poland as Nikolaus Gunther Nakszynski, established a reputation as a grade-B Peter Lorre in a number of West German film adaptations of Edgar Wallace mysteries during the 1960s. Although he appeared in major films, one of his most popular characterizations was that of the psychotic, hunchbacked gunslinger in Sergio Leone's *For a Few Dollars More* (1967). Kinski loved playing madmen whose barely suppressed hostilities suddenly exploded in a mad frenzy. The character of Steiner, however, displays all the frenetic energy of a department store mannequin.

Even more disappointing is the waste of Dennis Price as the sadistic homosexual. Price (1915–1973) delivered fine performances in such chillers as *No Place Like Homicide* (1962), *The Earth Dies Screaming* (1964) and *Curse of the Voodoo* (1965). His role in *Venus in Furs* requires him to leer and lick his lips while the script fails to offer him one word of dialogue.

There are also a few other dumb things, like Barbara McNair singing "Venus in Furs Is Smiling" after each of the deviates is killed off. Actually, McNair delivers the only good performance in the role of Rita who bows out after her lover becomes obsessed with the Wanda-Venus entity. (The mythological transformation of Wanda into Venus is pretty vague. You just have to be hip about it.) McNair is forced to recite some labored, slightly embarrassing dialogue which consists of purple prose that nearly drips off the screen.

Eclectic and confusing, *Venus in Furs* did poorly at the U.S. box office despite considerable promotion and frequent bookings at showcase theaters. The Italian version, supervised by Carlo Fadda and Milo G. Cuccia, contained a few atmospheric touches. Prints were processed in black-and-white for release in Italy, thus providing some pleasurably stark images in place of the occasionally gaudy excesses of Movielab Color. If *Venus in Furs* had dispensed with its surrealistically moronic treatment and presented itself as a modern gothic thriller, the film might have provided good entertainment.

War of the Zombies

Original title: *Roma contro Roma (Rome Against Rome)*. A.k.a. *Night Star, Goddess of Electra*. Galatea, AIP. 85 minutes (ORT: 95 minutes). 1965 (ORD: 1963). Eastman Color, Colorscope. Dir: Giuseppe Vari. Prod: Ferrucio de Martino, Massimo de Rita. Writ: Piero Pierotti, Marcello Sartarelli. Ph: Gabor Pogany. Mus: Roberto Nicolosi. Sp. fx.: Ugo Amadoro. Ed: Vari. Art Dir: Giorgio Giovannini. Cast: John Drew Barrymore, Ettore Manni, Susy (a.k.a. Susi) Andersen, Ida Galli, Mino Doro, Philippe Hersent, Matilde Colman, Rosie Zichel, Antonio Corevi, Livia Contardi.

Much like Mario Bava's *Hercules in the Haunted World* (1964), the visually colorful *War of the Zombies* attempts to merge fantasy epic with horror melodrama. The results are no more impressive than the Bava horror-spectacle hybrid, with *Zombies* being given a shot in the arm by the presence of its only name star—John Drew Barrymore.

The Roman war machine is required to suppress rebellions throughout the empire, clashing with a number of different cultures and their respective insurgents. Religious zealots often became rebels, as is the case involving a revolt in one of the Eastern provinces. Blows against the colonial regime have also resulted in the seizure of Roman treasures. A stalwart Roman officer named Gaius (Ettore Manni) is the commander of the force sent to restore order in the region.

His men first clash with dangerous but conventional forces.

224 War of the Zombies

Double feature: *The Lost World of Sinbad* and *War of the Zombies* (both 1965).

Burly opponents of peasant stock are a hardy breed, but they can be defeated by Roman steel in well-trained hands. Gaius comes upon a peasant girl, Tullia (Susy Andersen), who is about to be set upon by a band of grimy beggars. He drives away the brutal lot and earns the gratitude of the winsome maiden. Gaius quickly becomes enamored of the girl, a mysterious figure.

Tullia has been spied wandering the fields beyond the village at night, walking in a trance-like state. Gaius follows her one evening and emerges from behind a cluster of trees, startling the girl and breaking the trance. Her first instinct is to attack him, but she quickly comes to her senses and seeks comfort in his arms. Gaius learns that Tullia has been the psychic slave of the high priest Aderbal, whose rebellion against Rome is aided by the power of black magic.

Aderbal dwells in a cave that also contains the temple of an evil goddess. Resting on a pedestal is the huge idol of the goddess, which resembles a gaunt travesty of a woman's face and bears a single eye in the middle of its forehead. Aderbal swears an oath in blood to this fearful mistress of the night, whose aid he seeks in the creation of an empire. Aderbal has formed an alliance with a beautiful but ambitious young woman named Rhama (Ida Galli) who also craves power. Her nightly presence is felt in the village and nearby forest as she seeks information or searches out new followers to serve Aderbal.

The black magic rituals begin the invasion of the undead. The bodies of Roman soldiers, clad in full armor, rise from their tombs. Mounting their ghostly steeds, the legion of zombies rides against Roman forces. Attempts to combat the zombies prove futile as swords ineffectively strike undead flesh that seems hard as steel.

In the meantime, the inevitable confrontation between Aderbal and Gaius takes place in the stone chamber. The fiery eye of the goddess emits a beam of energy that saps the strength of an enemy, prompting Gaius to pursue a different strategy. Rather than directly confront Aderbal, the warrior strikes at the eye of the goddess and shatters the mystical orb. Aderbal emits a bitter scream and reaches for his own eyes. "Blind...blind!" he cries out. The vision of the goddess was his own vision and, with its destruction, he is now left sightless.

Aderbal craves revenge and his blindness will not dissuade him from striking back at Gaius. The mad priest settles into a half-crouch, searching the stone floor of the cave for a weapon. He finds a discarded sword just as Rhama, moved by Aderbal's plight, suddenly rushes forward to aid him. The priest strikes out with the blade, thinking that Gaius is attempting to engage him in combat. Rhama is fatally impaled by the blade.

Aderbal finds the lifeless form of his victim and realizes that it is his female accomplice. Stoically accepting the situation, he rises to his feet and prepares for a hopeless duel with the Roman. Aderbal awkwardly wields the sword, sweeping the area in wide arcs that Gaius can easily avoid. Resigned to his fate, the priest approaches the form of the goddess. His hands are outstretched toward the ruined eye of the idol in a final gesture of respect to the deity. With that, Aderbal falls backward and expires. His eyes are wide in death.

Tullia (Susy Andersen) seems mesmerized by the forces of black magic in *War of the Zombies* (1965).

Gaius and Tullia flee the cave as tremors shake the earth and the temple disintegrates. With the death of Aderbal and the destruction of the temple, the undead warriors are vanquished. Tullia is now free of the mad priest's influence and may give her love to Gaius without fear of retribution.

War of the Zombies received its American release early in 1965 after being picked up for double-billing by American-International.

The film became the co-feature of Toho's *The Lost World of Sinbad*, a colorful fantasy starring Toshiro Mifune. Despite some eerie sequences, *War of the Zombies* shows signs of frequent padding with mundane episodes that generate little interest. The weak love interest between Gaius and Tullia can easily be ignored, but the highly touted scenes depicting the "legions of the dead" fail to evoke a sense of terror or excitement. Advertising for *War of the Zombies* was inaccurate and exploitive in typical AIP fashion. Advertising inaccuracy can be tolerated, however, if the film itself manages to succeed on its own terms. *War of the Zombies* fails to do so as the lengthy build-up to the invasion of reanimated corpses never delivers the promised chills.

Instead, we see a brief glimpse of a zombie-warrior rising from the tomb, his head stiffly turning from left to right as he surveys his surroundings. There is also a long shot of the ghostly gathering of warriors galloping toward a confrontation with Roman soldiers. The actual clash between forces is presented in brief snippets. Amid a background of confusion, one soldier strikes a zombie with his sword and cries out, "They're invincible…invincible!" before being run through by the zombie's blade. These few scenes are red-tinted and largely photographed in slow motion. Though mildly creepy, they take up less than five minutes of screen time.

The scenes with John Drew Barrymore are fairly well done and benefit from good art direction by Giorgio Giovannini, plus some striking Gabor Pogany camerawork. Barrymore's Aderbal has a curious mixture of manic energy and solemn dignity. The actor skillfully delineates the role of a zealot who feels satisfaction at pursuing his "divine" purpose and explodes into mad rages when his purpose is thwarted. The enigmatic performance by Barrymore is the film's strongest asset.

Barrymore (born 1932) is himself an enigmatic figure, sensitive and highly talented while also afflicted with self-destructive tendencies. His numerous arrests for drunk driving, speeding and violent domestic disputes crippled his career and destroyed his marriage to actress Cara Williams. Barrymore began his film career while still in his late teens, often playing hysterical roles such as that of a suspected psychopath on the run in *High Lonesome* (1950). Most of his succeeding U.S. credits were mediocre efforts, including such titles as *High School Confidential* (1958) and *Night of the Quarter Moon* (1959).

Barrymore experienced far greater success in the European action market, mainly doing Italian costume dramas. He played Prince Youssoupoff in *Nights of Rasputin* (1960) and filled the role of Ulysses in *The Trojan Horse* (1962), starring Steve Reeves. *War of the Zombies* is the only solid horror credit for Barrymore. The film provides him with highly theatrical sequences featuring snatches of pseudo-Shakespearean dialogue. Perhaps we should expect such "classical" points of reference in a film featuring one of the Barrymores.

Barrymore left the acting profession for a while beginning in the late 1960s, becoming a Bohemian-styled intellectual devoted to meditation, detachment from personal ambition and the rejection of material values. His fine acting occasionally graces the TV screen, as he accepts roles that are unusual enough to pique his interest. Such roles are often accepted as favors to colleagues such as an appearance on television's original *Kung Fu* series at the request of actor-friend David Carradine. Barrymore's daughter, Drew has become an accomplished actress and further enriched the family legacy.

War of the Zombies has little else to recommend it. Ettore Manni is an adequate though unstriking hero while female leads Susy Andersen and Ida Galli also deliver acceptable performances. The two women may be familiar for their supporting roles in Mario Bava horror films. Manni earned an additional horror credit with his leading man role in a psychological thriller — Tony Richardson's *Mademoiselle* (1966), starring Jeanne Moreau. The score by Robert Nicolosi is unremarkable as is the pedestrian direction of Giuseppe Vari.

Like many other mediocre films, *War of the Zombies* still has something to recommend it. This effort's distinctive quality is its function as a showcase for the considerable talent of John Drew Barrymore. Although he never achieved the success of his father John or his Uncle Lionel, the younger Barrymore constantly rose above his material to deliver polished performances.

Werewolf in a Girls' Dormitory

Original title: *Lycanthropus*. A.k.a. *The Ghoul in School*. A.k.a. *Monster Among the Girls*. A.k.a. *I Married a Werewolf*. A.k.a. *Ghoul in a Girl's Dormitory*. Royal Films, MGM. 83 minutes. 1963 (ORD: 1961). B&W. Dir: Richard Benson Paolo Heusch). Prod: Jack Forrest (Guido Giambartolomei). Writ: Julian Berry (Ernesto Gastaldi). Ph: George Patrick. Mus: Francis Berman. Ed: Julian Attenborough. Cast: Barbara Lass, Carl Schell, Curt Lowens, Maureen O_Connor, Alan Collins (Luciano Pigozzi). Anini Steinert, Mary McNeeran, Maurice Marsac, Grace Neame, Joseph Mercer, Elizabeth Patrick, Lucy Derleth, Martha Marker, Patricia Meeker.

Can any flick be as bad as that title? Maybe...*Werewolf* is an example of a European thriller being pointlessly Americanized for the teen trade. The lurid retitling of this 1961 Italo-Austrian co-production, originally known as *Lycanthropus*, seems even more ludicrous with the addition of a laughable rock number ("The Ghoul in School") which accompanies the opening credits. Salability became the key word for this effort with a massive exploitation campaign and the gimmicky distribution of such items as Do-It-Yourself Werewolf kits, cardboard werewolf masks and werewolf "potions" (usually a mixture of water and food coloring).

However, the original film suffered from problems of its own before being loaded with extraneous gimmicks of the William Castle variety. Until the last 15 minutes, character motivations are so vague and the series of events that occur so eclectic that the film nearly emerges as *cinéma vérité* for the masses (apologies to Jean-Luc Godard!). Rather than confuse the reader with an incomprehensible summary of the story, let's just look at the basic scenario. The setting is a reform school for girls where a grisly murder has been committed. One of the girls, the promiscuous Mary Smith (Mary McNeeren), has met a gruesome demise amid the foreboding clusters of trees that surround the school. Voracious wolves are said to prowl the region at night, but the savage attack has actually been carried out by a slavering, beast-like man.

A variety of suspects are presented to the audience but, as the

**THERE'S MONEY IN MONSTERS—GOLD IN GHOULS!
LET THE FOLKS KNOW ABOUT THIS GREAT SHOW!**

Pressbook come-ons urged theaters to order lots of advertising materials for *Werewolf in a Girls' Dormitory* (1963) and *Corridors of Blood*.

ads blatantly claim, the werewolf is the one person you would least suspect. Is it Prof. Julian Olcott (Carl Schell), the handsome young teacher who may harbor a dark secret in his shadowy past? Or is it the crippled caretaker who is handy with a switchblade knife? Perhaps it is the aging, lecherous Sir Alfred, who was having a torrid affair with the murder victim. Or is it the mysterious young man who has been hired to act as chauffeur and porter at the school?

The murderous lycanthrope is none of these. The crippled caretaker turns out to be a sexually repressed brute who falls to his death from a rooftop after attempting to assault one of the girls. A suicidal bullet through the right temple ends the torment of the lecherous Sir Alfred. His wife Sheena falls victim to an embolism, the result of an air bubble injected from the syringe wielded by a mysterious figure clad in black. Prof. Olcott emerges as the film's hero when he saves one of the girls, Brunhilde (Barbara Lass), from the inhuman clutches of seemingly innocent school director Mr. Swift (Curt Lowens).

Cursed with lycanthropy, Swift has been protected by his mistress Leonore, who uses murder and blackmail to conceal her lover's terrible secret. She also seeks the cure for the beast-like transformations and finally discovers a vaccine that will control his lycanthropic interludes. Ironically, Leonore is mauled by Swift while still in his transformed state before a slavering dog finishes her off. Swift, wielding a metal bar, makes short work of the dog. Sadly, the transformations continue and Swift is released from his curse by well-aimed bullets from Olcott's pistol in the exciting finale.

This description of the plot is considerably more

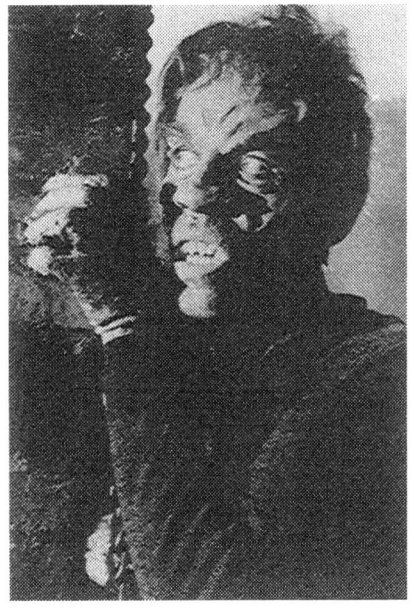

Werewolf in a Girls' Dormitory (1963): The werewolf (Curt Lowens) waits for an unsuspecting victim.

coherent than the muddled script written by "Julian Berry" (Ernesto Gastaldi) and based on his original story. Fans who do not strictly equate plot with film, however, will be able to enjoy a few high-powered shock sequences. There is an abundance of unbridled fury in the werewolf's fatal attacks on his two female victims. Subtlety, unfortunately, is not the trademark of director Paolo Heusch, who hides under the pseudonym of "Richard Benson," who generates little suspense. Typical of the film's "quiet moments" are the scenes dealing with the chauffeur, who never utters a word of dialogue. His first appearance is effectively punctuated by eerie organ music, but there's never any character exposition to heighten viewer interest. Heusch later insists on a closeup of the guy's face as his eyes shift from left to right. We already know that this is a furtive, shifty fellow, so why lay it on the line?

The director had similar problems with his 1959 SF-suspenser *La morte viene dallo spazio* (*Death Comes from Space*), released in

The slavering werewolf (Curt Lowens) seizes the hapless Brunhilde (Barbara Lass) in *Werewolf in a Girls' Dormitory* (1963).

the U.S. as *The Day the Sky Exploded*. This flick, dealing with a cataclysmic threat from deep space, was distinguished by grim black-and-white photography, sporadic bursts of violence (both natural and manmade) and a growing sense of impending doom. The austere power of such sequences vacillated with a stagey handling of quiet domestic scenes and weak romantic interludes.

Similarly, *Werewolf in a Girls' Dormitory* spares us nothing in the way of graphic physical violence, though we rarely see the depiction of positive human emotions. One can almost sense the impatience of the director, who apparently wanted to dispense with the mundane material as quickly as possible and concentrate on some good juicy mayhem. Paolo Heusch was always at his best when he attempted to portray the baser human emotions. He wisely switched to such gritty sociological studies as his dramatically convincing *Una Vita Violenta* (*One Violent Life*), released in 1962.

Beyond its well-done horrific episodes, *Werewolf in a Girls' Dormitory* features several competent performances, most notably by Curt Lowens in an effective, enigmatic portrayal of the tortured Swift. Lowens' smooth acting also enriched such major films as *Two*

Women (1961), *Tobruk* (1966), *Counterpoint* (1967) and *The Secret of Santa Vittoria* (1969). In supporting roles, impressive characterizations are achieved by Maureen O'Connor as Swift's outwardly innocent companion, Alan Collins (Luciano Pigozzi) as the guilt-ridden Sir Alfred and Barbara Lass as the vulnerable but courageous heroine. Lass acted with Karl Boehm in the caper flick *Rififi*, distributed by MGM almost simultaneously with their release of *Werewolf in a Girls' Dormitory* in the spring of 1963.

Carl Schell, the younger brother of Maria and Maximillian Schell, is well-cast physically as hero Julian Olcott, but he delivers an uninspired performance and seems bored with the whole thing. Schell proved himself to be lacking in the strength and versatility displayed by his more famous siblings. After acting in such major American films as *Escape from East Berlin* (1961) and *Freud* (1962), he settled into second-rate features, hitting rock-bottom with the awful *Quick Let's Get Married* (1964).

Werewolf in a Girls' Dormitory was widely released on a double-bill with Robert Day's *Corridors of Blood*. The latter flick, shot in 1958, had been languishing in the vaults for five years even though it boasted an excellent cast headed by Boris Karloff and Christopher Lee. Both films were ignored by many critics and panned by most others. The Heusch effort was especially ridiculed by those whose objectivity had been blurred by the lurid advertisements and bizarre (but amusing) gimmicks. Public exhibitions and private dinner parties, dressed up with horrific trappings, took place in major cities across the country.

One such invitation-only gathering was reported by New York columnist Mel Konecuff in *Motion Picture Exhibitor* on April 24, 1963. Konecuff was highly amused by the colorful doings at an "April Ghoul Luncheon" that he attended. This little feast not only provided a bit of nourishment for guests but also offered Do-It-Yourself kits which contained a vial of werewolf potion, wolf fur and a tube of witches' tears. A horse-drawn hearse arrived at the gathering, carrying a vampire-like female passenger who "refused to stay dead." A fellow in scary makeup and high hat arrived in a black limousine while a hidden record player played the lively rock 'n' roll number "The Ghoul in School." Newsreel crews and still photographers recorded the events.

Cub Records gave limited distribution to "The Ghoul in School" as a 45 RPM record which was occasionally given air play on rock music radio stations. The song was written by Marilyn Stewart and Frank Owens, with vocals by Adam Keefe. An up-and-coming nightclub performer, Keefe had gotten some TV exposure and was excited with the opportunity to do the recording. "It was as if "The Ghoul in School" was written with me in mind," Keefe stated in a 1963 interview. "The ghoul was me. I had been playing him since I was a kid."

Many other gimmicks and stunts were used at theaters where *Werewolf in a Girls' Dormitory* was booked. A typical lobby gag had a sheet-clad dummy on a stretcher bearing a sign that read "He couldn't take it!" Another stunt had a girl in a nurse's uniform wearing a placard reading "Nurse in attendance! Don't worry about shock!" In a few instances, an ambulance would be placed in front of the theater. A sign was taped on one (or both) sides of the vehicle and read: "Don't be afraid to faint! Our horror bill is packed with chills and thrills...but we're ready for an emergency! You'll enjoy fainting when you see *Werewolf in a Girls' Dormitory* and *Corridors of Blood*." Occasionally, the vehicle would cruise major streets for advance advertising purposes around town.

Obviously, promotion alone provides some mild entertainment value and may establish the proper frame of mind for fans who want to enjoy a mindless, scary horror flick. When examined objectively as a piece of horror entertainment, one may find *Werewolf in a Girls' Dormitory* no worse than many of its type.

What!

Original title: *La frusta e il corpo* (*The Whip and the Body*). A.k.a. *The Body and the Whip*. A.k.a. *Night Is the Phantom*. A.k.a. *The Way and the Body*. A.k.a. *Son of Satan*. Leone Film/Francinor, Futuramic. 77 minutes (ORT: 92 minutes). 1964 (ORD: 1963). Technicolor, Panoramic. Dir: John M. Old (Mario Bava). Prod: John Oscar (Elio Scardamagba). Writ: Julian Berry (Ernesto Gastaldi), Robert Hugo (Ugo Guerra), Martin Hardy (Luciano Martino). Ph:

Pressbook art for *What!* (1964).

David Hamilton (Ubaldo Terzano). Mus: Jim Murphy (Carlo Rustichelli). Ed: Bob King. Art Dir: Dick Grey (Ottavio Scotti). Cos: Peg Fax. Cast: Daliah Lavi, Christopher lee, Tony Kendall (Luciano Stella), Isli Oberon, Harriet White, Alan Collins (Luciano Pigozzi), Jacques Herlin, Dean Ardow (Gustavo de Nardo).

In its original form, this is one of Mario Bava's best films, certainly equal in quality to his masterful *Black Sunday* (1961). Due to extensive pruning, the U.S. release of *The Whip and the Body* (unimpressively retitled *What!*) became a generally fair chiller with some good ingredients.

A Medieval German castle becomes the scene of terror after a wayward son Kurt Menliff (Christopher Lee) returns after an absence of several years. Kurt had left after his affair with a servant girl, and his ultimate rejection of her, resulted in the girl's suicide. The vicious nobleman is an impressive figure, slim yet muscular and clad in black. He arrives late one day, riding a black stallion. Kurt's presence has been requested by his ailing father, Count Vladimir (Gustavo de Nardo), who wishes him to attend the wedding of younger brother Christian (Luciano Stella) and raven-haired Nevenka (Daliah Lavi).

The servants, as well as other family members, are far from delighted at the return of Kurt. Especially disturbed is Nevenka, whose life was nearly destroyed by Kurt, a former lover. Kurt's influence soon begins to affect Nevenka once again. Soon after her marriage, Kurt begins to make advances and concludes his seduction by giving her a sadistic flogging with a riding crop.

One night, as Kurt paces in his dimly lit quarters, he is stabbed by an unknown intruder. He manages to extract the dagger from his back and lives painfully for a few moments before the death rattle escapes his throat. Servants and family members are stunned by the murder, though none openly mourn his death. In the days that follow, Nevenka becomes convinced that Kurt's vengeful spirit still lingers in the castle. Strange figures move furtively in the night shadows while doors open seemingly by themselves. One night, Nevenka is awakened by strange noises and sees Kurt emerging from the darkness. Terrified, she buries her face in the pillow as the apparition's hand draws near. Her husband, alerted by her fearful cries, soon arrives and assures Nevenka that no one is lurking in the dark.

Christian later suggests that Nevenka may have harbored strong feelings for Kurt, despite his destructive nature. Enraged by the suggestion, Nevenka cries, "I hated him!" She flees to her bedroom as her husband becomes concerned over the growing rift between them.

Nevenka's fury is fanned higher by her suspicions that Christian has been unfaithful to her.

The nocturnal disturbances continue as Count Vladimir is awakened by the grating sound of a secret panel slowly opening to allow entry into his bedroom. The old man's eyes grow wide with horror as a knife-wielding intruder enters. Family members find his bloodied body the following morning.

One night, the vengeful "Kurt" strikes again — but it is actually Nevenka who wields the deadly dagger. She attacks her own husband, springing from the shadows and attempting to drive the deadly blade home. Still grasping the dagger, she flees down a shadowy corridor. Her husband enlists the aid of the servants in a search,

Nevenka enters the lower levels of the structure, where she hears Kurt calling out to her. An iron gate slowly creaks open, revealing the figure of Kurt, who waits behind a row of iron bars imbedded in a stone wall. They speak softly to each other while embracing — but Nevenka secretly raises a dagger that is poised to strike the middle of Kurt's back.

Christian, accompanied by a manservant (Luciano Pigozzi), arrives and sees Nevenka whispering aloud in the empty chamber. Her husband cries out as she thrusts the dagger into a figure that doesn't exist — and impales herself with the blade. As Christian takes Nevenka in his arms, she dies peacefully, ending both the reign of terror in the castle and her own torment.

What! is probably Mario Bava's most controversial film. It is certainly his most frequently banned effort, having been forbidden for a time in his native Italy as well as in other countries. In the United States, distribution was fairly limited and censors removed 15 minutes of "objectionable" material. In its original form, adult situations and elements of sadomasochism were important to the story (but were not exploited for their own sake). A closely detailed flogging of Daliah Lavi, for example, underwent various cuts in the U.S. version. This scene graphically depicted Kurt Menliff's desperate feelings of inadequacy, both sexually and socially. The desire to brutally degrade women as well as conquer them is necessary for a man who harbors doubts about his manhood and seems unable to assume socially defined responsibilities.

Kurt's excesses provoke the vengeful acts of Nevenka, who has retained a strange fascination for his dark charisma, his devilishly masculine projection and his noble position. Nevenka's love-hate attachment to Kurt, combined with a desire for wealth and power, are in conflict with the spark of decency that still dwells within her. Dwarfed by Kurt's destructive personality and haunted by memories of his cruelties, Nevenka becomes convinced that death cannot end his dominion over her. Nevenka's mind snaps and she strikes out compulsively at the men who exploited and abused her. The edited version doesn't make clear the fact that aging Count Vladimir, Nevenka's second victim, was also a former lover.

More appropriately titled *The Whip and the Body*, this Bava triumph effectively explores the conflict of power versus basic human needs and frailties. The Futuramic release, with its ruinous changes, becomes a good-looking film about creaking floorboards, strange shadows and clutching hands. Christopher Lee once remarked that he was puzzled by the extensive pruning of violent sequences and adult situations, while so much was allowed to remain in the James Bond films. Though we don't see quite enough of Lee, he delivers a nicely tuned performance as the lecherous, sadistic Kurt.

The film is Daliah Lavi's, however, as she dominates her every scene with a feverish portrayal of Nevenka. She is frightened yet ambitious, vulnerable but aggressive and always coursing with frustrated energy that is either barely suppressed or released abruptly in startling outbursts of fury. *What!* features the stand-out performance of Lavi's career. Her succeeding roles have allowed the actress to display her versatility in efforts that vary from the high drama of *Lord Jim* (1965) to the lightweight entertainment of *The Silencers* (1966), and *Those Fantastic Flying Fools* (1967).

It may be hard to believe that the intelligent script for *What!* was written by Ernesto Gastaldi, who also wrote the foolish *Werewolf in a Girls' Dormitory* (1963). Typically smooth camerawork by Ubaldo Terzano makes the most of the atmospheric sets; Bava's *What!* is also helped by an eerie Carlo Rustichelli score. American fans of period horror flicks are certain to enjoy the pleasurably creepy Gothic trappings, despite considerable damage to the film's continuity.

The Wild, Wild Planet

Original title: *I criminalli di gallasia* (*The Criminals of the Galaxy*). Mercury Film International/Southern Cross, MGM. 93 minutes. 1966. Eastman Color. Dir: Anthony Dawson (Antonio Margheriti). Prod: Margheriti, Joseph Fryd. Writ: Ivan Reiner, Renato Moretti. Ph: Richard Palton (Riccardo Pallotini). Mus: Angelo Francesco Lavagnino. Makeup: Euclide Santoli. Ed: Angle Coly (Otello Colangeli). Art Dir: Piero Poletto. Cos: Bernice Sparrow. Cast: Tony Russel, Lisa Gastoni, Massimo Serato, Franco Nero, Charles Justin (Carlo Giustini), Enzo Fiermonte, Umberto Raho, Isarco Ravaioli, Moha Tahi, Freddy Unger, Lino Desmond, Kitty Swan, Franco Ressel, Giuliano Raffaelli, Rodolfo Lodi, Victoria Zinny, Michel Lemoine.

This SF-horror is one of several features constructed from serialized adventures originally shown on Italian TV. The film is helped by a few colorful touches and a fairly novel premise, but TV-level production values finally destroy the illusion of a futuristic scenario.

In the Earth of the future, science has achieved great technological marvels. Interplanetary space flights, genetic engineering and experiments affecting the growth rate of life forms have forever changed the ways in which men live. The government's "above-the-law" trouble-shooters are forever vigilant under the leadership of Commander Mike Halstead (Tony Russel). He and his men must deal with many strange conflicts, often of a hi-tech nature. One of their most dangerous cases involves a series of kidnappings where brilliant, world-famous scientists are the victims.

The bizarre attacks occur swiftly and in broad daylight, with the perpetrators seizing their victims as they leave their offices or laboratories. The abductors disappear with their victims into waiting cars. Witnesses describe the kidnappers as bald-headed men with dark glasses and long coats.

The attempted seizure of one scientist goes awry, leaving him somehow reduced to a dwarfed state as the kidnappers flee the scene. Halstead and his men discover that the criminals possess a technological means of reducing people in size, after which the victims are stuffed into a suitcase! Their latest target is just partially reduced as circumstances failed to allow the shrinking process to be completed. Hospitalized under heavy guard, he has fallen into a coma. Halstead visits the unfortunate fellow and confers with members of a medical team who are mystified by the shrinking process. Even more startling is the recovery of the briefcase containing still-living scientists who are now the size of dolls.

Halstead's investigations lead him to brilliant scientist Nels Nurmi (Massimo Serato),whose bizarre biological experiments involve attempts to create a new type of human being. Moreover, Nurmi and his minions are involved in a conspiracy with hostile aliens from the planet Delphos. These furtive invaders need to procure vital information from scientific personnel and political leaders. Consequently, they have embarked on the series of kidnappings with the aid of the mad Nurmi, who has been promised great power as well as access to scientific secrets.

Connie Gomez (Lisa Gastoni), one of Halstead's agents, is abducted by Nurmi's followers. Halstead, his sidekick Jake (Franco Nero) and a crack unit of law enforcement officers launch an assault on the laboratory-stronghold of Nurmi in a bold attempt to rescue Connie.

The men use their hand-blasters, firing beams of destructive energy into the bald, unemotional automatons who defend Nurmi's stronghold. The raiders push deeply into the ultra-modern glass-and-steel structure and rescue Connie. Glass chambers and receptacles that contain the hideous results of biological experiments are destroyed. Nurmi himself perishes in the final conflagration.

Originally, *The Wild, Wild Planet* was done in serial form for the Italian TV series *Fantascienza (Science-Fiction)*. Many fans believe that the film provides ample evidence that television on movie screens is like mixing oil with water. Comic strip heroics aimed at juvenile audiences, inadequate sets and special effects sequences involving "tinker-toy" miniatures point to a less-than-elaborate production. There is one nightmarish closeup of the contents of the briefcase containing the shrunken scientists. Tiny chests rise and fall as normal respiration continues despite the shrunken state. There are times when the futuristic sets seem shrunken as well, with budget limitations failing to allow the scale of a George

Pal or Ray Harryhausen epic. However, there is some gaudy charm in the bizarre costumes and flame-spewing ray-guns that give the film a nice pulp flavor.

There are several good performances, the best being delivered by Tony Russel in the role of Mike Halstead. Russel, a competent actor with a muscular physique, had the distinction of prematurely gray hair much like Jeff Chandler. Actually, Russel resembles an unlikely cross between Chandler and Vince Edwards. Some of Russel's early film roles included the male leads in *War Is Hell* (1964), and the lightweight *Three Weeks of Love* (1964). The actor then turned to the European action market with such efforts as *The Secret of the Sphinx* (1964), a suspenser that cast him as a shrewd private investigator. He acted frequently on Italian TV, including roles in the serials that became the feature films entitled *The Wild, Wild Planet* and *The War Between the Planets*. Tony Russel also starred in a lively costume drama entitled *The Secret Seven* (1966), which featured Massimo Serato.

A fine character actor, Massimo Serato turns in a creepy portrayal of the mad scientist. Serato acted in a number of historical epics including *Cartouche* (1957), *David and Goliath* (1961) and *Constantine and the Cross* (1962). Some less typical efforts for Serato include a comparatively innocuous melodrama dealing with a group of card sharps—*The Gamblers* (1969), staring Don Gordon and Suzy Kendall. A quite different screen credit for the actor was *Camille 2000* (1969), an updating of the Dumas classic done as a soft-core tale of debauchery by Radley Metzger. *The Wild, Wild Planet* might be best known for featuring an early performance by Franco Nero as the second leading man. Nero also turned up in *War of the Planets, The Avenger* (1966) and John Huston's *The Bible* (1966). The actor filled roles in the spaghetti western *Django* (1966) and *The Tramplers* (1966), the latter starring former Tarzan Gordon Scott. A hard-bitten Franco Nero played a small-time hood in *The Hired Killer* (1967), starring Robert Webber. After playing a major supporting role in *Camelot* (1967), the lavish screen adaptation of the Lerner-Loewe musical, Nero settled into medium and big-budget film roles.

Antonio Margheriti went on to do adventure and horror-suspense films, including *The Young, the Evil and the Savage* (1969).

Although *The Wild, Wild Planet* remains a minor credit for director Margheriti, it gives some exposure to his "softer" side with its merger of comic strip sci-fi and horror melodrama of the Saturday matinee variety.

The Witch

Original title: *La strega in Amore (The Witch in Love)*. A.k.a. *Aura*. A.k.a. *The Strange Obsession*. Arco/G.G. Productions. 103 minutes. 1967 (ORD: 1966). B&W. Dir: Damiano Damiani. Prod. Alfredo Bini. Writ: Damiani, Ugo Libatore. Based on the novel *Aura* by Carlos Fuentes. Ph: Leonida Barboni. Mus: Luís Enrique Bacalov. Ed: Nino Bargli. Art Dir: Luigi Scaccianoce. Cos: Pier Luigi Pizzi. Chor: Robert Curtis. Cast: Richard Johnson, Rosanna Schiaffino, Sarah Ferrati, Gian Maria Volonté, Margherita Guzzenati.

Horror films sometimes place equal value on their horrific elements and subtext, presenting a philosophical statement to their audiences while trying to entertain people with a tale of terror. Roman Polanski's *Repulsion* (1965) created a chilling psychological horror tale that also made a valid statement about sexual morbidity. *Seance on a Wet Afternoon* (1964), with its psychological horrors, taught us that the crippling effects of emptiness could have terrifying consequences. Ingmar Bergman's *Hour of the Wolf* (1968) entered the mind of a tortured killer and portrayed truly frightening paranoid fantasies that had festered since a nightmarish childhood. Unfortunately, Damiano Damiani's *The Witch* is quite a different matter. Despite a good cast and an interesting premise, the film emerges as a pretentious, underdeveloped bore.

This "thriller" takes place in modern-day Italy where a writer named Sergio (Richard Johnson) is hired by a middle-aged widow (Sarah Ferrati) to organize the memoirs and curiously erotic writings of her late husband, a military man. Sergio accepts the work of historian and spends much of his time in the elegant old mansion of Consuelo (Ferrati). The woman's fetching young daughter Aura (Rosanna Schiaffino) soon works a spell on Sergio with her dark charisma and great beauty.

As Sergio's attachment to Aura grows stronger, he becomes quite hostile to the second male resident of the palatial home — Fabrizio (Gian Maria Volonté), another historian. Fabrizio, also trapped by his love for Aura, seems unable to leave the mansion. The situation becomes increasingly electric as Sergio is drawn into a claustrophobic existence laced with dark fantasies that the two women encourage.

Consuelo and her daughter are either unable or unwilling to expel Fabrizio from their private little world, and Sergio's hostility turns to open violence. He murders Fabrizio and is aided by the two women in disposing of the corpse. The full horror of his actions become more than Sergio can bear. As he pursues the seductive Aura throughout the mansion, the tormented "love slave" demands the truth about her furtive life and the terrible acts that she and her mother have manipulated him into perpetrating. As he seizes the girl, who has her back to him, the enraged man whirls her about — only to face the mother, Consuelo. The strange mystical link between the two women is as chilling and unearthly as the beauty of Aura.

Sergio realizes that Consuelo has hired yet another historian to replace him. He also realizes, that he will soon suffer the fate of the doomed Fabrizio. Sergio's instinct for self-preservation, combined with his loathing for the evil entities, force him to take drastic measures. He seizes Aura and binds her with strong cord before forcing her into the courtyard where he douses her with a flammable liquid. The woman, stunned by the sudden and violent rebellion, watches in horror as the match is struck. Encircled by flames, the untouched face of Aura is transformed into that of Consuelo's before fire consumes the witch completely.

This interesting, potentially frightening scenario is padded with snatches of boring dialogue and long stretches in which nothing of any consequence occurs. The film was attacked in some quarters as a vigorously sexist diatribe that presented women as cold-hearted creatures who feed upon the passions of men and destroy their lives completely. Certainly, such a strong statement against women wouldn't consciously be made by director and co-author Damiano Damiani, who is well known for his leftist sympathies. The script is based on *Aura*, the 1962 novel written by Mexican author Carlos Fuentes (born 1928). Rather than a message of male resistance and unity, Damiani tries (unsuccessfully) to emphasize the dangers of narcissism, unbridled passion and the resultant loss of humanity that destroys innocent lives.

A few competent cast members deliver substandard performances with the problem being miscasting in the case of Rosanna Schiaffino. The role of Aura requires the unearthly screen presence and exotic beauty of Barbara Steele, who would have been perfect as the female lead. Schiaffino usually does well as a heroine who is sensual yet possesses a core of sensitivity. She seems much too fragile for her role in *The Witch*. The actress (born in Genoa in 1939) delivered fine performances in more suitable roles provided by such films as *Blood on His Sword* (1961), *Two Weeks in Another Town* (1962) and *The Rover* (1967).

Richard Johnson (born 1927) is a versatile actor whose roles have ranged from the portrayal of Bulldog Drummond in *Deadlier Than the Male* (1967) to that of Creon in *Oedipus the King* (1968). Distinguished in both film and theater, he first gained attention for his exceptional performances as part of the Royal Shakespeare Company. Johnson is always at his best when portraying men of authority whose aggressive tendencies are tempered by compassion. He played such a character in a very good horror film, Robert Wise's *The Haunting* (1963). The role of Sergio, however, requires Johnson to do little more than scowl, furrow his brow and exhibit intermittent outbursts of uncontrolled rage. We see something of the forceful Johnson but the role doesn't permit him to deliver a polished performance.

Gian Maria Volonté, in contrast, is annoyingly passive in the role of Fabrizio. It was apparently intended for the viewer to see a man, drained of energy, who has accepted his fate and his inevitable end. Volonté was quite adept at portraying sullen, unpredictable characters who vacillated between languorous moments of self-examination and sudden outbursts of unbridled fury. The late actor (1933-1996) brilliant delineated such a role as the crazed, self-destructive Indio in Sergio Leone's *For a Few Dollars More* (1967). Neither Volonté or Johnson are allowed to portray multi-faceted characters in *The Witch* and subsequently, they only evoke occasional interest.

Damiano Damiani (born 1922), who began directing features

in the mid 1950s, soon concentrated on action movies with political overtones, such as *A Bullet for the General* (1967) and *Confessions of a Police Captain* (1971) with Martin Balsam. A sincere attempt at a tale of horror imbued with moral significance, *The Witch* remains a minor aspect of Damiani's career.

The Witch's Curse

Original title: *Maciste all'inferno* (*Maciste in Hell*). A.k.a. *The Witches Curse*. Cinematografica Italiana, Medallion. 1964 (ORD: 1961). Eastman Color, CinemaScope. 78 minutes (ORT: 90 minutes). Dir: Riccardo Freda. Prod: Luigi Carpentieri, Ermanno Donati. Ph: Riccardo Pallotini. Writ: Oreste Biancoli, Pierotti, Ennio de Concini, Eddie H. Given (Ermanno Donati). Original story: Donati (loosely based on the silent epic *Maciste in Hell* [1927]). Spfx.: Serge Urbislaglia. Mus: Carlo Franci. Ed: Ornella Micheli. Cast: Kirk Morris, Hélène Chanel, Andrea Bosić, Vira Silenti, John Karlsen, Mauro Donatella, Angelo Zanolli, Gina Mascetti, Charles Fawcett, Neil Robinson, Antonio Cianci, John Francis Lane.

Our old friend Maciste found his way into some unexpected locales during his wanderings. This flick places the quixotic crusader in 17th century Scotland, where he must combat a deadly curse invoked by a witch some 100 years earlier. The juxtaposition of sword-and-sandal fantasy with horror melodrama is never handled smoothly by director Riccardo Freda. Good moments are few and far between.

The story begins in a Scottish village during the 1500s. Angry peasants and townfolk gather in the village square to await the execution of a witch. Martha Gunt (Hélène Chanel) has been sentenced to death by a powerful local magistrate named Parris (Andrea Bosić)—a man who loved Martha during their youth. The woman cries out bitterly against what she sees as a terrible injustice made more painful since it is being perpetrated by a former lover. She places her dying curse upon the village. With that, the executioner lays a torch to the massive pile of wood encircling the woman.

A century has passed since the burning of Martha Gunt, and

the woman's curse seems to have remained potent. Famine, disease and fatal accidents have been attributed to her undead influence. The villagers' fears are fanned higher by the arrival of an aristocratic young couple who inhabit the large house once belonging to the Gunt family. The young bride (Vira Silenti) is a direct descendant of Martha. Word of their arrival spreads terror throughout a public inn. The men of the village quickly arm themselves and launch an assault on the Gunt estate. Although the bridegroom possesses a skill at swordplay, he is soon overwhelmed. Burly peasants armed with hoes and rakes make fierce opponents. The young man is knocked unconscious by a powerful blow to the head.

The young woman seems about to suffer the fiery fate of her ancestor when a lone champion arrives on a black charger. It is Maciste (Kirk Morris), defender of the oppressed, who quickly dismounts and enters the decrepit mansion. The hard-bitten villagers are strong, but their strength cannot match that of Maciste. The confrontation with the toga-clad hero concludes with the bruised and battered peasants accepting their defeat.

As peace is restored, the history of the village is explained to Maciste by the burgemeister (John Karlsen), who asks the hero's help in lifting the deadly curse. Maciste must confront the witch and convince her to bring the legacy of horror to an end. In order to do that, Maciste must enter Hell and seek out her spirit. The point of entry into the netherworld is an old tree that has grown over the spot where the witch was burned. Maciste approaches the tree and grasps its trunk. His muscles bulge as he uproots it and casts it aside. A fiery glow emanates from deep within a tunnel located beneath the tree — a tunnel that leads to a vast pit imprisoning tormented souls.

Maciste descends the sloping pathway until he reaches a flat stone surface. Looking down from a rocky precipice, he is able to view the tortures of the damned. Punishment is brutal and eternal for multitudes of condemned souls. Maciste is moved by the plight of a tattered, gray-bearded fellow who must bear the agonizing weight of a huge boulder upon his shoulders. The muscle-bound crusader enters the pit, seizes the boulder and heaves it onto a rocky shelf. Maciste expresses his desire to help all those in torment, but the old man stoically states that it is too late to help them. Out of

Pressbook art for *The Witch's Curse* (1964).

gratitude, the graybeard tells Maciste he must travel through a series of tunnels, dark passageways and caves to reach Martha Gunt.

Maciste's journey is suddenly interrupted by an agonized cry from atop a rocky ledge. An unfortunate fellow, chained to a flat rock, is being attacked by a voracious eagle. Maciste rushes to the top and seizes the bird of prey, hurling it against a stone wall.

After breaking the victim's heavy chains, Maciste is told that Martha is quite near. As Maciste continues his journey, he hears the man cry out once more. The doomed soul has been magically bound by chains once again, as another eagle attacks him. Maciste begins rushing to his aid a second time, but the man insists that Maciste continue on his quest. "Can you kill a thousand eagles?" he plaintively cries. "When my entrails are eaten, I will become whole again!" His horrendous fate is to be eaten alive for all eternity. Maciste realizes that this is yet another soul whose fate has long been sealed.

There are other physical obstacles for Maciste to overcome, the most difficult being a pair of enormous iron gates that are extremely hot to the touch. When the gates burst into flames, Maciste seizes two large rocks — one in each hand — and begins striking the pieces of stone against the gates. With Maciste's massive strength behind each blow, the stones serve the function of metal hammerheads. The gates are soon forced open, and the flames suddenly extinguish themselves. Though his strength seems to be waning, the stalwart crusader presses on. Shortly after his departure, the gates slam shut and once more erupt into flame.

Unknown to Maciste, his progress has been observed by Martha and Parris, who now share a strange kinship in death. As Maciste approaches, the two spirits discuss a course of action in confronting the intruder. Martha uses her powers to transform herself into the young, beautiful girl that she once was. Parris is suddenly aroused by the youthful image of Martha and attempts to embrace her. She pushes him away, regarding his amorous intentions as nothing more than foolish.

The revitalized Martha is a striking figure — slender, blond and clad in a flowing robe. She softly calls out Maciste's name and quietly comes to his side. This is no hideous wraith that Maciste faces, but he is not deceived by the superficial beauty. Martha assures him that she is not the monster portrayed in the village legend. She gently takes his hands in hers and, by casting a white magic spell, heals the burns that he suffered while opening the fiery gates.

Perhaps a spark of decency does indeed exist within Martha Gunt. Maciste softens his defensive posture as the woman embraces him. The curse can easily be lifted, claims Martha, by a gentle kiss. Their lips meet for one tender moment — before Martha crumbles into dust. Maciste is stunned by Martha's sacrifice as he ponders the soft robes that still rest in his arms. The startled Parris cries out in horror as he rushes forward and tumbles down a slope. An avalanche soon follows as the black-robed villain is buried under heavy rocks.

With the curse lifted, Maciste makes his way back to the surface world without being further assailed by dark forces. The Burgemeister is pleased that he and his people may once more lead peaceful lives, free of supernatural threats.

The final moments of *The Witch's Curse* provide a hint of bittersweet romance between Maciste and the rejuvenated Martha. If such a relationship had been developed as a subplot, then the film might have created the same sense of tragedy seen previously in Chano Urueta's 1957 thriller *La bruja* (*The Witch*). The latter flick has a disfigured necromancer being surgically transformed into a murderous beauty by a mad doctor. Urueta's witch carries out a campaign of vengeance against the surgeon's professional opponents until her love for a decent young man stirs her conscience.

The Witch's Curse occasionally contrasts the monstrous acts of "normal" men with the vengeful bitterness of tormented outcast Martha Gunt. Far more often, the script borrows ideas from other films or works of fiction. Several plot elements, for example, are taken directly from Mario Bava's *Black Sunday* (1961), with the condemned witch cursing a village while an innocent descendant suffers persecution because of her ancestor's deeds. Beyond the influence of the Bava and Urueta efforts, *The Witch's Curse* owes something to the classic horror story "The Ash-Tree," which has a huge, haunted tree growing over the spot where a witch was once burned. Ironically, the Freda film owes little to the effort that supposedly inspired it — Guido Brignone's 1927 epic *Maciste in Hell*. Freda's conception of hell doesn't conform to any mythos but becomes a generic pit of eternal punishment for those who violate Christian or pagan ethics.

One never quite accepts the intrusion of a toga-clad pagan hero into a 17th-century Scottish community. Also implausible is the fact that Maciste is immediately accepted by the Burgemeister, who would more likely see this interloper from the past as a minion of Satan.

A few striking images are provided by Freda in the midst of this disappointing film. The viewer often feels dwarfed by the cathedral-high stone ceilings and dark, cavernous spaces of the netherworld that even make an imposing figure like Maciste seem small in contrast. Probably the best sequence is Maciste's first look at the pit. The camera slowly pans over the nightmarish landscape inhabited by condemned souls, each of whom suffers a unique form of punishment. Such sequences benefit from the striking photography of Riccardo Pallotini, whose visual skills enriched other B-chillers (including Mel Welles' *Lady Frankenstein* [1971]).

One knows that a film is in trouble when the best thing about it is the camerawork. Even Pallotini's fine work is lessened in impact by garish color. This is a film that cries out for the stark images of black-and-white photography. On a technical note, there are other failings such as the sloppy editing that is definitely a cut below the average. Another problem is the intrusion of Italian architecture into what is supposedly a Scottish setting. Serge Urbislaglia's special effects work is fair at best. The savage eagle is a bit stiff, but the scene is pleasurably grisly as we are allowed to see glimpses of entrails being eaten. However, the worst single illusion has Kirk Morris "leaping" across a chasm; he sails limply through the air, obviously from a cable.

Though well-cast physically as Maciste, Morris seems unable to generate much in the way of emotion. Nevertheless, he continued to portray muscle-bound heroes who often found themselves in bizarre circumstances. One of his Maciste efforts, in *Atlas Against the Czar* (1964), has him aiding Russian peasants. *Hercules, Samson and Ulysses* (1966) finds Morris (as Hercules) shipwrecked in Judea with several Greek companions. They soon encounter Samson and Delilah in a silly story that merges Biblical adventure with Greek mythology. Morris also starred in *Colossus and the Headhunters* (1961), *Triumph of the Son of Hercules* (1962), *Conquerer of Atlantis* (1963), *Samson vs. the Giant King* (1963) and *Hercules of the Desert*

(1964). He finally spoofed his own image in *Maciste Against Hercules in the Vale of Woe* (1967), the story of two promoters who travel back in time to arrange a wrestling match between Maciste and Hercules. Though intended as a parody, the film wasn't as funny as some of the efforts that were played straight.

Remaining cast members of *The Witch's Curse* are merely adequate. Those whose credits are at least of peripheral interest to horror fans include Hélène Chanel, who acted in Riccardo Freda's *Samson and the 7 Miracles of the World* (1963). Second female lead Vira Silenti acted in such epics as *Son of Samson* (1962) and the biblical tale *Joseph and His Brothers* (1962) as well as a previous Maciste flick, *Atlas in the Land of the Cyclops* (1963). Trivia buffs will note the appearance of British film journalist John Francis Lane. His admiration of Italian culture and friendly ties with Italian filmmakers led to his cameo role as a coach driver.

Director Riccardo Freda soon redeemed himself with the enjoyable though hokey *The Horrible Dr. Hichcock* (1964). Several other period chillers followed, with competent actors, elaborate sets and sensible plotting lifting the level of quality. Despite some horrific moments, *The Witch's Curse* features a dark inferno that is fed only by erratic fire.

The Young, the Evil and the Savage

Original title: *Nude...si, muore* (*Nude...Yes Dead*). Super International/BGA, AIP. 82 minutes. 1969 (ORD: 1968). Perfect Color, Cromoscope. Dir: Anthony Dawson (Antonio Margheriti). Pro: Lawrence Woolner, Giuseppe De Blasio. Writ: Dawson, Frank Bottar (Franco Bottari). Ph: Frank (Fausto) Zuccoli. Mus: Carlo Savina. Cast: Michael Rennie, Mark Damon, Eleanora Brown, Franco De Rosa, Vivian Stapleton, Esther Masing, Valentino Macci, Aldo De Carellis, Sylvia Dionisio, Kathleen Parker, Paola Natale, Malisa Longo, Umberto Papiri, John Hawkwood. MPAA rating: R,

American-International released this third-rate horrer-suspenser as the bottom half of a double-bill with a teen gang thriller, *Born Wild*, early in 1969. Beyond two good performances and some impressive camerawork, *The Young, the Evil and the Savage* has little to offer. When one considers director Antonio Margheriti's skill at endowing ordinary material with great atmosphere and excitement value, this thriller comes off as especially dull and unimaginative.

Yet another European school for girls has become the setting for a series of murders — this time by strangulation. The mayhem begins when the body of a blond student is found nude in the trunk of a car. When another girl is found strangled on school grounds, the shrewd, steely-eyed Inspector Duran (Michael Rennie) comes upon the scene. There are the predictable handful of suspects, including a creepy, sexually repressed gardener named De Brazzi (Luciano Pigozzi) and a handsome, rather shiftless fellow named Richard (Mark Damon).

Lucille (Eleanora Brown), a wealthy student, has several near-fatal encounters with the mystery killer. She nearly falls victim to the murderer in a shower stall, but one of her sister students is claimed by the maniac instead. Lucille is aided by her roommate, a perky, Nancy Drew type named Jill (Sally Smith), who turns to amateur sleuthing. Jill seems to have developed a crush on Insp. Duran, who treats the girl kindly but with a patronizing attitude. Lucille feels drawn to Richard, despite his reputation as a young rake.

At first, Inspector Duran focuses his investigation on the strange gardener, De Brazzi. When the gardener is found strangled, however Duran comes up with another suspect: Richard.

There is an open confrontation with the murderer on a quiet night as Lucille and Jill venture out for a furtive meeting with Richard, who supposedly possesses information about the reign of terror afflicting the school and wishes to speak with them in the administration building. The two girls spy Richard peering through a window in the building and innocently enter to keep their engagement. As they arrive in the dimly lit office, they see Richard collapse — the victim of a gunshot wound. The killer reveals himself to be a distant cousin of Lucille's, a madman who disguised himself as a female administrator.

The murderer, wielding a pistol, prepares to open fire on the girls. Though wounded, Richard is able to intervene by knocking a desk-lamp to the floor. With the room plunged into darkness, the killer begins firing blindly until his vision adjusts to the dark. As he draws a bead on one victim, another shot rings out, and the murderous cousin falls dead. Duran stands in the office doorway, a smoking pistol in his hand.

The cousin, motivated by greed, embarked upon a series of murders to conceal the identity of the only necessary victim — Lucille. With the girl murdered, the cousin would have an excellent chance of seizing the family fortune. His plan has been foiled by the courage of the inspector, the plucky Lucille and her loyal friends. Richard recovers from his wound and is soon able to share a tender moment with Lucille.

Mark Damon and Eleanora Brown make an attractive couple, bringing a quiet charm and admirable restraint to their characters. There is a fair amount of tension in the film's final moments as the killer attempts to bring his ruthless plan for personal gain to a violent conclusion. This scene, in the darkened office beset by gunfire, is well photographed by Fausto Zuccoli. Some of the tension is lessened by the widescreen image in a story that would have been more effective if shot in 35mm.

There is little else of value in *The Young, the Evil and the Savage*, with its clichéd characters, predictable plot twists and largely unremarkable performances. The saddest thing about the film is the uninspired performance of Michael Rennie, who obviously hated the role. Rennie (1909–1971), a tall, slender and often monotone actor, filled leading man roles in many British and American films. He was best known as Klaatu, the benevolent alien of Robert Wise's *The Day the Earth Stood Still* (1951). The dignified strength that Rennie brought to the role was also expressed in his portrayal of Peter in *The Robe* (1953) and *Demetrius and the Gladiators* (1955).

A dark suspenser entitled *Tower of Terror* (1941) was Rennie's first horror credit, though he became a familiar face in the SF-horror field with his portrayal of Lord John Ruxton in Irwin Allen's remake of *The Lost World* (1960). Rennie's other SF-horror credits include *Cyborg 2087* (1966), George Pal's *The Power* (1968) and the Italo-Spanish *Assignment Terror* (1969). The latter film cast the actor as an alien who fabricates legendary monsters as part of a plan to conquer the world. *The Young, the Evil and the Savage* can only be remembered as the film that features Rennie's worst performance.

Appendix: Chronological List of Films

1960

Caltiki, the Immortal Monster

1961

Black Sunday
Ghosts of Rome
Goliath and the Dragon
Slaughter of the Vampires
The Thief of Baghdad
Uncle Was a Vampire

1962

The Vampire and the Ballerina

1963

Atlas in the Land of the Cyclops
Atom Age Vampire
Goliath Against the Giants
Hercules and the Captive Women
Mill of the Stone Women
The Minotaur, Wild Beast of Crete
Sex Party
Terror in the Crypt
Werewolf in a Girls' Dormitory

1964

Black Sabbath
Castle of Blood
Castle of the Living Dead
The Evil Eye
The Giant of Metropolis
Goliath and the Vampires
Hercules in the Haunted World
The Horrible Dr. Hichcock
The Last Man on Earth
The Long Hair of Death
My Friend Jekyll
The Planets Against Us
The Playgirls and the Vampire
The Vampire of the Opera
What!
The Witch's Curse

1965

Blood and Black Lace
The Ghost
Hercules Against the Moon Men
Horror Castle
Planet of the Vampires
The Possessed
Snow Devils
War of the Zombies

1966

An Angel for Satan
The Bloody Pit of Horror
The Embalmer
Kill Baby Kill
Libido
Nightmare Castle
She Beast
Terror-Creatures from the Grave
The Wild, Wild Planet

1967

The Murder Clinic
The Witch

1968

Fangs of the Living Dead
Satanik

1969

Assignment Terror
Ghosts, Italian Style
Hatchet for a Honeymoon
Isabel, Duchess of the Devils
Spirits of the Dead
The Unnaturals
Venus in Furs
The Young, the Evil and the Savage

Bibliography

Armstrong, Richard, and Armstrong, Mary. *The Movie List Book.* Jefferson, N.C.: McFarland, 1990.
Bowden, Liz-Anne. *The Oxford Companion to Film.* New York: Oxford University Press, 1976.
Cameron, Ian. *Adventures in the Movies.* Roxby, 1973.
Flynn, John L. *Cinematic Vampires.* Jefferson, N.C.: McFarland, 1992.
Hardy, Phil. *The Encyclopedia of Horror.* New York: Harper and Row, 1986.
Jones, Stephen. *The Illustrated Vampire Movie Guide.* Titan, 1993.
Katz, Ephraim. *The Film Encyclopedia.* New York: Putnam, 1979.
Lloyd, Ann, and Fuller, Graham. *The Illustrated Who's Who of the Cinema.* Portland House, 1987.
Marrero, Robert. *Vampire Movies.* Fantasma, 1994.
Nicholls, Peter, ed. *The Science-Fiction Encyclopedia.* Roxby, 1979.
Parish, James Robert. *Film Actors Guide: Western Europe.* Metuchen, N.J.: Scarecrow, 1977.
Pitts, Michael. *Horror Film Stars.* Jefferson, N.C.: McFarland, 1981.
Tomlinson, Doug. *Actors on Acting for the Screen.* New York: Garland, 1994.

Magazines:

Castle of Frankenstein, #1-#10 (1960-1969)
Famous Monsters of Filmland, #31-#56 (1964-1969)
Monster World, #1-#10 (1964-1969)
Scary Monsters, #18, #20 (1996)
Spacemen, #4 (July 1962)

Index

Abbott and Costello Go to Mars 78
Un' accetta per la luna di miele see *Hatchet for a Honeymoon*
Ackerman, Forrest J 94, 95, 137
Acquari, Giuseppe 7, 202
Addessi, Giovanni 55
Addobbati, Giuseppe 163, 217–219
Adios Sabata 132
Adorf, Mario 82–84
The Adventures of Martin Eden 143
Agar, John 77, 170
Agent 383: Passport to Hell 119, 131
Agliani, Giorgio 154
The Agony and the Ecstasy 20
Alfonsi, Lydia 22, 25
The Alien Within 93
All the King's Men 97
Allen, Irwin 253
Allied Artists (AA) 47, 113, 124, 131, 163, 217
Alone Against Rome 130, 180
Alonso, Chelo 13
Alton, Laura 109, 110
Amadio, Silvio 154, 158
Amadoro, Ugo 14, 105, 109, 223
Amanti d'oltretomba see *Nightmare Castle*
Amber(t), Audrey see Ambessi, Adrianna
Ambessi, Adrianna 75, 78, 202
Ambrosiana Cinematografica 98
Amendola, Mario 131
American-International Pictures (AIP) 9, 12, 22, 23, 30, 31, 37, 38, 61, 67, 68, 71, 74, 79, 85, 88, 96, 98, 102, 114, 132, 137, 142, 146, 150, 160, 167, 171, 172, 176, 184, 189, 194, 202, 204, 219, 220, 223, 227, 251
The Americano 162
Amidei, Sergio 85
Among Vultures 153
L'amore primitivo see *Primitive Love*
Anchisi, Piero 179
Anders, Helga 213
Andersen, Susi/Susy 22, 27, 223, 224
Anderson, Howard A. 220
Anderson, Reginald Price 80
André, Gaby 97
Andronica, Enzo 131, 132
Angel, Nick see Angelini, Nando
An Angel for Satan 7–9, 256
Angelini, Nando 43
Un angelo per Satana see *An Angel for Satan*
Angels of Darkness 8
The Angry Red Planet 170
Anton, Edoardo 210
Any Wife's Enemy 162
Anzio 31, 147
Apache Gold 153
The Ape Woman 162
Appointment in Honduras 189
Arabella 147
Aranda, Angel 95, 166, 167, 172
Arcalli, Franco 194
Arco 242
Arden, Mary 39
Ardes, Robert see Ardis, Robert
Ardis, Robert 43, 198
Ardisson, George see Ardisson, Giorgio
Ardisson, Giorgio 114, 115, 119, 147, 149
Arditi, Mario 177

Index

Ardow, Dean *see* de Nardo, Gustavo
Arnold, Frank 43
Arrivederci Roma 211
Artists and Models 78
Assignment Outer Space 192, 253
Assignment Terror 9–12, 255
El ataque de los muertos sin ojos see *Tomb of the Blind Dead*
Athena 209
Atlas Against the Cyclops see *Atlas in the Land of the Cyclops*
Atlas Against the Czar 185, 250
Atlas in the Land of the Cyclops 13, 14, 251, 255
Atom Age Vampire 14–22, 38, 70, 157, 255
Attack of the Blind Dead see *Tomb of the Blind Dead*
Attack of the Crab Monsters 189
Attack of the Robots 221
Attenborough, Julian 229
Aura see *The Witch*
The Avenger 94, 241
The Awful Dr. Orloff 221
An Axe for a Honeymoon see *Hatchet for a Honeymoon*

Bacalov, Luís Enrique 82, 242
Bachelor of Hearts 38
The Bad and the Beautiful 172
Baggarrini, Francesco 68
Baker, Roy Ward 204
Balbo, Ennio 200
Baldini, Renato 131, 132, 192
Baldwin, Peter 80, 179–181
Ballanti, Adriana 88
Balsam, Martin 245
Balstracci, Angelo 215, 217
Baracco, Adriano 82
Baratto, Luisa 43, 44
Barbarella 162
Barbone, Leonida 179, 181, 242
Barboni, Enzo 163
Bardot, Brigitte 194, 196
Bargli, Nino 242
Barilla, Giuseppe 39
Barilla, Joe *see* Barilla, Giuseppe
Barker, Lex 197
Baron, Susanne 194
Barrett, Louise *see* Baratto, Luisa
Barrymore, John Drew 153, 184, 223, 227, 228
Bartok, Eva 39, 42

Batista, Henry 220
Battaglia, Rik 154, 157, 163, 165, 166
Battistella, Antonio 205
Battle of the Worlds 176, 192
Bava, Mario 1, 7, 9, 14, 20, 22, 30, 31, 36–39, 42, 43, 47, 53–55, 60, 71, 73, 75, 96, 97, 102, 104, 109, 114, 115, 118, 119, 132, 133, 136, 137, 143, 144, 147, 149, 150, 152, 154, 160, 166, 167, 172, 176, 180–182, 185, 187, 190, 198, 201, 205, 209, 219, 223, 234, 236, 238, 249
Baxter, Les 22, 31, 37, 71, 74, 97
Bazzoni, Luigi 179
BCR Produzione 179
Beach Party Italian Style 8
Beast with a Million Eyes 175
Bebo's Girl 88
Beebe, Ford 186
Bell, Edward 200
Belty, Frank *see* Vicario, Marco
Benda, Georges 205
Bengell, Norma 166, 167, 172
Bennet, Carol 80
Benussi, Eufemia 43, 102
Benussi, Femi *see* Benussi, Eufemia
Benvenuti, Jolande 82
Benvenuti, Leo 82
Berger, William 158, 159
Bergman, Ingmar 242
Berman, Francis 229
Bernar, Francisco 95
Bernardi, Nerio 154
Berry, Jul(i/y)an *see* Gastaldi, Ernesto
Berta, Roberto 14, 17, 21
Berti, Aldo 7
Berti, Marina 7
Beswick, Martine 132
Betti, Laura 102, 103
Bettoia, Franca *see* Bettoja, Franca
Bettoja, Franca 137, 140
Between Heaven and Hell 30
Bevilacqua, Alberto 22, 166
Beyond the Law 185, 191
BGA 251
Bianchi, Tino 31
Biancini, Liliana 7
Biancoli, Oreste 13, 245
The Bible...in the Beginning 241
Biddlewood, Clement 194
Big Deal on Madonna Street 88
The Big Gundown 185
Bigazzi, Gianpaolo 152
Bilbao, Fernando 75

Index

Billiteri, Salvatore 22
Bindi, Clara 31
Bini, Alfredo 242
Black Angel see *Venus in Furs*
Black Christmas see *Black Sunday*
The Black Duke 43
Black Friday 208
Black Magic 75
Black Sabbath 22–31, 37, 75, 102, 136, 154, 219, 255
The Black Stallion Returns 201
Black Sunday 7, 9, 30, 31–38, 43, 54, 55, 113, 115, 149, 152, 165, 190, 201, 209, 236, 249, 255
The Black Torment 108, 217
The Blade in the Body see *The Murder Clinic*
Blanc, Erika 133, 134, 137
Blood and Black Lace 1, 37, 39–43, 104, 136, 143, 150, 160, 209, 256
Blood and Roses 202
Blood Bath 104, 153
Blood Beast from Outer Space 74
Blood Beast Terror 124
Blood Brides see *Hatchet for a Honeymoon*
Blood Feud 147
Blood for a Silver Dollar 153
Blood Money 77
Blood on His Sword 244
The Blood-Spattered Bride 204
The Bloody Pit of Horror 43–47, 162, 256
Bloody Silk see *Blood and Black Lace*
Blutige Seide see *Blood and Black Lace*
The Bob Mathias Story 157
Boccianti, Alberto 13
The Body and the Whip see *What!*
The Body Stealers 124
Boehm, Herbert 152
Bohr, Robert see Valeri, Bruno
Il boia scarlatto see *The Bloody Pit of Horror*
Boido, Rico 166
Bolmengen, Rudolphe 154
Bolognesi, Bruno 215, 217
Bolognini, Manolo 179
Borden, James 125
Borelli, Rosario 205
Borgese, Salvatore 131, 132
Born Wild 251
Boschero, Dominique 145, 146, 213
Bosić, Andrea 245
Botta, Leonardo 177

Bottar, Frank see Bottari, Franco
Bottari, Franco 251
The Bounty Hunters 132
Bradley, Wilbert 192
The Brain from Planet Arous 170
Brandi, Walter 43, 44, 177, 179, 190, 191, 200, 201, 215, 216
Brando, Marlon 94
Brandt, Walter see Brandi, Walter
Brazzi, Rossano 9, 94
Brest, Harry 39
Brice, Pierre 152, 153
Brignone, Guido 249
Brignone, Lilla 85
Brochero, Eduardo M. 181
Brotto, Alba 68
Brown, Charles see Di Palma, Carlo
Brown, Eleanora 251–253
Brown, Maureen Litgard 68, 70
La bruja 249
Brunelli, Ugo 177, 179, 190, 191, 217
Buazzelli, Tino 85
Buchanan, Robert 71, 72
A Bucket of Blood 70
Bufi-Landi, Aldo 13
A Bullet for the General 245
El buque maldito see *Horror of the Zombies*
Burton, Richard 46, 124
Butterfield 8 26
Byron, Michael see Reeves, Michael

The Cabinet of Dr. Caligari 154
Cabiria 2
Caesar the Conqueror 43, 146
Cahn, Edward L. 170
Caiano, Carlo 163
Caiano, Mario 163, 166
Call Me Bwana 78
Callegari, Paolo Gian 154
Caltiki, il mostro immortale see *Caltiki, the Immortal Monster*
Caltiki, the Immortal Monster 3, 47–54, 123, 255
Calvo, Armando 181, 183
Camaso, Claudio 213
Camelot 241
Camille 2000 241
Campos, José 202
Canale, Gianna Maria 98, 99, 101
Il cappotto see *The Overcoat*
La cara del terror see *Face of Terror*
Carey, John 147

Carlini, Carlo 109, 112
"Carmilla" 78, 202, 203, 205
Carpentieri, Luigi 13, 80, 120, 245
Carpet of Horror 214
Carr, Patricia 158
Carradine, John 30, 94, 183
Carrel, Dany 152
Carroll, Barbara 95
Cartouche 241
Carusa, Elmo 68
Casanova '70 94
Casaravilla, Carlos 75
Casetti, Tiziana 154
Castellani, Renato 82, 83
Castilla Cinematografica 166
Castle, William 70, 102, 130, 186
Castle of Blood 1, 9, 27, 38, 55–61, 115, 123, 125, 129, 133, 148–150, 152, 165, 183, 201, 215, 255
"Castle of Frankenstein" 30, 67, 257
Castle of the Living Dead 60–68, 180, 188, 255
Cavedon, Giorgio 131
Cavelli, Catla 217
CCC 152
Cecci, Andrea 31, 32
Cei Incom 209
Celano, Guido 98
Centro 88
The Centurion 176
Cevenini, Alberto 166, 167
Chabrol, Claude 185
Chamarat, Georges 205, 206
Chanel, Hélène 245, 251
Chaney, Lon, Jr. 7, 12
Cheaper by the Dozen 11
Chekhov, Anton 22
Chianetta, Maria 145
Chicago Syndicate 162
Chimenz, Alberto 172
China Doll 158
Christianson, Al 120
Christie, Donna *see* Micheli, Ornella
Christina, Katia 194
Christmas, Robert *see* Natale, Roberto
Ciampaglia, Marissa 215
Cianci, Antonio 245
Ciani, Sergio 105, 106, 108
Cinecittà Studios 88
Cinegai 147
Cinematografica Italiana 245
Cineproduzioni Associati 95, 219
Cinesecolo 131

Cinque tombe per un medium see *Terror-Creatures from the Grave*
Cinquini, Renato 163
Ciuffino, Sabatino 88
Clair, Jany 105, 106, 172, 176
Cleopatra 70
Clerici, Fabrizio 194
Clift, Lawrence 163–165
Clouzot, Henri-Georges 81
The Cobra 79
Cobra Films 75, 79
Cocinor 194
Code Name: Wild Geese 215
Coffin of Terror see *Castle of Blood*
Coffins of Terror see *Terror-Creatures from the Grave*
Colangeli, Otello 125, 192, 239
Colli, Franco Delli 137
Colli, Ombretta 192, 193
Colli, Tonino Delli 82, 84, 85, 194, 205
Collins, Alan *see* Pigozzi, Luciano
Collins, Amber *see* Colli, Ombretta
Collins, John *see* Trasatti, Luciano
Colman, Matilde 223
Colossus and the Headhunters 250
The Colossus of Rhodes 114, 172
Coly, Angel *see* Colangeli, Otello
The Comedy of Terrors 22, 88
Comptoir Français 104, 109
Confessions of a Police Captain 245
The Conformist 219
Conjiu, Nela 202
Connery, Sean 12
Conqueror of Atlantis 250
The Conqueror Worm 188, 189, 194
Conquest of Mycene 176
Consorzio Italiano 22
Constantine and the Cross 87, 241
Constantine the Great see *Constantine and the Cross*
Constantino il grande see *Constantine and the Cross*
Contardi, Livia 223
Contero, Mario 68
Contero, Roberto 68, 70
Continenza, Alessandro 109, 114, 154, 210
Contronatura see *The Unnaturals*
Copernices 181
Corbucci, Bruno 131, 133
Corbucci, Enzo 71
Corbucci, Sergio 55, 98, 101, 131, 133
Corevi, Antonio (Tony) 137, 223

Corman, Roger 22, 25, 31, 37, 55, 61, 70, 85, 88, 113, 133, 146, 157, 188, 194
Coronet 71
Corridor of Mirrors 211
Corridors of Blood 233
Cortes, Fernando 177, 178
Cortese, Valentina 71, 72, 74, 75, 179, 180
Cortez, Bella 88, 91, 94
Cosulich, Callisto 166
Cottafavi, Vittorio 97, 98, 109, 112–114
Cotten, Joseph 46
Coubert, Chana 71
Count Frankenstein's Castle of Freaks 93
Courtland, Christi 137
Cousin, Pascel 194
Cramer, Richard *see* Pallotini, Riccardo
Crawford, Broderick 97
Creature of the Walking Dead 178
Crime at Porta Romana 133
Criminal in the Mirror see Sex Party
The Criminals of the Galaxy see The Wild, Wild Planet
The Crimson Executioner see The Bloody Pit of Horror
The Crimson Pirate 42
La cripta de l'incubo see Terror in the Crypt
Cristaldi, Franco 88
Croccolo, Carlo 161
Crossed Swords 94
Cry of the Banshee 37
The Crypt and the Nightmare see Terror in the Crypt
Crypt of Horror see Terror in the Crypt
Crypt of the Demon see Terror in the Crypt
The Crypt of the Vampires see Terror in the Crypt
Cuccia, Milo G. 219, 223
Cum, quando e con chi? see How, When and with Who?
Curse of Frankenstein 130, 212
Curse of the Blood-Ghouls see Slaughter of the Vampires
Cruse of the Crimson Altar 9
Curse of the Dead see Kill Baby Kill
Curse of the Doll People 68
Curse of the Ghouls see Slaughter of the Vampires
The Curse of the Karnsteins see Terror in the Crypt
Curse of the Living Dead see Kill Baby Kill

Curse of the Vampire see The Playgirls and the Vampire
Curse of the Voodoo 222
Curtis, Robert 242
Cushing, Peter 124
Cyborg 2087 11, 253
The Cyclops 14

Dahlberg, Hannes 213
D'Alberti, Dalia 105, 106
Dali, Fabienne 133, 134
Damiani, Damiano 157, 242, 244, 245
Damiani, Tilde 177
Damon, Mark 22, 27, 30, 31, 251–253
Damon, Peter 9
Damon and Pythias 94
Dane, Peter 173
Danger: Diabolik 9, 104, 181
Dangerous Exile 87
Danieli, Emma 137, 139
Danse macabre see Castle of Blood
Dantes, Claudia 39, 40, 42
Darcy, Jeffrey 147
Da Roma, Eraldo 98
Darren, James 220–222
Dassin, Jules 185
The Daughter of Dr. Jekyll 77
Daughters of Darkness 204
David and Goliath 185, 241
Davidson, Robert 80
Davis, Ursula *see* Quaglia, Piera Ana
Day, Robert 233
Day for Night 75
The Day the Earth Stood Still 11, 253
The Day the Sky Exploded 38, 231
The Day the World Ended 157
Dead End 191
The Dead Eyes of London 214
Deadlier Than the Male 212, 244
de Agostini, Fabio 163
Dean, Max *see* Righi, Massimo
De Benedetto, Gianni 71, 73
de Benedictus, Maria Luisa 75
De Bernardi, Piero 82
De Blasio, Giuseppe 251
de Blas, Manuel 9
De Carellis, Aldo 251
DeConcini, Ennio 31, 71, 245
de Cortes, Antonio 212
De Filippo, Eduardo 82, 85, 86
Del Carmen, Mario 202
del Castro, Viki 68
Del Grosso, Remigio 152

de Lirio, Carmen 95
Delitto allo specchio see *Sex Party*
Dell'Era, Gaetano 68
Dell'Orco, Sandro 133
del Monte, Rafaele 215
Delon, Alain 150, 194, 196
Delon, Betty 7
del Pozo, Angel 9
de Martino, Antonio 61
De Martino, Feruccio 223
De Martino, Romolo 205
De Masi, Franco 158
Demetrius and the Gladiators 253
Demichelli, Tullio 9, 12
De Nardo, Gustavo 235
De Ossorio, Amando 75, 77
De Paolo, Dane see Di Paolo, Dante
De Piso, Arpod 95, 105
De Rita, Massimo 31, 223
Derleth, Lucy 229
De Rosa, Franco 251
De Sabata, Eliana 71
de Sade, Marquis 44
De Santis, Gino 14
Desires of the Vampire see *The Playgirls and the Vampire*
Desmond, Lino 239
De Teffé, Antonio 7–9
de Tejada, Luis 181
De Toth, André 124
The Devil's Commandment 179
The Devil's Night 153, 154
The Devil's Nightmare 137
The Devil's Wedding Night 31
de Witt, Emina 131
De Wolff, Francis 82
The Diabolical Dr. Z 221
Diabolique 81, 146
Dialina, Rica 22, 27
di Benedetto, Gianni 71, 73
di Centa, Erika 177
Diciottenni al sole see *Beach Party Italian Style*
Die! Die! My Darling 68
Dimensions of Death see *Castle of Blood*
Dionesio, Sylvia 251
Di Palma, Carlo 198, 201
Di Paolo, Dante 13, 39, 71, 72
Discobolo Cinematografica 7
Disorder 185
Il disordine see *Disorder*
Divorce Italian Style 88, 181

Divorzio all'italiana see *Divorce Italian Style*
Django 133, 241
Dr. Goldfoot and the Girl Bombs 104, 118, 144
Dr. Jekyll and the Wolfman 12
Dr. Jekyll y el hombre lobo see *Dr. Jekyll and the Wolfman*
Dr. Terror's House of Horrors 68
Dolce, Ignazio 95
La dolce vita 78, 87, 103, 181, 197, 201
Dolen, Jim 71, 87, 103, 181, 197, 201
Dominici, Arturo 32, 38, 205, 206, 209
Dominici, Franco 133
Dominici, Germana 31
Donatelli, Mauro 245
Donati, Ermanno 13, 80, 120, 245
La donna dei faradina see *The Pharaoh's Woman*
La donna del lago see *The Possessed*
Dor, Karin 9–12
Doro, Mino 114, 223
Doro, Virginia 71
The Double Bed 146
Douglas, Kirk 2, 114, 212
Draco, Ely 114
Dracula jagt Frankenstein see *Assignment Terror*
"The Dreams in the Witch-House" 9
Dreyer, Carl 202
The Driver's Seat 181
Drops of Blood see *Mill of the Stone Women*
Duel of the Titans 100, 101
Duel Without Honor 8, 94

The Earth Dies Screaming 222
Eastwood, Clint 197, 214
Edo Cinematografica 213
Edwards, Blake 26
Eichberg Film 9
8½ 87
Eighteen in the Sun see *Beach Party Italian Style*
Ekberg, Anita 75, 78, 79
Elliott, Leonard see Jotta, Elio
The Embalmer 68–71, 256
Embassy 209
Emmanuele, Luigi 7
Emmeci 163
Emmepi Cinematografica 22, 39
End of Desire 185
Eppler, Dieter 190, 191

Equini, Arrigo 152
Ercole al centro della terra see *Hercules in the Haunted World*
Ercole alla conquista di Atlantide see *Hercules and the Captive Women*
Esdra, Micaela 133
El espejo de la brujo, see *The Witch's Mirror*
Esther and the King 21, 157
Europix 68, 75, 133, 158, 186
Evans, Maurice 124
The Evil Eye i, 39, 71–75, 180, 255
Experiment in Terror 26
Explorer 152

Fabioloa 2, 86
Face of Fire 43
The Face of Fu Manchu 12
The Face of Terror 183
The Faceless Monster see *Nightmare Castle*
Fadda, Carlo 219, 223
Fairbanks, Douglas 205
"Famous Monsters of Filmland" 95, 257
Fanfare 177
Fangs of the Living Dead 75–80, 256
Fanny Hill 74
Fantascienza 240
La fantasma del convento see *The Phantom of the Convent*
Fantasmi a Roma see *Ghosts of Rome*
Fantoni, Sergio 14, 16, 20
Faro 152
The Fascist 162
Fashion House of Death see *Blood and Black Lace*
Fava, Otello 22
Fawcett, Charles 245
Fax, Peg 235
Il federale see *The Fascist*
Felix 75
Fellini, Federico 3, 75, 78, 87, 181, 194, 196, 197
Ferrari, Marco 162
Ferraro, Ralph 186
Ferrati, Sarah 242
Ferreri, Romano 172, 176
Ferronao, Edda 190
Ferroni, Giorgio 152–154
Field, Anne 158
Fields, Samuel see Chairi, Mario
Fiermonte, Enzo 239
55 Days at Peking 180

La figlia de Frankenstein see *Lady Frankenstein*
Finger, William 192
Fisher, Kay 210
Fisher, Terence 154, 177, 211, 215
A Fistful of Dollars 214
Fitzgerald, Teresa see Vianello, Maria Teresa
Five Graves for a Medium see *Terror-Creatures from the Grave*
Fixed Bayonets 11
Flaiano, Ennio 85
Flavio 13
Fleming, Rhonda 93
Flemyng, Robert 120
The Flight That Disappeared 15
Flight to Fury 15
Flight to Mars 43
Flynn, Sean 12
Foan, John see Bava, Mario
Follow the Boys 11, 12
Fonda, Jane 162, 194–196
Fonda, Peter 194, 195
Fondat, Marcel see Fondato, Marcello
Fontaine, Corinne 177
Footsteps in the Fog 87
For a Few Dollars More 114, 222, 244
For Love or Gold 9
For Those Who Think Young 222
Forest, Mark 97
Forever My Love 21
Forrest, Jack see Giambartolomei, Guido
Forster, Elisabeth 131
Forsyth, Stephen 102–104
Fort Yuma Gold 153
Fortini, Romano 133
Forty Guns 172
Foscari, Carla 190
Four for Texas 78
Four Girls in Town 214
Franchetti, Rina 14
Franci, Carlo 105, 245
Francicor 234
Franciosa, Tony 61
Francis, Freddie 68, 81
Francis of Assissi 172
Francisci, Pietro 2, 209
Franco, Jess see Franco, Jesús
Franco, Jesús 219, 221
Franju, Georges 152–154, 160
Frankenstein's Bloody Terror 77, 78
Frankenstein's Monster 2
Frassineti, Augusto 205

Freda, Riccardo 2, 13, 47, 53, 54, 77, 80, 81, 101, 120, 123, 124, 129, 148, 179, 180, 215, 245, 249–251
The French Connection 96
Frozen Alive 214
The Frozen Ghost 7
La frusta e il corpo see *What!*
Fryd, Joseph 192, 239
Fuchs, Gianni 97
Fuchsberger, Joachim 213, 214
Fuentes, Carlos 242, 243
Ful Films 133
Fuller, Sam 11
Fumagalli, Franco 120
Furnari, Salvatore 109
The Fury of Achilles 93
The Fury of Hercules 96
Fury of the Pagans 130
Futuramic 234

Gabel, Scilla 152
Galatea 22, 31, 71, 85, 223
Galli, Ida 85, 114, 223, 225
Gallitti, Alberto 158, 160
The Gamblers 241
The Gamma People 43
Gargano, Omero 88
Garrani, Ivo 14, 31, 33, 38, 109, 113
Garret, Richard see Garrone, Riccardo
Garrón, Ramón see Garroni, Romolo
Garrone, Riccardo 198, 201
Garroni, Romolo 145, 146
Gasparri, Gianfranco 95
Gasper, Luciano 68
Gassman, Vittorio 82, 83, 85, 87
Gastaldi, Ernesto 120, 123, 145–147, 150, 158, 160, 202, 203, 215, 217, 218, 229, 231, 234, 238
Gastoni, Lisa 239, 240
Gay, Felice Testa 147, 150
Gazzotto, Alcide 68
Geerk, Antie 210
Gengarelli, Amerigo 186
Gentilomo, Giacomo 98, 101, 105, 109, 143, 217
Germani, Gaia 61, 62, 66
Germi, Pietro 181
Gessler, Ella 9
G.G. Productions 102, 142
The Ghost 1, 38, 54, 80–82, 123, 124, 180, 183, 184, 256
The Ghost of Dr. Hichcock see *The Horrible Dr. Hichcock*

Ghosts Italian Style 82–85, 87, 88, 255
Ghosts of Rome 84–88, 255
GI Blues 74
Giacobini, Franco 114, 115, 118
Giambartolomei, Guido 229
Giannini, Giancarlo 145, 147
The Giant of Marathon 21, 54, 209
The Giant of Metropolis 14, 88–95, 186, 255
Gidget 222
Gidget Goes Hawaiian 222
Gidget Goes to Rome 9, 222
Gigante, Marcello 68
Il gigante di Metropolis see *The Giant of Metropolis*
Gilbert, Lewis 12
Gimead, Antonio 166
Gimmy, Gena 190
Giordani, Aldo 14, 20, 154, 157
Giorsi, Mario 114, 163
Giovannini, Maria 177
Girolami, Marino 161
Giulietta degli spiriti see *Juliet of the Spirits*
Giustini, Carlo 239
Giustini, Massimo 158
Given, Eddie H. see Donati, Ermanno
The Glass Sphinx 79
Glenn, Montgomery see Tranquilli, Silvano
Gloriani, Tina 215
Goddess of Love 9
Gogol, Nicolai 31
Gold, William 158
Gold for the Caesars 124
The Golden Arrow 130, 132, 146
The Golden Blade 78
Goliath Against the Giants 95, 96, 132, 172, 185, 255
Goliath and the Barbarians 14, 97, 209
Goliath and the Dragon 96–98, 112, 255
Goliath and the Giants see *Goliath Against the Giants*
Goliath and the Island of Vampires see *Goliath and the Vampires*
Goliath and the Vampires 98–102, 109, 255
Goliath contra las gigantes see *Goliath Against the Giants*
Goliath contro i giganti see *Goliath Against the Giants*
Gomez, Ramiro 95
Gondola Film 68

Gora, Claudio 7–9, 85
Gordon, Albert 43
Gordon, Bert I. 14, 95, 102
Gordon, Don 241
Gori, Mario Cechi 210
Gorilla at Large 43
Gorine, Arianna 39
Governor 104, 181
Gragnani, Ugo 215
El gran amor de Conde Dracula see *Dracula's Great Love*
Granata, Graziella 190
Granger, Stewart 201
Grani, Trini 22
Grassi, Antonio 68
Green, Donald see Masciocchi, Raffaele
Greville, Edmond 124, 129
Grey, Dick see Scotti, Ottavio
Grimaldi, Gianni 55
Grimaldi, Hugo 109
Grimaud, Jean see Grimaldi, Gianni
Grunewald, Allan see Caiano, Mario
Guerra, Ugo 234
Guglielmi, Marco 152, 173
Gunmen of the Rio Grande 12
Guzzenati, Margherita 242

Una hacha para la luna de miel see *Hatchet for a Honeymoon*
Hagar, Freddy see Unger, Goffredo
Hamilton, David see Terzano, Ubaldo
Hamilton, John see Medici, Gianni
Hamilton, Michael see Scardamaglia, Elio
Hammer Films 38, 68, 81, 119, 130, 132, 137, 191, 204, 210, 218
The Hangman of London see *The Mad Executioners*
Hape Film 131
Hard Times for Vampires see *Uncle Was a Vampire*
Hardy, Martin see Martino, Luciano
Hargitay, Mickey 43, 44, 46, 47
Harley, Nat 120
Harris, Brad 95, 96
Harrison, Richard 94, 146, 150
Harryhausen, Ray 120, 241
Hart, John 14, 133
Hart, Susan 172
Hatchet for a Honeymoon 102–104, 255
The Haunted Palace 188
The Haunting 244
Hawkwood, John 251

Hayward, Louis 166
The Head 191
Helen of Troy 130
The Hell from Manitoba see *A Place Called Glory*
Der Henker von London see *The Mad Executioners*
Hercules 2, 101, 115, 132, 212
Hercules Against Rome 108
Hercules Against the Moon Men 104–109, 176, 256
Hercules and the Black Pirates 108
Hercules and the Captive Women 98, 109–115, 118, 132, 185, 255
Hercules and the Conquest of Atlantis see *Hercules and the Captive Women*
Hercules and the Masked Rider 108
Hercules and the Treasure of the Incas 108
Hercules at the Center of the Earth see *Hercules and the Captive Women*
Hercules in the Haunted World 37, 39, 55, 97, 102, 114–120, 149, 223, 255
Hercules of the Desert 250
Hercules, Samson and Ulysses 183, 250
Hercules Unchained 21, 115, 132, 212
Hercules vs. the Vampires see *Hercules in the Haunted World*
Herlin, Jacques 235
Hersent, Philippe 97, 158, 223
Herter, Gerard 47, 50
Hessler, Gordon 189, 194
Heston, Charlton 20, 144
Heusch, Paolo 39, 160, 229, 231, 233
High Lonesome 227
High School Confidential 227
Highway Patrol 98
Hill, Craig 9–11
Hill, Jack 104, 153
The Hired Killer 150, 241
Hispamer Films 202
Histoires extraordinaires see *Spirits of the Dead*
Hitchcock, Alfred 25, 80, 102, 122
Die Hölle von Manitoba see *A Place Called Glory*
Holt, Seth 81
Holzer, Ivy 177
El hombre que vino de Ummo see *Assignment Terror*
Homicidal 102
Honeymoon with a Stranger 9
Honore, Jean-Pierre 105, 106
Hornet's Nest 21, 143

The Horrible Dr. Hichcock 1, 13, 38, 54, 67, 80, 120–124, 160, 165, 184, 251, 255
The Horrible Mill Women see Mill of the Stone Women
The Horrible Secret of Dr. Hichcock see The Horrible Dr. Hichcock
The Horrible Stone Women see Mill of the Stone Women
Horror Castle 61, 67, 124–131, 256
Horror Chamber of Dr. Faustus 153, 160
Horror of Dracula 130, 177, 210–212, 215, 216
Horror of the Stone Women see Mill of the Stone Women
Horror of the Zombies 77
Hour of the Wolf 242
House of Usher 25, 30, 31, 37
House of Wax 70
The House on Haunted Hill 186
How, When and with Who? 86
Howard, Barbara *see* Howerd, Barbara
Howard, Tom 205, 209
Howerd, Barbara 217
Hugg, Mike 219
Hugo, Robert *see* Guerra, Ugo
Hunchback of the Morgue 78
Hunter, Max *see* Pupillo, Massimo
Huston, John 241
Hypnosis 8

"I Am Legend" 137, 144
I Deal with Danger 191
I Married a Monster from Outer Space 175
Ikaria XB-1 see Voyage to the End of the Universe
The Incredible Mr. Limpet 208
Indief 131
Ingles, Rufino 95
Innocenzi, Carlo 13, 95, 152
Institute Luce 179
International Entertainment 43
International Jaguar 9
Invasion 1700 176
Invasion of the Body Snatchers 46
The Invisible Creature 68
The Invisible Dr. Mabuse 12, 153
Invisible Invaders 170
Ippoliti, Silvano 181, 183
Isabel, Duchess of the Devils 131–133
It Happened in Athens 158
Italian International 166

Jailbait 209
Jamaica Inn 122
Johnny Yuma 31
Johns, John Charlie *see* Giannini, Giancarlo
Johnson, Richard 242, 244
Jolly 31
El jorobado de la morgue see Hunchback of the Morgue
Joseph and His Brethren 251
Josipovici, Jean 184–186
Jotta, Elio 80, 82
Journey to the 7th Planet 170
Judd, Jack 68
Juliet of the Spirits 75, 87, 181
Just, Phillip *see* Sanjust, Filippano
Justice, James Robertson 194
Justin, Charles *see* Giustini, Carlo

Karamesinis, Vassili 7
Karloff, Boris 22, 23, 28, 30, 37, 188, 233
Karlsen, John 186, 189, 245, 246
Karnstein see Terror in the Crypt
The Karnstein Curse see Terror in the Crypt
Karson, Phil 55
Kechler, Carlo (Charles) 80, 82
Kendall, Tony *see* Stella, Luciano
Kill Baby Kill 31, 133–137, 172, 198, 219, 256
Killer Fish 215
King, Bob 235
King of Kings 103
Kinski, Klaus 61, 220, 222
Kiss the Other Sheik 162
Klein, Rita 43
The Knife in the Body see The Murder Clinic
Knives of the Avenger 185
Koch, Mariann(a/e) 213, 214
Konopka, Magda (Madge) 181, 182
Koscina, Sylva 210, 212
Kronos 88, 89
Kruger, Henry 55, 57
Krugher, Lea 39

Il ladro di Bagdad see The Thief of Baghdad
Lady Frankenstein 46, 250
Il lago di Satana see She Beast
The Lake of Satan see She Beast
La lama nel corpo see The Murder Clinic
Lancaster, Burt 42, 150, 153

Lane, Abbe 161
Lane, John Francis 245, 251
Lane, Mark *see* Masciocchi, Marcello
Lang, Fritz 94, 95
Lass, Barbara 229, 230, 233
Lassander, Dagmar 102, 103
The Last Days of Pompeii 172
The Last Man on Earth 137–145, 255
The Last Mohican see *The Last Tomahawk*
Last of the Renegades 153
Last of the Vikings 101, 109, 119, 143, 149, 217
Last Prey of the Vampire see *The Playgirls and the Vampire*
The Last Tomahawk 8
Last Victim of the Vampire see *The Playgirls and the Vampire*
Lastretti, Adolfo 220
Lattanzi, Tina 154
Lavagnino, Angelo Francesco 98, 192, 239
Lavi, Daliah 235–238
Law, John Phillip 181
Lawrence, Max 133
Lazenby, George 38
Le Borg, Reginald 37
Lee, Belinda 85, 87
Lee, Christopher 61–63, 66–68, 114, 116, 118, 119, 125, 129, 131, 191, 202, 204, 210–212, 216, 233, 235, 236
Lee, Margaret 82, 83, 220
Le Fanu, Joseph Sheridan 78, 202–205
Leibl, Marianne 213
Leicester, William P. 137, 144
Leith Films 186
Lemoine, Mich(a)el 173, 175, 176, 184, 185, 239
Leone, Sergio 114, 214, 222, 244
Leone Film 13, 158, 234
Leonviola, Antonio 13
The Leopard 150
Leroux, Gaston 217, 218
Leroy, Philippe 61–63, 66, 179, 180
Der letze Mohikaner see *The Last Tomahawk*
Lewis, Jerry 78, 162
Libatore, Ugo 152, 242
Libido 145–147, 256
Licudi, Maurizio 109
Life Begins at 17 30
Lindstrom, Pia 179, 180
Liné, Helga 163, 165

Lion's Film 14
Lippert, Robert L. 137
Lisi, Virna 147, 179, 191
The Little Shop of Horrors 189
Llimera, Veronica 102
Lodi, Rodolfo 239
Lolli, Franco 109
London, Jack 143
The Long Hair of Death 1, 38, 61, 119, 147–150, 255
The Long Night of Terror see *Castle of Blood*
A Long Ride from Hell 201
Longo, Germano 13
Longo, Malisa 251
Longo, Tiziano 177, 179
Lopez, Soledad 102
Lord Jim 238
Loren, Sophia 82, 83, 87, 147, 180
Loret, Susanne 14, 16, 17, 19, 20, 154, 157, 210, 212
Lorre, Peter 141, 222
Lorys, Diana 75
Lost Souls 191
The Lost World 253
The Lost World of Sinbad 227
Lotti, Angelo 219
Love and Marriage 46, 103
Lovecraft, H. P. 9
A Lovely Way to Die 212
Lovers Beyond the Tomb see *Nightmare Castle*
The Loves of Hercules 46
Lowens, Curt 229, 230, 232
Lozzi, Edmondo 95
Lualdi, Antonella 184, 185
Lubin, Arthur 85, 205, 208, 209
Lucidi, Maurizio 97
Lucisano, Fulvio 166
Lugosi, Bela 160
Lulli, Piero 133, 134
La lunga notte del terrore see *Castle of Blood*
I lunghi capelli della morte see *The Long Hair of Death*
Lupi, Roldano 88, 89, 93
Lupo, Albert(o) 14, 16, 18–22, 154, 157
Lust for a Vampire 204
Lux Films 85, 205
Luz, Maria 173

McCallum, David 201
Macci, Valentino 82, 251

Maccuri, Ruggero 85
McDouglas, John *see* Addobbati, Giuseppe
McDowall, Roddy 209
Maciste Against Hercules in the Vale of Woe 251
Maciste Against the Men of Stone see Hercules Against the Moon Men
Maciste Against the Vampires see Goliath and the Vampires
Maciste all'inferno see The Witch's Curse
Maciste contre les hommes de pierre see Hercules Against the Moon Men
Maciste contro gli uomini della luna see Hercules Against the Moon Men
Maciste contro gli uomini pietri see Hercules Against the Moon Men
Maciste contro il vampiro see Goliath and the Vampires
Maciste e la regina di Samar see Hercules Against the Moon Men
Maciste in Hell (1927) 2, 245, 249
Maciste in Hell see The Witch's Curse
Maciste in the Land of the Cyclops see Atlas in the Land of the Cyclops
Maciste vs. the Vampire see Goliath and the Vampires
McNair, Barbara 220, 222
McNamara, Richard 129
McNeeran, Mary 229
The Mad Executioners 153
Madame Death 183
Mademoiselle 228
Madison, Guy 12
Mafioso 172
Magherini, Flavio 205
Magna 80
Mainwaring, Daniel 154
Majano, Anton Giulio 14, 21
Malagoli, Milo 154, 156
Malatesta, Guido 95
La maldición de los Karnsteins see Terror in the Crypt
Malenka see Fangs of the Living Dead
Malenka, la nipute del vampiro see Fangs of the Living Dead
Malenka, la sobrina del vampiro see Fangs of the Living Dead
Malle, Louis 194, 196
A Man Called Noon 77
The Man Who Never Was 124
The Man with the Yellow Eyes see The Planets Against Us
Mancori, Alvaro 98
Man-Eater of Hydra 143
Manghini, Gino 13
Mangione, Giuseppe 7–9
Maniac 180
Maniac Mansion 158
Manley, Walter 68
Mann, Louis *see* Carpentieri, Luigi
Mann, Manfred 219
Manni, Ettore 109, 110, 114, 223, 228
Mannino, Franco 80
Mansfield, Jayne 44, 46, 158
Maracaibo 162
Marandi, Evi 166, 168, 172
Maravidi, Mirella 200, 201
La marca del hombre lobo see Frankenstein's Bloody Terror
La marca del muerto see Creature of the Walking Dead
Marco, Luis 95
Maretti, Sandro 97
Margheriti, Antonio 1, 27, 55, 60, 61, 115, 123–125, 129–133, 143, 146–150, 152, 176, 183, 188, 191–193, 205, 213, 215, 239, 241, 242, 251, 252
Mariani, Marco 217, 218
Marietto 88, 89
Marin, Luciano 109, 110
Marini, Alexandra 85, 87
Marinuzzi, Gino, Jr. 109, 166
Marion, Marc *see* Mariani, Marco
Mark of the Dead see Creature of the Walking Dead
Mark of the Wolfman see Frankenstein's Bloody Terror
Marker, Martha 229
Marriage Italian Style 180
Marsac, Maurice 229
Mart, Gin 68, 70
Martell, Peter 79, 192
Martin, Femi *see* Benussi, Eufemia
Martin, Ross 26
Martínez, Ramón 202
Martino, Luciano 158, 234
Martino, Ray 95
Marturano, Luigi 95
Marvel, Christian 68
Maryl, Mara *see* Chianetta, Maria
Marzi, Franca 85
Mas, Antonio 102
Mascetti, Gina 205, 245

Index

La maschera del Demonio see *Black Sunday*
Masciocchi, Marcello 158, 160
Masciocchi, Raffaele 80, 81, 120, 184
Masing, Esther 251
Mask of the Demon see *Black Sunday*
Maslansky, Paul 61, 67, 186, 188
Mason, Frank see De Masi, Franco
Mason, James 214
Masson, Diego 194
Mastrocinque, Camillo 7–9, 78, 134, 202, 204
Mastroianni, Marcello 78, 82, 83, 85, 94, 181
Mastroianni, Ruggero 194
Maté, Rudolph 11
Matheson, Richard 137, 144, 146
Mathias, Bob 154, 155, 157, 158
Mauri, Roberto 190, 191
Maurin, Delphine 158, 159
Maxim Film 209
MBS Cinematografica 43, 198
Mecaci, Piero 137, 144
Medallion 13, 95, 245
Medea 181
Medici, Gianni 75, 76
Meeker, Patricia 229
Melchior, Ib 166, 170, 171
Melecco, Marta 71
Mellone, Amedeo 105, 215
Melrose, Maureen see Berti, Marina
Men in Space 171
Menghi, Jenner 190
Meniconi, Furio 88, 192
Mercer, Joseph 229
Mercier, Michèle 22, 25, 27, 61
Mercury 102, 190, 192, 239
Merivale, John 47, 51
Merle, Frank see Merli, Francesco
Merli, Francesco 43, 198
MES Cinematografica 202
Metro-Goldwyn-Mayer (MGM) 82, 85, 192, 193, 205, 217, 229, 233, 239
Metropolis (1925) 94
Metropolis see *The Giant of Metropolis*
"Metzengerstein" 194–196
Metzger, Radley 241
Micheli, Ornella 80, 245
Midnight Lace 26
Mifune, Toshiro 227
The Mighty Ursus 8
Migliorine, Romano 43, 198, 200
Milian, Tomás 9

Mill of the Stone Maidens see *Mill of the Stone Women*
Mill of the Stone Women 150–154, 176, 184, 185, 255
Mill of Torments see *Mill of the Stone Women*
Milland, Angel see Minervivi, Angeli
Milland, Gloria 95, 96, 184, 186
Miller, Paul see Muller, Paul
Miller, Thomas see Mastrocinque, Camillo
Milo, Sandra see Marini, Alessandra
Milone, Luciana 125, 127
Minervini, Angeli 202
Minnesota Clay 102, 131, 133
The Minotaur, Wild Beast of Crete 20, 154–158, 165, 255
Mio amico, Jekyll see *My Friend Jekyll*
Mirabel, Alfred see Mirabili, Alfredo
Mirabili, Alfredo 39
Les Misérables 54
Mission Stardust 219
Mr. Ed 208
Mitchell, Cameron 39, 43, 102, 119, 131, 133, 143, 146, 149, 185
Mitchell, Gordon 13, 88, 89, 93, 95
Mitchell, Marilyn see Maravidi, Mirella
El Mito see *The Myth*
Modugno, Lucia 71
Moffa, Paolo 98
Molina, Antonio 9
Molina, Jacinto 9, 10, 12
Moll, Giorgia 205, 206
Molteni, Ambrogio 88, 185, 186
Monarchia 39
Moncada, Santiago 102
Mondello, Luigi 105
Monflour Film 209
I mongoli see *The Mongols*
The Mongols 78, 124
The Monster of London City 214
Monster of the Island 30
The Monster of the Opera see *The Vampire of the Opera*
The Monster of Venice see *The Embalmer*
The Monster with Yellow Eyes see *The Planets Against Us*
Monsters of Terror see *Assignment Terror*
Los monstruos del terror see *Assignment Terror*
Montauri, Mario 97
The Monte Carlo Story 211
Montes, José I. 202

Monti, Milli 22, 23
Montini, Luigi 181
Monviso, Piero 14
Moore, Roger 188
Morales, Mario 166
Mordini, Dino 154
Morelli, Marco 213
Moretti, Renato 239
Morgan the Pirate 70
Morigi, Franco 71
Morris, Kirk 114, 245, 246, 250
Il mostro dell'isola see *The Monster of the Island*
Il mostro dell'opera see *The Vampire of the Opera*
Il mostro de Venezia see *The Embalmer*
Le Moulin des supplices see *Mill of the Stone Women*
Muller, Paul 75, 77, 154, 163, 165, 220
Mulligan, William 202
The Murder Clinic 150, 158–160, 255
The Murder Society see *The Murder Clinic*
Muretta, G. 68
Murphy, Audie 215
Murphy, Jim see Rustichelli, Carlo
Mussolini, Romano 181
Musy, Mario 102
My Blood Runs Cold 172
My Friend Jekyll 161–162, 255
My Pal Jekyll see *My Friend Jekyll*
The Myth 172

Naked Terror see *The Last Man on Earth*
Nannuzzi, Nella 154
Naschy, Paul see Molina, Jacinto
Natale, Paola 251
Natale, Roberto 43, 133, 198, 200, 201
Nathan, Peggy 71
Navajo Joe 183
Neame, Grace 229
Nelli, Barbara 43
Neri, Monica 114
Nero, Franco 133, 150, 239, 240
Neumann, Kurt 183
"Never Bet the Devil Your Head" 196
Newman, Raoul see Raho, Umberto
Nicholson, Jack 22, 113, 208
Nicolosi, Roberto 30, 37, 223
Nicos, Antoine 177
NIF 270
The Night Evelyn Came Back from the Grave 8
Night Is the Phantom see *What!*

The Night Monster 186
Night of Lust 176
Night of Terror see *The Murder Clinic*
Night of the Doomed see *Nightmare Castle*
Night of the Living Dead 143
Night of the Quarter Moon 228
The Night of the Seagulls 77
"Night of 21 Hours" 166
Night People 214
Night Star, Goddess of Electra see *War of the Zombies*
Nightmare 81
Nightmare Castle 38, 77, 157, 163–166, 255
A Nightmare on Elm Street 74
The Nights of Lucretia Borgia 87
Nights of Rasputin 101
Nike Cinematografica 104
No Place Like Homicide 222
No Room to Die 8
La noche de los gaviotas see *Night of the Seagulls*
La noche del terror ciego see *Tomb of the Blind Dead*
Nord Film Italiana 177
La notte dei diavoli see *The Devil's Nightmare*
Le notti bianche see *White Nights*
Le notti di lucrezia see *The Nights of Lucretia Borgia*
Novelli, Mario 131
Nucci, Laura 147
Nucleo Film 145
Nude...si, muore see *The Young, the Evil and the Savage*
Nude...Yes, Dead see *The Young, the Evil and the Savage*
The Nutty Professor 162
Nuyen, Laureen see Nucci, Laura

Oberon, Isli 235
The Oblong Box 189
O'Connor, Maureen 229, 233
Oedipus the King 244
Ogilvy, Ian 186–188
Olca, Antonio Perez 166
Old, John M. see Bava, Mario
The Old Dark House 186, 214
Olivieri, Enrico 33
The Omega Man 144
Omri, Nira 186
On Her Majesty's Secret Service 38

Index

Once Upon a Tractor 9
One Million B.C. 38
One Million Years B.C. 38, 132
One Silver Dollar 153
One, Two, Three 162
00-2 Most Secret Agent 132
Operation Counterspy 119
Operation Fear see Kill Baby Kill
Operation Scotland Yard 38
Operation Terror see Kill Baby Kill
Operazione Paura see Kill Baby Kill
Orfei, Liana 88, 89, 94
Orlak, el infierno de Frankenstein see Orlak, the Hell of Frankenstein
Orlak, the Hell of Frankenstein 183
Oronato, Glauco 22, 27
Orphée 158
L'orribile segreto del Dr. Hichcock see The Horrible Dr. Hichcock
Ortas, Julio 202
Ortiz, Angel 95
Ortolani, Riz 55, 60, 125
Ouspenskaya, Maria 11
Outlaw Planet see Planet of the Vampires
The Overcoat 185, 211

Pacemaker 43, 47, 190, 191, 198
Pacheco, Godofredo 9
Padinotti, Aldo 13
Pal, George 11, 120, 240, 241, 253
Palance, Jack 143
Palella, Oreste 88
Pallotini, Riccardo 13, 55, 60, 124, 125, 129, 147, 150, 192, 193, 213, 215, 239, 245, 250
Palmara, Mimmo 95, 109, 131, 132
Pamphili, Mirella 220
Pan Latina Films 102
Panda Film 80, 120
Papi, Giuliano 13
Papiri, Umberto 251
Parade 152
Paranoiac 180
Paris Holiday 78
Paris When It Sizzles 146, 172
Park, Reg 109, 112, 114, 115, 118, 119, 149
Parker, Kathleen 251
Parolini, Gianfranco 95
Pasolini, Pier Paolo 181
Pasquale, Fortunato 102
Passante, Mario 31
Patrick, Elizabeth 229

Patrick, George 229
Patrizi, Massimo 39
Pavoni, Pier Ludovico 152, 172, 176
Pavoni, Vico 172
Pazzafini, Nello 95
Pearl, Gay 47
Peck, Gregory 214
Peguri, Gino 43
Pellegrini, Giuseppe 215
Pena, Julio 181
Pepe, Nico 154
Per un pugno di dollar see A Fistful of Dollars
Perego, Didi 47, 53
Perez, Manuel 95
Peruzzi 97
Pestiniero, Renato 166
Petri, Mario 109
Phantom Lovers see Ghosts of Rome
Phantom of the Convent 214
Phantom of the Opera 208, 217, 218
The Pharaoh's Woman 70, 176
PI Cinematografica 184
Il pianeta degli uomini spenti see Battle of the Worlds
I pianeti contro di noi see The Planets Against Us
Piazzi, Achille 97, 114
Pica, Antonio 181
Piccolo, Marco 97
Pierfederici, Antonio 31
Pierotti, Piero 172, 223
Pierreux, Jacqueline 22, 23, 25
Pietrangeli, Antonio 85–87
Piga, Aldo 177, 190, 191, 198, 215, 217
Pigozzi, Luciano 61, 102, 103, 145, 146, 200, 201, 213, 214, 229, 233, 235, 237, 252
Pintoff, Ernest 82
The Pirate and the Slave Girl 14
Pirates of Tortuga 74
The Pit and the Pendulum 9, 55, 146, 165
Pitoni, Daniel 47, 48
Pizzi, Pier Luigi 242
A Place Called Glory 153
A Place for Lovers 181
The Planet of Extinguished Men see Battle of the Worlds
Planet of Terror see Planet of the Vampires
Planet of the Vampires 31, 37, 96, 166–172, 176, 256

Planet on the Prowl see *War Between the Planets*
The Planets Against Us 172–176, 185, 255
The Playgirls and the Vampire 70, 176–179, 191, 255
Plebani, Alberto 154
Plemiannikov, Helene 194
Podestà, Rossana 125, 130
Poe, Edgar Allan 37, 55, 61, 88, 146, 194, 197
Pogany, Gabor 223, 227
Polani, Anna Maria 105, 106
Polanski, Roman 242
Poletto, Piero 82, 154, 239
Polselli, Renato 177, 215, 218, 219
Ponti, Carlo 82
Pontius Pilate 74
The Poppy Is Also a Flower 185
The Possessed 179–181, 256
The Power 11, 253
Pozen, Mike 220
Prades, Jaime 9
Prado, Vittoria 217, 218
El precio de un hombre see *The Ugly Ones*
Prehistoric Women 132
Preiss, Wolfgang 152, 153
Prévost, Françoise 158, 159, 194
Price, Dennis 220, 222
Price, Vincent 22, 94, 104, 118, 137, 143, 144, 188, 189
The Price of One Man see *The Ugly Ones*
The Pride and the Passion 77
Primitive Love 44
Prisoner of the Iron Mask 176
Prisoner of the Volga 157
Procusa 95
Prodromides 194
Promises, Promises 46
Prospero, Franco 71, 114
Prucaccini, Marietta 190
Psycho 102, 104, 123
Puente, Jesús 102
Può una morta rivivere per amore? see *Venus in Furs*
Pupillo, Massimo 43, 44, 46, 198, 201
Purdom, Edmond 94, 158
The Purple Gang 172
Pyro 172

Quaglia, Pier Ana 7, 202
Quattrini, Marisa 177
Queen of Babylon 8, 93
Queen of Blood 74
Queen of the Nile 144
Quesada, Milo 71
Questi fantasmi see *Ghosts Italian Style*
Questi, Giulio 179, 181
Quick, Let's Get Married 233
Quinn, Anthony 8

Raffaelli, Giuliano 39, 147, 150, 239
Rafferty, Jean see Raffaelli, Giuliano
La ragazza di Bube see *Bebo's Girl*
Rage of the Buccaneers 94, 144
Raho, Umberto 55, 80, 137, 181, 183, 239
Raho, Umi see Raho, Umberto
Rains, Claude 192
Rains, Robert 147
Ranchi, Federica 97
Randall, Tony 46
Randolph, Ed 186
Randone, Salvo 55, 179, 194
Ranieri, Giuseppe 68, 70, 177
Raptus see *The Horrible Dr. Hichcock*
Rascel, Renato 86, 210–212
Rasmino, Antonio 205
Rasona, Ubaldo 137
Rassimov, Ivan 166
Rau, Umberto see Raho, Umberto
Ravaioli, Isarco 181, 183, 192, 193, 215, 239
The Raven 22, 85
Reflections in a Golden Eye 93
Regnoli, Piero 177, 179
Reiner, Ivan 239
Reiner, Thomas 39, 40, 192
Rémy, Hélène 215, 217
Rennie, Michael 9–11, 251–253
Renoir, Claude 194, 196
Reptilicus 170
Repulsion 242
Ressel, Franco 239
The Restless Years 74
The Return of Dr. Mabuse 153
Return of the Blind Dead see *Tomb of the Blind Dead*
Revenge of the Blood Beast see *She Beast*
Revenge of the Gladiators 95
Revolt of the Ghosts 86
Rey, Fernando 95, 96, 183
Reyes, Gene 9
Rhapsody 87
Ribotta, Ettore 137
Ribotta, Hectore see Ribotta, Ettore
Ricci, Antonio 7

Ricci, Luciano 61, 67
Rice, Alfred *see* Rizzo, Alfredo
Richardson, John 31, 32, 38
Richardson, Tony 228
Righi, Massimo 13, 22, 27, 39, 158–160, 166
Riley, Jay 186
Rinaldi, Antonio 102, 133, 166
Rivelli, Luisa 184, 185
Rivière, Georges 55, 61, 125, 131, 133
Rizzo, Alfredo 43, 177, 179, 190, 191, 200
The Robe 253
Robinson, Neil 120, 145
Robinson, Steve 200
Robsahm, Margaret 55, 58
Roc 184
Rocca, Daniela 47, 48, 177, 179, 181
Rocca, Lyla 177, 179
Rodiacines 181
Rohm, Maria 220, 221
Rolando, Maria Luisa 215
Roma contro Roma see *War of the Zombies*
Roman, Antonio 166
Roman, Leticia 71, 74
Romatelli, Sante 102
Rome Against Rome see *War of the Zombies*
Romero, George 143
Rosales, Lina 95
Rosi, Leopoldo 215
Rossellini, Franco 179, 181
Rossi, Vittorio 109
Rossi-Stuart, Giacomo 47, 133, 134, 137, 138, 143, 192, 193
Il rosso segno della follia see *Hatchet for a Honeymoon*
Rota, Nino 194
Rotundo, Giuseppe 194
Rotunno, Giuseppe 85, 88
The Rover 244
Royal Films 229
Rubio, José 95
Ruffo, Eleanora 97
Ruffo, Leonora 114, 116
Ruggiero, Gene 137, 205
Run for Your Wife 191
Russel(l), Tony 239, 241
Russo, Carlo 68
Rustichelli, Carlo 39, 133, 134, 154, 157, 205, 209, 235, 238

Sabatini, Stefania 215
Sabbatini, Enrico 82
Sabu 205
Sacco and Vanzetti 114, 183
Saga of Dracula 165
Sagal, Boris 144
The Saint 188
The Saint vs. Dr. Death 165
Salerno, Enrico Maria 109
Salerno, Vittorio 145
Salkow, Sidney 137, 143, 144
Salvatore, Alberto 158
Salvi, Emimmo 88
Salvia, Rafael J. 166
Samson and the Seven Miracles of the World 190, 251
Samson and the Slave Queen 108
Samson vs. the Giant King 250
Sancho, Fernando 95
Sanciriaco, Manuel Cano 102
Sanders, George 124, 215
Sandokan the Great 185, 209
Sanjust, Filippano 47, 205
Sanjust, Filippo *see* Sanjust, Filippano
Sansoni, Mario 95
Sant'ambrogio, Dino 190
Santo contra el Doctor Muerte see *The Saint vs. Dr. Death*
Santoli, Euclide 14, 239
Santonocito, Carlo 95
Sapphire 38
Sarch, Walter *see* Addessi, Giovanni
Sartarelli, Marcello 223
Satanic see *Satanik*
Satanik 181–183, 255
Savage, Archie 192
Savina, Carlo 251
Sawtell, Paul 137, 144
Saxon, John 30, 71, 72, 74
Scaccianoce, Luigi 242
Scardamaglia, Elio 158, 234
The Scarlet Hangman see *The Bloody Pit of Horror*
Scarmadagba, Elio *see* Scarmadaglia, Elio
Scarnicci, Giulio 161
Scarpelli, Marco 210, 212
Scarpelli, Umberto 88
Schell, Carl 229, 230, 233
Schiaffino, Rosanna 154, 157, 242, 244
Schneider, Samuel 47
Schrei in der Nacht see *The Unnaturals*
Scola, Ettore 85
Scolaro, Nino 104
Scondurra, Franco 210

Scott, Gordon 98, 100, 101, 108, 241
Scotti, Andrea 14, 154
Scotti, Ottavio 235
Scotti, Tino 131
Scream 26
Scream in the Night see *The Unnaturals*
Scream of Fear 81
The Screaming Eagles 30
Screaming Mimi 78
Scuccuglia, Leo 88
The Sea Pirate 185
Seance on a Wet Afternoon 242
Sears, Heather 108, 217
Seated at His Right 103
Seccia, Cesare 95
Secret Agent Fireball 146, 150
The Secret of Dr. Hichcock see *The Horrible Dr. Hichcock*
The Secret of Santa Vittoria 88, 147, 211, 233
Secret of the Sphinx 241
The Secret Seven 93, 241
The Secret War of Harry Frigg 212
Seddok: L'erede di Satana see *Atom Age Vampire*
Seddok: The Heir of Satan see *Atom Age Vampire*
See Naples and Die 54
Sei donne per l'assassino see *Blood and Black Lace*
La señora muerte see *Madame Death*
Sensi, Mario 88, 93
Serandrei, Mario 13, 31, 71, 114
Serato, Massimo 239–241
Serena Films 61
Sernas, Jacques 98
Servais, Jean 137
Seven Arts 88, 95
The Seven Tasks of Ali Baba 186
Severini, Luigi 125
Sex Party 184–186
She 38
She Beast 38, 70, 186–189, 200, 255
She Devil 183
Shefter, Bert 137, 144
Shepard, Patty 9, 10
Sherman, Anne 158
Sherman, Richard M. 219
Ship of Evil see *Horror of the Zombies*
Siege at Red River 11
Sigma III 120
The Sign of Rome see *Sign of the Gladiator*

Signoret, Simone 81
The Silencers 238
Silenti, Vira 13, 245, 246, 251
Simonelli, Giovanni 7, 95
Sinatra, Frank 21, 153
Sinclair, Charles 192
Sins of Rome 54
Sister of Satan see *She Beast*
Six Women for the Murderer see *Blood and Black Lace*
Skay, Brigitte 131, 132
Slaughter Hotel 179
Slaughter of the Vampires 22, 70, 179, 190–192, 255
Slaughter on 10th Avenue 46
The Slave 133
Smith, Sally 252
Smokecocks, Frank see Fumagalli, Franco
Snow Demons see *Snow Devils*
Snow Devils 132, 150, 183, 192, 193, 255
Snyder, Howard 22
Sodom and Gomorrah 130, 157, 183
Solbelli, Olga 152
Sollima, Sergio 95
Solvay, Paolo 190
Sombrero 87
The Son of Captain Blood 12
Son of Samson 251
Son of Satan see *What!*
The Sorcerers 188
Sordi, Alberto 87
La sorella di Satana see *She Beast*
Sorrente, Silvia 55
Sortolda, Victor 192
Southern Cross 192, 239
SPA Cinematografica 55, 109, 114
Spain, Fay 109, 110, 113
Sparrow, Bernice 239
The Spectre see *The Ghost*
Sperli, Nicola 109
Lo spettro de Dr. Hichcock see *The Horrible Dr. Hickcock*
Spirits of the Dead 3, 85, 194–198, 256
The Spooks of Castle Speisert 86
Das Spuksschluss im Speisert see *The Spooks of Castle Speisert*
Spy in Your Eye 132, 133, 176
Stacy, John 71
Stafford, Gino 88
Im Stahlnetz der Dr. Mabuse see *The Return of Dr. Mabuse*
Stamp, Terence 181, 194, 196, 197

Stanislawski, Jacques 61
Stapleton, Vivian 251
Starly, Inoa 120
Steele, Alan *see* Ciani, Sergio
The Steel Power of Dr. Mabuse see The Return of Dr. Mabuse
Steele, Barbara 7, 9, 31, 33, 37, 38, 47, 55, 56, 60, 80–82, 113, 119, 120, 123, 146–150, 163, 165, 166, 180, 186, 188, 191, 200, 244
Steffen, Anthony *see* De Teffé, Antonio
Steffen, Ben 55
Stegani, Giorgio 152, 184–186
Steiger, Rod 113
Steinert, Anini 229
Stella, Luciano 235, 236
Steno, Stefano *see* Vanzina, Stefano
Stevenson, Robert Louis 161
Stoker, Bram 204, 210
Storff, Victor *see* Salerno, Vittorio
Strahl, Franca Parisi 14, 16, 21
"The Strange Case of Dr. Jekyll and Mr. Hyde" 161
The Strange Obsession see *The Witch*
La strega in amore see *The Witch*
Le streghe see *The Witches*
Stribling, Melissa 216
Stuart, Jack *see* Rossi-Stuart, Giacomo
Sullivan, Barry 166, 167, 171, 172
Sullivan, Didi *see* Perego, Didi
Summer Love 74
Super International Pictures 213, 251
Suran, Mark 39
Suspicion 123
Sutherland, Donald 61, 63, 68
Swan, Kitty 239
Swanson, Logan *see* Matheson, Richard
The Sweet Body of Deborah 146
Swept Away by an Unusual Destiny in the Blue Sea of August 181
The Sword and the Cross 101
The Swordsman of Siena 9, 201

Tagliaferri, Pasquale 184, 185
Tahi, Mona 43, 239
Tales of Mystery and Imagination see *Spirits of the Dead*
Tamberlani, Carol 154
Tamberlani, Nando 105, 106
The Taming of the Shrew 46
Tammy and the Bachelor 11
The Tartars 94, 185
Tarzan and the Lost Safari 100

Tarzan the Magnificent 100
Tarzana, Herman *see* Tarzana, Ubaldo
Tarzan's Fight for Life 100
Tarzan's Greatest Adventure 100
Tarzan's Hidden Jungle 100
Taste for Women 191
Taur the Mighty 94
Die tausend Augen des Dr. Mabuse see *The Thousand Eyes of Dr. Mabuse*
Tavella, Dino 68
Taylor, Elizabeth 46, 181
Taylor, Robert 79
Teenage Doll 113
"The Telephone" 22, 25, 27, 136
Teleworld 172
Tempestini, Giotto 13
I tempi duri per vampiri see *Uncle Was a Vampire*
Teorama 181
Terra Film Kunst 219
The Terrace 162
Il Terrazza 162
The Terrible People 12, 214
The Terrible Secret of Dr. Hichcock see *The Horrible Dr. Hichcock*
The Terror 22, 23
Terror-Creatures from the Grave 38, 46, 47, 181, 198–201, 255
Terror in Space see *The Planet of the Vampires*
Terror in the Crypt 7, 8, 78, 134, 201–205, 255
The Terror of Dr. Hichcock see *The Horrible Dr. Hichcock*
The Terror of Rome Against the Son of Hercules 166
Terrore nello spazio see *The Planet of the Vampires*
Terzano, Ubaldo 22, 31, 36, 39, 74, 235, 238
Teseo contro il minotauro see *The Minotaur, Wild Beast of Crete*
Tessari, Duccio 98, 101, 102, 109, 114
Testi, Fulvio 75
Theodora, Slave Empress 54
These Ghosts see *Ghosts Italian Style*
Theseus Against the Minotaur see *The Minotaur, Wild Beast of Crete*
The Thief of Baghdad (1961) 38, 70, 85, 205–209, 255
Thief of Baghdad (1978) 209
Thierry, Richard *see* Pallotini, Riccardo
The 39 Steps 38

Those Fantastic Flying Fools 238
The Thousand Eyes of Dr. Mabuse 153
The Three Avengers 108
Three Bites of the Apple 201
Three Faces of Terror see *Black Sabbath*
Three Weeks of Love 241
Thriller 22
Throne of Blood 96
Thunder Island 113
Tichy, Gérard 102, 103
The Tiger and the Pussycat 87
Till, Tilde 200
The Time Travelers 170
The Time Tunnel 222
Titanus 205
To Commit a Murder 219
"Toby Dammit" 3, 194, 196, 198
Todesco, Anita 68, 70, 205
Tognazzi, Ugo 161, 162
Tolstoy, Leo 22, 153
Tom Corbett, Space Cadet 171
Tomb of Ligeia 194
Tomb of the Blind Dead 77
Tombs of Terror see *Castle of Blood*
Tonti, Aldo 61, 66
Topaz 14
Torture Chamber of Dr. Sadism 191
Tosi, Otello 172
Tosi, Piero 82
Toto all'inferno see *Toto in Hell*
Toto in Hell 8
Toto in the Moon 212
Touch of Larceny 124
Tourneur, Jacques 54, 189
Tower of Terror 253
Towers, Harry Alan 219
Towers of London 219
Tragedy of a Ridiculous Man 201
The Train 153
The Tramplers 100, 241
Tranquilli, Silvano 55, 57, 120, 123
Trapped in Tangiers 54
Trasatti, Luciano 43, 46, 161, 162
I tre volti della paura see *Black Sabbath*
Triton Filmindustria 75
Triumph of the Son of Hercules 250
The Trojan Horse 153, 185
Trojani, Oberdan 105
Trovajoli, Armando 14, 88, 93, 109, 114
Trunk to Cairo 215
Turner, John 108, 215, 217
12 to the Moon 175
24 Hour Lover 132

Twice Told Tales 144
Twilight Zone — The Movie 162
Twins of Evil 209
Twitch of the Death Nerve 103, 132
Two Nights with Cleopatra 114
Two Weeks in Another Town 244
Two Women 83, 233

Ugarte, Julian 75, 77
The Ugly Ones 9
Ulloa, Alejandro 95
Ulmer, Edgar G. 77
L'ultima preda del vampiro see *The Playgirls and the Vampire*
L'ultimo uomo della terra see *The Last Man on Earth*
Ulysses 2, 114, 130
Una lunga fila di croci see *No Room to Die*
Uncle Was a Vampire 66, 86, 209–212, 255
The Undead 189
Under Ten Flags 191
Unger, Freddy see Unger, Goffredo
Unger, Goffredo 105, 192, 193, 239
The Unguarded Moment 74
United Artists (UA) 144, 154, 215
Universal 12
The Unnaturals 213–215, 256
Uno dollaro bucato see *One Silver Dollar*
Die unsichtbaren Krallen des Dr. Mabuse see *The Invisible Dr. Mabuse*
Upstairs and Downstairs 38
Urbisaglia, Serge 245, 250
Ursus in the Valley of the Lions 157
Urueta, Chano 249
Ustinov, Peter 209

Vaccari, Paolo 68
Vadim, Roger 162, 194, 195, 202
Valdemarin, Mario 109, 184, 185
Valentin, Mirko 61–63, 66, 67, 125, 131
Valeri, Bruno 147, 202
Valeri, Valeria 133
Valmont, Vera 202
The Vampire and the Ballerina 22, 177, 183, 191, 215–219, 255
The Vampire Lovers 204
The Vampire of the Opera 217–219, 255
The Vampires see *Goliath and the Vampires*
The Vampires (1956) 3, 54, 77, 101, 179, 215

The Vampire's Crypt see *Terror in the Crypt*
The Vampire's Last Victim see *The Playgirls and the Vampire*
The Vampire's Niece see *Fangs of the Living Dead*
Vampires vs. Hercules see *Hercules in the Haunted World*
I vampiri see *The Vampires* (1956)
Vampyr 37, 202
Van Cleef, Lee 185
Vanguard 152, 172
Vanzina, Stefano 209, 212
Vargas, Daniele 205
Vari, Giuseppe 184, 223
Vaser, Vittorio 154
Veidt, Conrad 205
The Velvet Vampire 204
La vendetta de ercole see *Goliath and the Dragon*
The Vengeance of She 38
Vengeance of the Mummy 12
Venus im Pelz see *Venus in Furs*
Venus in Furs 17, 219–223, 256
Veo, Carlo 161
Verde, Dino 210
Vessel, Edy 205, 207
Vialati, Bruno 205
Vianello, Maria Teresa 120, 124
Vianello, Raimondo 161, 162
Vicario, Marco 55, 124
Victory Films 75
Vides 85
Villasanti, José 202
Villena, Fernando 166, 167
The Violent Four 114
Viridiana 96
Visconti, Luchino 88, 150
Visconti, Luigi 205
Vite perdite see *Lost Souls*
Vitelloni 46
Vittet, Lucien 152
Vivaldi, Gianna 133, 134
Vivarelli, Piero 181
Vivo per la tua morte see *A Long Ride from Hell*
Le Voleur de Bagdad see *The Thief of Bagdad* (1961)
Volonté, Gian Maria 109, 111, 113, 242–244
Von Ryan's Express 21, 153
Von Sacher-Masoch, Leopold 219, 221

Voodoo Island 37
Voyage to the End of the Universe 170

Waggner, George 11
Wald, Marvin 219
Wallace, Edgar 160, 222
Wallace, Frank see Mannino, Franco
Walsh, Raoul 205
Walter, Pietro 68
Walton, Patrick 125
The Wandering Jew 21
Wanted 153
War and Peace 78
The War Between the Planets 147, 150, 193, 241
War Is Hell 241
War of the Planets 193, 241
War of the Satellites 175
War of the Zombies 114, 184, 223–238, 256
Warlord of Crete see *The Minotaur, Wild Beast of Crete*
Warren, Jerry 178
The Warrior and the Empress 101
The Warrior and the Slave Girl 114
Watson, Richard 186
The Way and the Body see *What!*
Way...Way Out 78
Web of Passion 185
Web of the Spider 26, 61, 215
Webber, Robert 241
Weine, Robert 154
Welles, Mel 186–189, 250
Wentworth, Nicholas 200
Werewolf in a Girl's Dormitory 39, 145, 160, 203, 229–234, 238, 255
Wertmüller, Lina 147
Whale, James 186, 213, 214
What! 1, 150, 160, 209, 234–238, 255
Where the Hot Wind Blows 185
The Whip and the Body see *What!*
White, Harriet 80, 82, 120, 158, 160, 235
White Nights 88
White Slave Ship 21, 158
The White Spider 12, 214
White Voices 191
The White Warrior 132, 209
The Wild, Wild Planet 3, 150, 176, 183, 193, 239–242, 255
Wilde, Cornel 162
Will Success Spoil Rock Hunter? 46
"William Wilson" 85, 194, 196
Williams, Cara 227

Williams, Fred 131, 132
Williams, Guy 94
Williams, Spencer 120
Wilson, Barbara 158
Wilson, Gordon, Jr. *see* Corbucci, Sergio
"Window Panes" 30
Wisberg, Audrey 192
Wise, Robert 11, 130, 244, 253
The Witch 114, 157, 242–245, 255
The Witch of Vampires see *Slaughter of the Vampires*
The Witches 88, 103
The Witches Curse see *The Witch's Curse*
The Witch's Curse 129, 147, 245–251, 255
The Witch's Mirror 183
With Hercules to the Center of the Earth see *Hercules in the Haunted World*
Wolfe, Rene 200
The Wolfman 11
Woman of the Lake see *The Possessed*
Woman Times Seven 87
Woolner, Bernard 55
Woolner, Lawrence 51
Woolner Bros. 39, 55, 109, 114, 115
"The Wurdulak" 22, 27, 153
Wuthering Heights 60
Wynter, Paul 13

X…The Man with the X-Ray Eyes 37

Yanni, Rossana 75, 78
Yeux sans visage see *Horror Chamber of Dr. Faustus*
You Only Live Twice 12
Young, Mary 158, 159
The Young Racers 31
The Young, the Evil and the Savage 11, 133, 241, 251–253, 256
The Young Torless 9

Zahler, Gordon 109
Zalewska, Halina 147, 149, 150, 192
Zanolli, Angelo 245
Zapponi, Bernardo 194
Zarfati, Giancarlo 205
00-2 Most Secret Agent 132
Zichel, Rosie 223
Zinny, Victoria 239
Zita, Antonietta 152
Zocchi, Nietta 82
Zodiac 124
Zoppelli, Lia 210
Zounds, Archibald, Jr. 97, 109
Zuccoli, Fausto 131, 133, 251, 253
Zuccoli, Frank see Zuccoli, Fausto
Zucker, Ralph see Pupillo, Massimo

 www.ingramcontent.com/pod-product-compliance
Ingram Content Group UK Ltd.
Pitfield, Milton Keynes, MK11 3LW, UK
UKHW041929140426
5217IPUK00014B/380